Prices and Wages in U.S. Manufacturing

Prices and Wages in U.S. Manufacturing

A Factor Analysis

Nancy Smith Barrett

Geraldine Gerardi

Thomas P. Hart

The American University

Lexington Books
D.C. Heath and Company
Lexington, Massachusetts
Toronto   London

Library of Congress Cataloging in Publication Data

Barrett, Nancy Smith.
   Prices and wages in U.S. manufacturing.

   Bibliography: p.
   1. Inflation (Finance)–United States–Mathematical models. 2. Prices–
United States–Mathematical models. 3. Wages–United States–Mathematical models. I. Gerardi, Geraldine, joint author. II. Hart, Thomas P., joint
author. III. Title.
HG538.B28   332.4'1'0973   72-3546
   ISBN 0-669-84079-3

The most curious part of the thing was, that the trees and the other things round them never changed their places at all: however fast they went, they never seemed to pass anything. "I wonder if all the things move along with us?" thought poor puzzled Alice. And the Queen seemed to guess her thoughts, for she cried "Faster! Don't try to talk!"

Alice looked round her in great surprise. "Why I do believe we've been under this tree the whole time! Everything's just as it was!"

"Of course it is," said the Queen. "What would you have it?"

Lewis Carroll, *Through the Looking Glass*

Contents

List of Figures   xi

List of Tables   xiii

Preface   xv

Acknowledgments   xvii

Chapter 1   **The Theory of Inflation and Its Policy Implications**   1

Introduction   1
The Keynesian Legasy   2
The Phillips Curve: An Empirical Relationship   5
Wages and the Labor Market   6
Recent Controversies   6
Summing Up   9
Industry Studies   9

Chapter 2   **Methodology**   13

Recent Empirical Studies   13
The Factor Analytic Model   15
Interpreting the Results   19

Chapter 3   **The Data, Variable Transformations, and Alternative Samples**   21

Variables   21
Data Problems   25
Alternative Specifications and Samples   26

viii

Chapter 4 **Results for Total Manufacturing and Durables** 29

The Factors and Their Interpretation 29
The Price Equation—Total
  Manufacturing 45
The Price Equation—Durable
  Manufacturing 53
The Wage Equation—Total
  Manufacturing 55
The Wage Equation—Durable
  Manufacturing 56
Interaction of Wages and Prices—Total
  Manufacturing 60
Interaction of Wages and Prices—
  Durable Manufacturing 61
Secular Trends in the Inflationary
  Process for Total Manufacturing 62
The Policy Variables 64
Relation to the Theoretical Models 67

Chapter 5 **The Industry Results** 69

Choice of Industry Classification 69
Interpreting the Results 70
General Remarks about the Factors 70
The Price Equations 71
Unassigned Industries 91
Relation of Market Structure to
  Price Behavior 91
General Observations 97
The Policy Variables 98

Chapter 6 **Summary and Conclusions** 101

Methodological Considerations 101
Description of the Inflationary
  Process 102
Relation to Other Studies 105
Policy Conclusions and
  Recommendations 108

Appendixes 111

Appendix A   Sources of Data 113

Appendix B   Rotated Factor Loadings for the
Industry Variables 117

Bibliography 207

Index 211

About the Authors 213

List of Figures

1-1   Price-Employment Relationship in
            the Keynesian Model   3

1-2   Price Adjustment to an Increase in
            Demand at Full Employment   4

1-3   A Typical Phillips Curve   5

List of Tables

4-1   *Total Manufacturing:* Rotated Factor
        Loadings for the Full Sample—
        Percent Change over Four Quarters   30

4-2   *Total Manufacturing:* Rotated Factor
        Loadings for the Full Sample—
        Quarterly Percent Change   33

4-3   *Durable Manufacturing:* Rotated
        Factor Loadings for the Full
        Sample—Percent Change over Four
        Quarters   36

4-4   *Durable Manufacturing:* Rotated
        Factor Loadings for the Full
        Sample –Quarterly Percent Change   39

4-5   *Total Manufacturing:* Factor
        Loadings for Alternative Samples
        and Specifications–Percent Change
        over Four Quarters   47

4-6   *Total Manufacturing:* Factor
        Loadings for Alternative Samples
        and Specifications–Quarterly
        Percent Change   49

4-7   *Durable Manufacturing:* Factor
        Loadings for the Wholesale
        Price Index for Alternative
        Specifications and Data
        Transformations   53

4-8   *Total Manufacturing:* Factor
        Loadings for Average Hourly
        Earnings for Alternative Samples—
        Percent Change over Four Quarters   57

4-9   *Total Manufacturing:* Factor
        Loadings for Average Hourly

Earnings for Alternative Samples—
Quarterly Percent Change   58

4-10   *Durable Manufacturing:* Factor
            Loadings for Average Hourly
            Earnings and Average Weekly
            Earnings   59

4-11   *Total Manufacturing:* Selected
            Factor Loadings for 1961:1 to
            1970:4—Percent Change over Four
            Quarters   63

4-12   *Total Manufacturing:* Factor Loadings
            for the Policy Variables in the
            Full Sample—Percent Change over
            Four Quarters   65

4-13   *Durable Manufacturing:* Factor Loadings
            for the Policy Variables—Percent
            Change over Four Quarters   66

5-1 to 5-18 *Industry Variables:* Factor
            Loadings for WPI for Alternative
            Specifications and Data
            Transformations   73-93

5-19   Explanatory Variables for
            Cross-section Analysis of Price
            Behavior   95

5-20   Cross-section Regressions on the
            Factor Loadings for F_1, F_2,
            and F_3 96

B-1 to B-38 *Industry Variables:* Rotated Factor
            Loadings for 1959:1-1971:3   119-206

Preface

We began this study in the summer of 1971, a time of much concern in both academic and government circles over the persistent upward creep in wholesale and consumer prices as restrictive monetary and fiscal measures pushed the overall unemployment rate above 6 percent. One major reason for the consternation, particularly among academic economists, was the failure of the orthodox policy model, based on Keynesian theory and Phillipsian empiricism, to produce the predicted, stabilizing results. Reminiscent of a similar situation in the early 1930s, when the unemployment rate stubbornly refused to fall in response to downward pressure on wages, the conventional wisdom was forced to bow to a series of ad hoc, intuitive, piecemeal policy measures designed more to keep the boat from sinking than to change the mode of transportation.

The experience of the early thirties did produce a new policy model and, in the capitalist world at least, the Marshallian ship was abandoned for a new vessel. In the current situation, however, our reluctance to abandon ship stems largely from the failure of economic theorists to come up with a consistent model of the inflationary process to provide the basis for a new brand of anti-inflation policy. This is not to say that much has not been accomplished since our study began. But that particular form of eclectic theorizing born of computerized econometric analysis—which, for better or worse, was not technologically feasible in 1935—is not readily conducive to the development of the type of revolutionary paradigm that was represented by *The General Theory*.

This study does not purport to be such a paradigm. In fact, it could be argued that ours is the reverse of theorizing—that we have been on an ex post fishing expedition. Our aim has been to examine the inflationary process through every possible quantitative perspective, both to test the prevalent theories as well as to suggest new ones. But we view our work primarily as providing an empirical overview of the economic interrelationships that have influenced prices in the manufacturing sector for the past two decades, an overview which can provide the empirical basis for such heated theoretical and policy discussions that have dominated the economics literature since that summer when our project began. This we see as our contribution to the yet-unborn, but hopefully, imminent reconstruction of the theory of inflation.

Acknowledgments

We are grateful to many individuals for their technical, critical, financial, and emotional support to this project. Many of the data were unpublished. George Hay Brown and Ralph Eichelberger of the Census Bureau provided us with new orders and unfilled orders for the two-digit industries. John Stinson and others in his office at the Bureau of Labor Statistics filled in many gaps in our unemployment rates series. Otto Eckstein made available to us his updated series for input and output prices for the two-digit industries.

Jama Martin of the American University Computer Center spent many long hours helping us catalog the data into machine-readable form. Walter Davis of the Federal Reserve Board of Governors provided us with an extremely efficient seasonal adjustment program. Maria Tokić typed the manuscript and assisted with some of the mathematical computations. All of these people helped to smooth over a number of rough spots that we cannot even begin to enumerate.

Ms. Gerardi and Mr. Hart received financial support from the American University Graduate School which made life, if not pleasant, at least bearable during the course of the project. The Graduate School also provided funds for computer time.

Finally, we owe a great debt of gratitude to Gary Fromm, Cynthia Taft Morris, and Richard H. Puckett for their valuable comments on and criticisms of the many versions of our manuscript. Although they are in no way responsible for our conclusions, their suggestions greatly improved both our methodological design and the interpretation of our results. Professor Bo Södersten and the students in a seminar on inflation and labor market policy at the University of Gothenburg, Sweden, during the spring of 1973 provided additional insights that we incorporated.

A project that takes two years and involves approximately 1722 variables (with multiple observations on each) can become, at times, extremely frustrating and exhausting. To all those of our patient friends who listened to our troubles and helped us put them into perspective we owe the greatest debt.

**Prices and Wages in U.S.
Manufacturing**

The Theory of Inflation and its Policy Implications

Introduction

Recent experience with inflation in the United States economy has led many economists to question the universal validity of the Keynes-Phillips model of the inflationary process and the efficacy of aggregate demand measures for controlling the rate of price increase. One difficulty for evaluating alternative models and their policy implications is that the empirical evidence is consistent with a number of hypotheses. This is because multicollinearity in the potential set of explanatory variables requires that some variables be excluded from the so-called structural model. The problem is intensified when theoretical models which cannot be rejected on the basis of empirical evidence contain conflicting policy implications.

Aside from the basic theoretical framework on which the policy model is based, it is well known that many variables influence price level changes and that the relative importance of these variables is different depending on the level of economic activity and other economic considerations. The social and political climate as well as expectations about the future may also affect the relationship between economic conditions and the price level. Again, if potential explanatory variables are highly correlated, it is impossible to separate their respective influences on the basis of empirical evidence.

Thus, the choice of a structural model describing the inflationary process as well as an assessment of the impact of individual variables—including policy instruments—cannot always be accomplished on the basis of empirical evidence alone. This poses a serious dilemma if anti-inflation policy is to be derived from such models. If economists cannot agree on the appropriate remedy, the decision is often left to the political process.

In view of the difficulties in testing the validity of structural models, this study examines the inflationary process from a different perspective. If we can ascertain the channels through which the inflation is transmitted, regardless of its initial causes, we will be able to assess the potential efficacy of aggregate demand remedies, wage-price controls or other measures.

We have analyzed the principal components of 82 quarterly economic time series for the period 1953 to 1970 and for subperiods within those years. These components, which are linear combinations of groups of the variables in the explanatory set, are used as factors in an analysis of movements in the wholesale price index and certain wage variables. This methodology allows us to investigate

1

the relationship between price and wage changes and categories of explanatory variables. Before describing the statistical methodology, we shall review in more detail some alternative theories of inflation and their policy implications.

The Keynesian Legacy

In view of the observed insensitivity of the rate of inflation to slack demand conditions since the recession of 1969, it has become fashionable to reject the Keynesian model of inflation as a structural description of the contemporary scene. However, it is important to keep in mind that Keynesian policy remedies, at least in the capitalist countries, have a certain political and intellectual respectability that others lack. *The General Theory*[1] provided the intellectual rationale for government intervention in an economic system rooted in a laissez-faire ideology. The supposed neutrality of Keynesian activities in the public sector with respect to private resource allocation—this being the point of Keynes' discussions of pyramid-building, cathedrals, and masses for the dead[2] — provided the basis for their political acceptance.

The idea that inflation is due to an excessive growth of demand relative to supply and that an "inflationary gap" can be eliminated by reducing aggregate demand is perhaps an oversimplified interpretation of Keynes' contribution to the theory of prices. But it is, nevertheless, the conventional wisdom at the heart of his legacy. In order to pinpoint the model's failure to explain the recent inflationary process it is necessary to examine its underlying assumptions.

Keynes viewed the aggregate level of employment as determined by the level of aggregate demand, and his model emphasizes product market conditions. The Keynesian theory of inflation essentially ignores the labor market altogether. The economy is either at full employment or not. If not, an increase in aggregate demand increases employment with no price changes. At full employment, the elasticity of price changes with respect to aggregate demand becomes unity. Thus, there is a relationship between price changes and employment, but it is the extremely simple one shown in Figure 1-1.

If short-run price changes are proportional to changes in unit labor costs, that is

$$p = \frac{W}{MP}$$

where p is the product price, W, the wage, and MP is marginal labor productivity, it is implied that unit labor costs are invariant to the level of employment. In his chapter on inflation[3] Keynes implies that both money wages and marginal labor productivity will remain constant until full employment is reached, although in earlier chapters he treats marginal labor productivity as a decreasing function of employment.

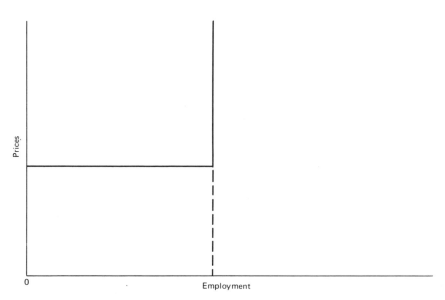

Figure 1-1. Price Employment Relationship in the Keynesian Model

A second important legacy of Keynes was his use of the comparative statics methodology. His economy is always moving toward an equilibrium[a] and this is true even at full employment. In Figure 1-2, the economy is initially in equilibrium at full employment, Y_F, with aggregate demand at a level represented by IS. In (a), an increase in demand shifts IS to IS'. Since real income cannot increase when the economy is at full employment, equilibrium is restored by a price increase that shifts LM leftward to LM', shown in (b). A new equilibrium can be attained as long as the monetary authorities allow interest rates to rise to i'. If they increase the money supply to ease credit conditions, equilibrium will not be achieved, prices will continue to rise, and a dynamic inflationary process will set in.

Post-Keynesian developments in the theory of inflation have been heavily influenced by the comparative statics approach. Although the Phillips model turned attention from price levels to rates of change, the idea that the relationship between prices and employment is stable with respect to changes in aggregate demand and that anti-inflation policy could be designed in terms of movements along that function has persisted until very recently.

[a]Keynes viewed equilibrium in a comparative statics sense, not as a situation in which all markets are necessarily cleared. National income equilibrium can be viewed as Samuelsonian, not Marshallian. Some Keynesian scholars dispute this interpretation, however, arguing that unemployment is always a disequilibrium state. See, for example, Axel Leijonhufvud, *On Keynesian Economics and the Economics of Keynes* (New York: Oxford University Press, 1968), Chapter 2.

4

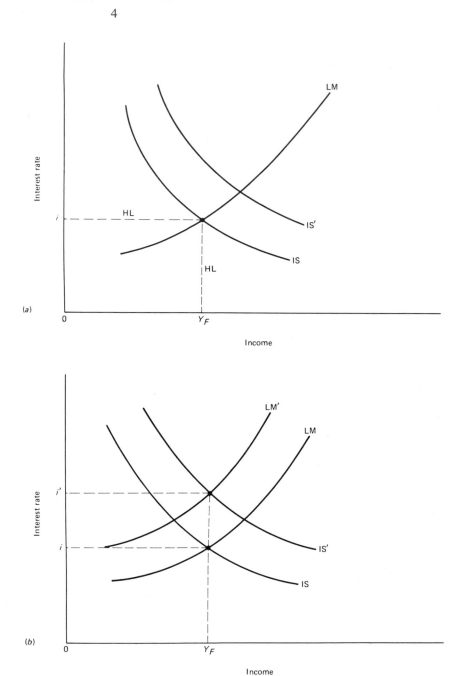

Figure 1-2. Price Adjustment to an Increase in Demand at Full
Employment

The Phillips Curve: An Empirical Relationship

The idea that there is a stable relationship between unemployment and inflation was tested empirically by A.W. Phillips in 1958.[4] Although the so-called Phillips curve—an inverse relation between money wage changes and the unemployment rate—was originally an empirical relationship, it has a theoretical basis as well. The major policy implication is that there is a trade-off between inflation and unemployment, at least in the range of socially acceptable unemployment rates. As seen in Figure 1-3, money wages increase as labor markets tighten, even before full employment is reached. Prices will rise in response to increasing unit labor costs, as unemployment falls. Unlike the Keynesian model, the definition of full employment is no longer unequivocal, but is related to the amount of unemployment associated with the highest allowable inflation rate.

Although the Phillips model emphasizes the role of labor market conditions in the inflationary process, it can be viewed as the logical extension of the Keynesian model both methodologically and from a policy perspective. We can no longer achieve full employment without inflation, but we can always return to the original starting point once an inflationary process is set in motion.

Suppose we begin with stable prices and an unemployment rate of 4.5 percent. An increase in demand reduces the unemployment rate to 4 percent, but prices rise at a rate of 3 percent. The Phillips model suggests that price stability can be achieved by reducing demand to its previous level and maintaining an unemployment rate of 4.5 percent.

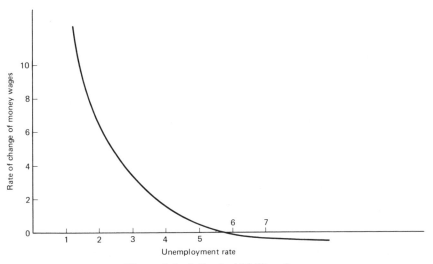

Figure 1-3. A Typical Phillips Curve

6

Wages and the Labor Market

Whereas the Keynesian model ignores the impact of labor market conditions on wages and hence of wages on prices, the Phillips approach suggests that money wages are highly sensitive to the unemployment rate in the relevant policy range. This means that the principal way that aggregate demand affects the price level is through the labor market. Although the policy conclusions are the same, the Phillips approach shifted attention away from the Keynesian concern with product markets and returned to the neoclassical view of unemployment as a labor market problem.

However, if we keep in mind that prices depend on wages, we must also recognize that price changes may affect the wage bargain. The Phillips model implies a total money illusion on the part of workers, since the relationship between money wage changes and unemployment is viewed as independent of the actual rate of inflation.[b]

While the assumption of money illusion may be reasonable in the early stages of inflation, an inflationary psychology that destroys money illusion may eventually develop. If workers begin to bargain for real, rather than money wages, then the elasticity of wage change with respect to inflation approaches unity. Since short-run wage changes will be passed on in price increases, loss of money illusion will produce an inflationary spiral regardless of the level of aggregate demand or unemployment.

To the extent that some money illusion persists, inflation can be slowed down by reducing demand and producing slack labor market conditions, because then money wages will fall. But as long as the elasticity of money wages with respect to the inflation rate is unity, aggregate demand measures cannot halt the inflationary spiral.

Recent Controversies

Any theoretical model must be consistent with empirical relationships, particularly when such relationships persist over a reasonably long period of time. The rate of inflation in the United States after 1968 has shown a striking insensitivity to aggregate demand conditions. While restrictive fiscal and monetary measures pushed the unemployment rate above 6 percent, prices continued to rise at record rates. Indeed, the rate of inflation exhibited an upward trend in this period of slack labor markets with the monthly increase in the wholesale price index surpassing the record high of the Korean War period during the first half of 1973.

---

[b]Phillips actually found his relationship to be affected by changes in the price of food, which, in nineteenth-century Britain could serve as a proxy for perceived changes in the cost of living. But this aspect of his study has been overlooked in most interpretations.

This evidence has led many economists to question the existence of a trade-off between inflation and unemployment as well as the efficacy of aggregate demand remedies for stabilizing prices. Recent theoretical developments have suggested that fundamental changes have occurred in the structure of the economy in recent years and that these changes have altered the so-called Phillips relationship.

The Shifting Phillips Curve

One such view, associated with George Perry, is that there is a trade-off between unemployment and inflation, but that the Phillips curve has shifted rightward since 1968, increasing the unemployment rate associated with any rate of inflation.[5] Perry attributes this rightward shift to changes in the demographic composition of the labor force characterized by increasing participation of women and young people. Coupled with this increased participation is an increase in the unemployment rates of these groups relative to central-age males. When the unemployment rate is adjusted for these changes, that the period since 1968 has uniformly been characterized by tight labor markets and the observed high rate of inflation has been consistent with a Phillips trade-off based on the adjusted unemployment rate.

Perry argues that inflation can be slowed down by aggregate demand remedies, but that a concerted effort must be made to improve labor market conditions for women and young people. Emphasis on selective labor market policy to improve the lot of these groups will serve to improve the inflation-unemployment trade-off so that price stability will be consistent with a socially acceptable level of unemployment.

The Accelerationist View

Other economists reject the usefulness of the Phillips curve for explaining recent inflation in the United States or for designing anti-inflation policy. They argue that a model in which unexplained shifts in the price-unemployment trade-off supposedly account for the recent acceleration of inflation is based on ex post reasoning. In fact, Perry seems to have experimented with a number of adjustments to the unemployment rate before finding one that was consistent with the evidence. Furthermore, although his econometric model explains the data within the sample from which it was estimated fairly well, it did not predict the upsurge in inflation in late 1972 and early 1973.

The accelerationist view is that we have observed no relationship between inflation and unemployment because of the development of a psychology of inflationary expectations that have reduced or eliminated money illusion.[6] Since at least some workers now bargain in terms of real rather than money wages, this has produced a wage-price spiral that is relatively unaffected by labor market conditions. If the development of inflationary expectations or, equivalently, the loss of money illusion is a function of the length as well as the level of past inflation, the rate of increase of money wages will accelerate, producing an accelerated rate of price inflation as unit labor costs rise.

As long as there is some money illusion in the labor market, past inflation will not be completely passed on in money wage increases, and aggregate demand remedies may have some impact on money wages at the prevailing rate of inflation. But since an inflationary psychology is more likely to develop the higher the inflation rate and the longer the period of inflation, aggregate demand remedies become weaker the longer the inflation has been allowed to persist.

Accelerationists advocate the use of wage-price guidelines, or controls, to break the inflationary psychology. It is interesting to note that the concept of price control policy advocated by the accelerationists is different from the guidelines practiced in the Kennedy-Johnson era or the so-called incomes policies followed by some Western European countries. In the latter the emphasis has been on holding wages to gains in productivity, thereby stabilizing unit labor costs. Such guidelines are typically not applied across the board, but only in highly concentrated and basic industries. The accelerationists, on the other hand, see price controls primarily as a means of breaking an inflationary psychology which will have an indirect effect on money wage increases and unit labor costs.

The so-called Phase II price policy of the Nixon administration emphasized the consumer-participation aspect of price controls. Retail stores were required to list pre-control prices, and consumers were requested to report illegal price increases to a price commission set up to receive such complaints. In the popular view, a one-cent increase in the price of cigarettes at a local drugstore was to be handled in much the same way as a general rise in steel prices. Although the commission could not possibly process all the complaints it received, the very idea that he was involved in the enforcement process was supposed to convince the consumer *qua* worker that prices would no longer rise.

Although both the Perry view and the accelerationist model are consistent with the empirical evidence,[c] the policy conclusions they draw are very different. Perry argues that there is excess demand for certain types of labor and that solutions must be found in selective labor market policy together with restrictive fiscal and monetary measures. The accelerationists, on the other hand, call for more expansionary monetary and fiscal measures to reduce the excessive unemployment and to stimulate investment and productivity growth (which will reduce the rate of growth of unit labor costs). At the same time, they advocate tighter enforcement of wage-price controls to reduce inflationary expectations.

Because of these conflicting policy implications, the choice of models is

[c]We shall examine empirical tests of these hypotheses in Chapter 2.

crucial for designing anti-inflation policy. In Chapter 2, we shall discuss empirical tests of these hypotheses as well as the relevance of the methodology used in this study.

Summing Up

The theory of inflation can be viewed as a model for evaluating alternative policy remedies. In this context, tests of alternative hypotheses are important when they suggest conflicting anti-inflation programs. Although the traditional demand-pull-cost-push controversy has often been centered around the initial causes of inflation, the important underlying issue is whether aggregate demand remedies will reduce the rate of price increase once inflation is underway.

The accelerationists, who reject the use of Keynesian remedies once a psychology of inflationary expectations has developed, attribute the recent inflation to an attempt to push unemployment below its "natural rate," that is, the rate at which demand for and supply of labor are in balance. Thus, although the initial inflation was caused by excess demand, the persistent inflationary process is transmitted by an interaction between money wages and prices due to the loss of money illusion on the part of workers. A reduction in the demand for labor will not cause money wage increases to decline unless the expectations of inflation are reduced or eliminated.

For the neo-Keynesians, such as Perry, however, the ongoing inflationary process is transmitted by an excess demand for labor which causes money wages to rise. A reduction in the demand for labor will slow the rate of increase in money wages and thereby stabilize prices through the effect on unit labor costs.

Thus, it is important to assess the significance of the interaction of wages and prices in an inflation relative to the effect of changes in demand conditions. The stronger the feedback of prices to wages, the less favorable will be the tradeoff between inflation and unemployment. As the social cost of price stability increases, the issue of appropriate targets as well as of instruments becomes of major concern.

Industry Studies

There is growing support for the view that the relationship between prices, costs, and demand must be viewed as a microeconomic process. The theory of the firm suggests that price behavior will vary with the structure of the product market and that the wage bargain will depend on both product market and labor market conditions. Furthermore, there is empirical evidence that firms' pricing decisions are much more sensitive to conditions within the industry than to macroeconomic variables.[7] Thus, although stabilization policy in the United States has traditionally relied on aggregate measures, the inflationary process may be transmitted differently in different industries and sectors of the economy.

Models of Price Behavior

Several models of price behavior are available from the theory the firm. It is generally assumed that the more competitive the market structure the more sensitive prices and wages will be to demand conditions. Highly concentrated industries, on the other hand, are presumed to follow administered or mark-up pricing practices that are less sensitive to changes in demand. Powerful labor unions are expected to achieve more favorable wage bargains than in competitive labor markets. Thus, the theory suggests that in an industry with little competition in either the product or the labor market, price increases are most likely to interact with wages and other production costs. In competitive industries with competitive labor markets, on the other hand, price changes will be more closely associated with changes in demand conditions.

The results of an industry analysis are of both theoretical and practical concern. From a theoretical perspective we are interested in testing alternative hypotheses from the theory of the firm concerning the relationship between the structure of both product and labor markets and price and wage behavior. In addition, understanding the structure of price and wage determination at the industry level will provide insights into the microeconomic processes that transmit inflation throughout the manufacturing sector.

From a policy viewpoint, if Keynesian remedies are to be supplemented by wage-price policies that can be applied with respect to industry-specific conditions, industry studies will be useful for designing these policies. Moreover, since prices in primary-products industries represent production costs in others, it is particularly important to identify the inflationary mechanism in these basic industries for assessing the efficacy of Keynesian remedies for the manufacturing sector as a whole.

Because of the relevance of industry studies for testing hypotheses about price behavior, we have disaggregated our data to the two-digit level of the standard industrial classification (SIC), in addition to our macro-analysis of data for total manufacturing and durables. In Chapter 2, we shall examine alternative techniques for testing hypotheses about price behavior and the problems associated with structural estimation. After a review of the literature we shall discuss our own methodological approach.

Notes

1. John Maynard Keynes, *The General Theory of Employment, Interest, and Money* (New York: Harcourt Brace Jovanich, Inc., 1965). Originally published in 1936 by Macmillan and Co., Ltd.

2. Ibid., p. 131.

3. Ibid., Chapter 21, pp. 292-309.

4. A.W. Phillips, "The Relation Between Unemployment and the Rate of Change of Money Wage Rates in the United Kingdom, 1861-1957," *Economica*, 25 (November 1958), pp. 283-99.

5. George L. Perry, "Changing Labor Markets and Inflation," *Brookings Papers on Economic Activity* (1970:3), pp. 411-48.

6. For a review of the accelerationist literature see Robert J. Gordon, "Wage-Price Controls and the Shifting Phillips Curve," *Brookings Papers on Economic Activity* (1972:2), pp. 385-421.

7. See Otto Eckstein and David Wyss, "Industry Price Equations," *Conference on the Econometrics of Price Determination*, Washington, D.C., 30-31 October 1970.

Methodology

The traditional approach to empirical analysis of price behavior is to hypothesize a theoretical relationship and to test its empirical validity by applying regression analysis to a set of variables that are supposed to represent the hypothesized structure. But it is well known that economic variables, particularly time series, are interrelated, so there is bound to be collinearity in the potential explanatory set. Thus, it is likely that several different structural models will be consistent with the empirical evidence. In this chapter we shall review briefly some cases in which this problem has resulted in a policy dilemma. Then we shall discuss the methodology employed in this study as a way of dealing with the collinearity problem.

Recent Empirical Studies

Empirical tests of the hypotheses described in Chapter 1 have always been plagued with the problem of collinearity. Collinearity becomes a problem when the principal explanatory variables in alternative structural specifications are highly intercorrelated. In essence, one structure can be viewed as a proxy for another in an empirical context. When the theoretical models represented offer conflicting policy remedies, the empirical approach leaves us in a dilemma, since we have nothing but an a priori basis for choosing between them.

In his 1966 study of wage behavior, George Perry found the coefficients on the unemployment rate (UN) and the consumer price index (CPI) to be highly sensitive to the choice of variables included in the same equations.[1] For example, he experimented with both the profit rate and a dummy variable for direction of unemployment change as proxies for changes in the level of economic activity. Since these two variables were highly collinear they could not be introduced together. When the profit rate was entered in place of the direction of unemployment, the elasticity of wage change with respect to the CPI rose from 0.29 to 0.37 and the coefficient in the unemployment rate increased from 13.35 to 14.71. Gordon does not speculate on which structure has the better a priori justification, but he implies that the structure accounting for the largest proportion of the variance in the dependent variable (or technically, the one with the highest R^2) should be selected. For small differences in the R^2, however, there is no justification for this procedure. That is, a significant R^2 may allow us to reject a null hypothesis, but marginal differences in (significant) R^2s for two equations are not criteria for selecting one and rejecting another.

Eckstein and Fromm also encountered difficulty with multicollinearity in their study of alternative microeconomic pricing models.[2] The variables reflecting demand conditions were so highly intercorrelated that when two were included in the same equation one would become insignificant or take the wrong sign. Eckstein and Fromm as well as Perry select the variable that accounts for the greatest percent of the variance, but whether such an equation can be called a structural model is questionable.

The recent controversy over the existence of the Phillips curve has also been plagued with the multicollinearity problem. Gordon[3] summarizes the various empirical relationships offered by Perry[4] (who supports the Phillips model), Eckstein and Brinner[5] (accelerationists), and Gordon[6] (who attempts to test both hypotheses simultaneously). Gordon concludes that all the models explain the data equally well even though there are marginal differences in their explanatory power in different samples. However, the structural significance of the most important variables such as the unemployment rate and a guideposts dummy depends on which other variables are included in the equation.

The impact of the consumer price index on wages depends on which unemployment rate is included in the equation. When the conventional unemployment rate is used, the coefficient on the CPI is much higher than when the unemployment rate is adjusted for structural changes in the labor market. Perry is able to explain wage changes without the CPI at all. Since the magnitude of the elasticity of wage change with respect to the CPI is of crucial importance for gauging the efficacy of aggregate demand remedies for inflation, the policy conclusion is left up in the air.

Because the choice between the so-called structural equations must be left to a priori justification, the selection of anti-inflation remedies becomes a matter for individual subjective interpretation. The argument is often couched in technical econometric jargon, as is the case with Gordon's review article,[7] giving the appearance that the issue is beyond the layman's comprehension. But it boils down to a choice between two rather simple structural models. Money wages are either sensitive to slack labor market conditions or they are not. The secondary issue of whether to use the unadjusted unemployment rate as a measure of labor-market slack is also straightforward. If the CPI is entered in the wage equation with the unadjusted unemployment rate the structural model explains about as much of the variance in wages as Perry's equation without the CPI and adjusted unemployment rate.

Applying Components Analysis

Components analysis is a method of grouping variables that are highly correlated in a sample. Principal components of a set of data are orthogonal (independent) linear combinations of the original variables. Since economic variables are often intercorrelated, there will generally be a few principal components that account for most of the variance in the original set.[a] In fact, one way to interpret the components is that they identify the true dimensions of variation in the original set of variables. Thus, a components analysis will indicate the maximum number of variables that can be used in a regression equation without encountering collinearity for a stipualted R^2.

Instead of specifying the relationship between certain explanatory variables and the rate of change in prices and wages, we use the most important principal components of the full explanatory set as independent variables. This technique permits us to examine the ability of certain groups of interrelated variables to account for changes in prices and wages. In addition, we can examine the relationship of our 19 policy variables to the principal components.

Since all potential explanatory variables are included in the analysis, there are no alternative structures to test. It could be argued, of course, that our methodology can tell us nothing about structure. But it is hardly appropriate to label a model "structural" simply because its parameters reflect relationships between individual variables rather than groups of variables. This is particularly true when there are several empirical structures that can account for changes in the dependent variable.

In this study we find that 82 variables can be reduced to four components that explain over 78 percent of the variance in price level changes and over 91 percent of the variance in wage changes. Furthermore, when the relationship between these components and the original explanatory variables is examined, we are able to interpret the components in economic terms. Thus, our regressions of price and wage changes on the components can be used to support certain a priori views of the inflationary process.

Whether our equations can be interpreted as a structural model of the inflationary process will be left to the judgment of the reader. It is important, however, to bear in mind that our methodology must be evaluated with respect to a data set containing multiple degrees of collinearity, making it consistent with alternative theoretical structures in regression analysis. We shall return to a discussion of interpretation after we have described the statistical properties of our method in more detail.

The Factor Analytic Model

The use of principal components in a single-equation model is a special case of factor analysis. Factor analysis is a technique for examining relationships between variables in a set. Each variable, X_i, is assumed to be a linear function of

---

[a]As we shall see, there will generally be as many principal components as variables, but only a few of these components will account for most of the variance in the original set of variables.

some orthogonal (uncorrelated) factors, which are linear combinations of the variables, as well as of some specific variables not in the set.[b] Allowance for residual variation unaccounted for by the linear relationship is specified as an error term. Thus

$$X_i = \sum_j a_{ij}f_j + \sum_k s_{ik}Y_k + e_i \qquad (2.1)$$

where the f_j are factors and the Y_k are explanatory variables not in the set.

Our study is a factor analytic model in which all the s_{ik} are zero. That is, no variables outside the initial set are introduced into the equation for X_i. This does not imply that excluded variables would not account for some of the residual variation in X_i. We are simply concerned with the explanatory power of the common influences within the original set (communality) rather than with specifying a more elaborate structure. Consequently, our model takes the form

$$X_i = \sum_j a_{ij} f_j + e_i \qquad (2.2)$$

The factors are orthogonal weighted averages of the variables in the set. One method of obtaining such factors is a principal components analysis of the data, the principal components becoming the factors, $f_1 \dots, f_n$. Principal components have the property of accounting for as much of the variance of the original variables as possible while maintaining the correlation between the original variables.

Thus, if

$$Z = KX \qquad (2.3)$$

where Z is a vector of principal components of the matrix of variable observations and where the X_i's are in standardized form, then the variance of Z can be expressed as

$$E(Z'Z) = E(K'X'XK) = E(K'RK) \qquad (2.4)$$

where R is the correlation matrix of the variables, X. Also since the K's are orthogonal,

$$K'K = I \qquad (2.5)$$

[b]One variable may be a function of only one other in the set, in which case it may be treated as a function of a factor which has a nonzero weight for only one variable.

Maximizing the variance of Z, subject to the orthogonality constraint

$$\frac{\partial V}{\partial K} = K'RK + \lambda(I - K'K) = 0 \qquad (2.6)$$

we obtain

$$(R - \lambda I)K = 0 \qquad (2.7)$$

Thus, the weights forming the principal components are the eigenvectors of the correlation matrix of the original variables.

Since

$$RK = \lambda K \qquad (2.8)$$

and the variance of Z is

$$E(Z'Z) = E(K'RK) = E(K'\lambda K) = E(\lambda K'K) = E(\lambda) = \lambda \qquad (2.9)$$

the variance of each principal component, Z_i, is equal to the corresponding eigenvalue, λ_i. By extracting the largest eigenvalue we can then determine the component that contributes the most to the explained variance by weighting the variables with the associated eigenvector.

Clearly, the greater the degree of multicollinearity in the original set, the smaller will be the number of components required to account for some portion of the variance, since linear dependence produces eigenvalues close to zero. In a statistical analysis components are generally extracted until no component adds more than 5 percent to the variance.[c]

Once the factors are extracted from the data set by the method of principal components they are rotated orthogonally so as to obtain the most distinct factor pattern possible. The procedure is admissible, since there are an infinite number of ways in which a set of $(n-m)$ orthogonal factors can be situated n-space.[d] The intent is to be able clearly to associate certain variables with a certain component and to avoid multifactor association of variables wherever possible. Thus, the rotation is designed in such a way as to maximize the number of near-zero weights (a_{ij}) or factor loadings.

Although components or factors thus derived are merely mathematical constructs, they can often be identified or defined in terms of the groups of

---

[c]Some procedures discontinue extracting eigenvalues when the eigenvalue is less than one. This implies the component adds less to the variance than a single standardized variable.

[d]For a complete discussion of rotational procedures see H.H. Harman, *Modern Factor Analysis* (Chicago: University of Chicago Press, 1960), Part 3.

variables most highly associated with them, that is, which have the highest weights, a_{ij}, for

$$f_j = \sum_i a_{ij}X_i \qquad (2.10)$$

when the X's are standardized. Thus, if there are high loadings on the variables measuring labor market conditions and near-zero loadings on the other variables, the factor could be designated a "labor market factor" interpreted as an index of variables reflecting labor market conditions.

The Factor Regression Equations

Since the factors are orthogonal and the variables are in standardized form, the factor loadings are equivalent to least-squares regression coefficients for the equation

$$X_i = a_{i1}f_1 + a_{i2}f_2 + a_{i3}f_3 + a_{i4}f_4 + e_i \qquad (2.11)$$

where the coefficient of multiple determination, R^2, is given by

$$R^2 = a_{i1}{}^2 + a_{i2}{}^2 + a_{i3}{}^2 + a_{i4}{}^2 \qquad (2.12)$$

The a_{ij} are also equivalent to beta-coefficients.
   A test of significance for the regression coefficients is

$$F = \frac{a_{ij}{}^2 (n-k)}{(1-R^2)} \qquad (2.13)$$

where

   n = number of variables

   k = number of factors rotated

and for the coefficient of multiple determination,

$$F = \frac{R^2}{(1-R^2)} \frac{(n-k)}{(k-1)} \qquad (2.14)$$

Methodological Considerations

Previous experience with applying factor analysis to economic data has shown the a_{ij} coefficients or *factor pattern* can be affected by peculiarities in the sample.[8] Consequently, for total manufacturing and durable manufacturing we analyzed the data for 10 sample periods (9 subsamples of the full sample). In addition, we tested our results for spuriousness by omitting some variables in certain runs for all the data sets. In most cases, we found the interpretation of our factors invariant to the omission of data and change of sample. For all nineteen industries as well as the manufacturing aggregates, we also tried alternative specifications of our data, both quarterly percent change (PCH) and percent change over four quarters (PCH/4), as well as four different lag patterns, and found no change in the economic interpretation of our factors.

The criterion we selected for determining the number of factors to be used in our analysis was somewhat unorthodox. When the criterion of selecting all eigenvalues greater than unity was used, about fourteen factors were rotated. However, it was obvious in all the runs that only the first four factors reflected meaningful economic relationships. The others were associated with only 2 or 3 variables each and in all cases the association was weak. Consequently, we rotated only the four factors we could interpret. These four factors accounted for 66 percent of the variance of 82 variables in the PCH/4 specification and 51 percent in the PCH specification in the full sample for total manufacturing. In the regressions, these four principal components of the explanatory set accounted for over 78 percent of the variance in price level changes and over 91 percent of wage changes. This method of selecting the number of variables to be rotated is not new. It is suggested in Harman[9] and used in an econometric study by Adelman and Morris.[10]

Interpreting the Results

This study reduces a large set of potential explanatory variables to four principal components. The components are given an economic interpretation based on the variables most highly correlated with them. In turn, regressions of the four components on prices and wages in total manufacturing, durables manufacturing, and for 19 two-digit manufacturing industries are examined.

Although these regression equations are not structural in the usual sense, they identify channels through which the inflationary process is transmitted. We have suggested earlier that analysis of the on-going inflationary process is as important for designing anti-inflation policy as is understanding its initial causes. Furthermore, in view of the availability of several conflicting but plausible theoretical hypotheses and the high degree of multicollinearity in the potential explanatory set (as evidenced by the few significant eigenvalues in the correlation matrix in our study), the possibility of identifying the actual structure is doubtful.

Some econometricians such as Kendall have argued that structural estimates can be obtained from a factor analysis.[11] Kendall interprets the product of the factor regression coefficient on the kth factor when X_i is the dependent variable and the factor loading on X_j for the kth factor as a structural coefficient for a regression of X_i in X_j.[e] Although this interpretation is somewhat controversial, we used this approach to test our results against other structural models.

The major focus of this study, however, was not to identify structural parameters but to use the components analysis to determine the number and nature of independent dimensions in the set of explanatory variables we used. We drew heavily from other empirical studies in an effort to encompass the full potential explanatory set. Then, once these dimensions were isolated, we determined how much of the variance in our dependent variables was accounted for by each component. There is no attempt to test causal hypotheses, although our results might be used to support certain a priori views, but only to identify the channels through which the inflationary process was transmitted in U.S. manufacturing industries between 1953 and 1970.

Notes

1. George Perry, *Unemployment, Money Wage Rates, and Inflation* (Cambridge, Mass.: The M.I.T. Press, 1966), pp. 49-51.

2. Otto Eckstein and Gary Fromm, "The Price Equation," *The American Economic Review*, 58 (December 1968), pp. 1177-1179.

3. Robert J. Gordon, "Wage-Price Controls and the Shifting Phillips Curve," *Brookings Papers on Economic Activity* (1972:2), pp. 385-421.

4. George L. Perry, "Changing Labor Markets and Inflation," *Brookings Papers on Economic Activity* (1970:3), pp. 411-41.

5. Otto Eckstein and Roger Brinner, *The Inflation Process in the United States*, A study prepared for the use of the Joint Economic Committee, 92d Cong. 2d Sess. (1972).

6. Robert J. Gordon, "Inflation in Recession and Recovery," *Brookings Papers on Economic Activity* (1971:1), pp. 105-58.

7. Op. cit., *Brookings Papers*, 1972.

8. For example, see Irma Adelman and Cynthia Taft Morris, *Society, Politics, and Economic Development* (Baltimore: Johns Hopkins Press, 1967).

9. H.H. Harman, *Modern Factor Analysis* (Chicago: University of Chicago Press, 1960), p. 363.

10. Op. cit., pp. 145-47.

11. Maurice Kendall, *A Course in Multivariate Analysis* (New York: Hafner Publishing Company, 1961), pp. 71-75.

---

[e]The kth factor is selected to maximize the structural regression coefficient.

3

The Data, Variable Transformations, and Alternative Samples

Although the components analysis permits us to incorporate an unlimited number of variables, we included only those variables with some a priori relationship to the behavior of prices and wages. Our data set for the two-digit industries was further limited by the nonavailability of certain variables at that level of disaggregation. In this chapter we shall discuss the data and the various transformations we analyzed. In addition, we shall describe the different lag specifications for our price regression equations and the alternative sample periods for estimation.

Variables

One focus of our study is to locate the independent dimensions of variation in the potential explanatory set. Consequently, we borrowed heavily from other studies of inflation to examine the interrelationships between variables used to support alternative hypotheses about the structural determinants of price and wage behavior. For instance, we incorporated the standard unit labor cost (*SULC*) and inventory disequilibrium variables of the Eckstein and Fromm study,[1] the direction of unemployment dummy from Perry's early work,[2] and labor force composition variables from Perry's later analysis.[3]

There were 82 variables in the components analysis for total manufacturing, and some of these were entered in different forms. For durable manufacturing and the two-digit industries, we included as many of these 82 as were available. For durables, we sometimes included the total manufacturing variable where a durables variable was unavailable. Similarly, for the two-digit industries we sometimes used total manufacturing or durables (nondurables) variables where appropriate.

Rather than discuss each of the 82 variables, we shall outline the general rationale for including certain groups of variables. A detailed list of the individual variables and their sources is in Appendix A. For the individual industries the variables actually included in the component analysis are listed in Tables B-1 through B-38. The variables analyzed for total manufacturing and durables are listed in Tables 4-1, 4-2, 4-3, and 4-4.

Labor Market Variables

In view of the Phillips-Perry hypothesis that labor market conditions affect wages and prices, we incorporated a number of labor market variables. Although

21

we are primarily interested in labor market conditions in the manufacturing sector, we took into account the possibility that the unemployment situation in other sectors will affect manufacturing due to a spillover effect. Consequently, for total manufacturing and durables as well as at the industry level, we included economy-wide unemployment and labor force participation rates.

As one measure of labor market tightness, we used the unemployment rate in a variety of forms, including the reciprocal specification of the Phillips relationship. Both the industry-specific and economy-wide unemployment rates were entered as levels for all data transformation in addition to being transformed with the other data. For instance, when quarterly percent changes of the data set are analyzed, unemployment rate levels as well as percent changes are included. This is because of the Phillips-Perry hypothesis that rate of change of prices and wages are inversely related to the *level* of the unemployment rate (rather than to its rate of change).

As a test of the hypothesis that labor market conditions affect prices and wages with a lag, we entered the various unemployment rates both current and with a one-quarter lag. Because of the possibility that economic variables behave differently in different phases of the business cycle, we included for both total manufacturing and durables a dummy variable that equals one when the unemployment rate increased from the previous quarter and zero when it decreased. The industry unemployment rates were too volatile from quarter to quarter to use this approach. Consequently, we tried a dummy that would reflect a longer trend in labor market conditions. For each industry we included two dummy variables. The first ($UN \uparrow$) equals one when the unemployment rate for the industry increased for three successive quarters, and the other ($UN \downarrow$) equals one when the unemployment rate for the industry decreased for three successive quarters. Both are zero otherwise.

Perry has suggested that labor force characteristics are important when the unemployment rate is used as a measure of labor market slack. The more women, teenagers, blacks, and inexperienced workers in the labor market, the higher the overall unemployment rate associated with any given rate for white males.[4] Consequently, the composition of the labor force should affect the rate of wage increase associated with any given unemployment rate. In addition to variables reflecting labor force composition, we included such indicators of labor market conditions as accession, quit, and layoff rates in both lagged and unlagged form.

Three different wages variables are included. Average hourly earnings (*AHE*) represents hourly take-home pay of production workers. Average weekly earnings (*AWE*) takes overtime hours into account. Compensation per manhour (*MHC*) includes supplements and fringe benefits paid by the employer and represents hourly labor cost from the point of view of the firm.[a]

---

[a]Manhour compensation is only available for total manufacturing.

Demand Variables

According to the Keynesian view, labor market conditions depend upon the level of product demand. In a real sense, increases in output require additional workers, resulting in an increased demand for labor. The inflationary impact is due in part to rising wages as labor markets tighten. In addition, increasing product demand can be inflationary due to declining marginal factor productivity as firms move along a rising short-run supply curve. We incorporated a number of variables measuring real and money demand both for manufacturing (or for durables or a specific industry) and the whole economy. These include *GNP*, output, and sales. We also used output per manhour as a measure of labor productivity.

The relationship between demand and output capacity is likely to affect the rate of increase in prices. Consequently, we included such variable ratios as new orders to sales, unfilled orders to sales, capacity utilization and output to previous peak output.[b]

Investment can affect prices in a number of ways. As a component of demand, increases in investment should be directly related to price increases. Furthermore, if investment takes place in response to *expected* increases in demand, it should be a leading indicator of price level increases, due to the effect on labor productivity. We included not only actual plant and equipment investment, but also approved capital appropriations for manufacturing. We introduced inventory investment lead one quarter, interpreting it as an expectational variable. Assuming that stock prices reflect expectations about economic conditions we included the Standard and Poors index of 425 industrial stock prices, lead one quarter. For the industries we included inventory investment and the Standard and Poors stock price index for the industry-specific product, both in their concurrent form.[c]

Financial Variables

Keynesian theory suggests that tight credit conditions are deflationary since they tend to restrict demand. However, tight money might be associated with rising prices for several reasons. First, increasing demand for goods and services creates an increased transactions demand for money which may result in a direct

---

[b]Output to previous peak output is a rough measure of excess capacity which is much easier to construct than the standard capacity index. We were interested in investigating its association with the other capacity variables.

[c]We tried variations in the lag structure of some variables in the industry analyses (rather than run multiple analyses of the same data set) in order to test the sensitivity of our results to the lag specification.

relationship between interest rates and demand. In addition, the monetary authorities may be following a tight money policy as an anti-inflationary measure. These types of association are spurious, however, and not inconsistent with the Keynesian view. On the other hand, firms may view higher interest rates (particularly on short-term borrowing) as increased production costs and may mark them up into higher prices.

We included several interest rate variables and unborrowed reserves of Federal Reserve member banks as a measure of credit market slack. The impact of external credit market conditions on price and investment policies of individuals depends also on the cash flow position and leverage of firms. Consequently, we introduced cash flow (retained earnings, depreciation, and inventory valuation adjustment) and the ratio of liabilities (less cash flow) to assets as a measure of leverage.[d]

Prices and Cost Variables

Our principal dependent variable is the wholesale price index, *WPI*. When an appropriate wholesale price index for the major product of a particular industry was not available, we used the indices[e] of output price for those industries that were developed by Otto Eckstein and David Wyss.[5] *WPI* was entered in various runs with different lag patterns to test both the timing of the hypothesized relationship with the factors, as well as the possibility of a distributed lag relationship with the explanatory variables.

One hypothesis about price behavior suggests that rising materials and labor costs are marked up by firms into price increases. For total manufacturing we used an index of materials costs based on the methodology used by Faith Halfter Ando.[6] Her technique uses input weights from the 1963 U.S. input-output table. These weights are applied to the wholesale price indices for the various materials used by each industry to obtain an index of materials cost. For total manufacturing and durables, we also included the wholesale price index for iron and steel both because iron and steel are important inputs for manufacturing and because this industry has been a principal target of anti-inflation policy in the period studied. For the specific industries we used the index of input price developed by Eckstein and Wyss[7] as a measure of materials cost. For industries for which input prices were not available, we used the wholesale price index of the major product used as an input to the industry.[f]

We included the ratio of manhour compensation to manhour productivity as

---

[d]In the durables and industry runs, the leverage variable was entered in inverse form.

[e]Such an index was not available for industry 27, printing and publishing, and, consequently, we have no price equation for that industry.

[f]For instance, the WPI for textiles was used as the materials cost index for apparel, that of lumber and wood for paper and furniture, and that of paper for printing and publishing.

a measure of unit labor cost (*ULC*) for total manufacturing. For durables and the industries, since manhour compensation was not available, we approximated *ULC* by the ratio of average hourly earnings to manhour productivity. Standard unit labor cost (*SULC*) is a twelve-quarter moving average of *ULC* that removes the influence of short-run swings in productivity.

In the accelerationist model, money wages are influenced by the consumer price index as money illusion loses its importance in wage bargains. Consequently, we included the *CPI* in our potential explantory set.

Policy Variables

One of the important aspects of this study is the impact of public policy on price level changes. In addition to federal government purchases and expenditures as a whole, we looked also at the proportion of government expenditures allocated to national defense, in response to the popular notion that our involvement in the Korean and Vietnam wars was responsible for the inflation experienced during the early 1950s and late 1960s. To gauge the impact of the relative size of the public sector we examined the ratio of government purchases to national income.

A measure of the expansiveness of fiscal policy is the full employment surplus. Since inflation is sometimes attributed to deficit financing, we also included the ratio of federal debt to *GNP*.

We incorporated effective tax rates, both personal and corporate as well as tax receipts from these sources. Social security benefits and the effective indirect tax rates were also introduced.

We considered two money supply variables, both excluding (M_1) and including (M_2) time deposits. Because of an expected lag in the effectiveness monetary policy, both were lagged one quarter.[g]

We included two policy dummies. The first is a political dummy that is zero during Republican administrations and one during Democratic administrations. This dummy was entered in concurrent form and also lagged one year to reflect the lag in the effect of changing public policy on the economy. We also entered a dummy to reflect the contribution of the wage-price guidelines. This dummy is zero except for the period 1962:1 to 1966:4, where it is one. Following Perry we implicitly assumed that the guidelines were equally effective in all quarters.[8]

Data Problems

There were basically two types of data problems. The first is that certain series were unavailable for certain industries. For example, we could not obtain the

[g]We experimented with longer (undistributed) lags for the money supply variables, but the one-quarter lag relative to the other explanatory variables produced the most meaningful results.

unemployment rate for six industries (tobacco, paper, petroleum, rubber and plastics, leather, and instruments). In some situations we were able to substitute another series for an unavailable series. For example, we used the output prices of certain basic industries as input prices in others.

The second type of problems related to the series that were available. One such problem was seasonal adjustment of unadjusted series. We adjusted all unadjusted series using the Census Bureau XII Q seasonal adjustment program. Another was that some series were reported in composite form only. For example, there is a single wholesale price index for textile products and apparel and one for apparel only. Consequently we had to construct the *WPI* for textiles by weighting the *WPI* for apparel by the percent of apparel and textile sales attributable to apparel and subtracting the weighted series from the *WPI* for textiles and apparel.

For the index of input price for primary metals we had the opposite problem. Input prices were available for primary ferrous metals and for primary nonferrous metals but not for primary metals. We constructed an index of input price for primary metals by weighting the indices of primary ferrous and primary nonferrous by the percent of sales attributable to each, and then we combined the resulting weighted indices.

Alternative Specifications and Samples

Data Transformations

Initially we analyzed the data in four different transformations—levels, quarterly first differences, quarterly percent change, and percent change over four quarters. The high degree of multicollinearity in the levels data resulted in nearly all variables loading on a single factor, so we omitted this specification for most runs. First differences and quarterly percent change gave nearly the same results, so we selected the percent change specification for our later runs and for presentation in this monograph.

Percent change over four quarters was subject to less-random variation than quarterly percent change, but provided sufficient independent dimensions of variation for distinct factor separation. However, the overlapping of four-quarter price changes is likely to introduce autocorrelation into the regression residuals, which is a problem if the R^2 is relatively low. Thus, it could be argued that quarterly percent change is a more powerful analytical transformation, despite the likelihood that the factor loadings (beta coefficients) and R^2 will be lower. Consequently, we will report our results for both percent change over four quarters and quarterly percent change.

Lag Specifications

The wholesale price index was introduced into the analysis in four different forms. We included the concurrent and lagged form in the same equation and the concurrent and lead in another. In addition, we tried *WPI* alone and WPI_{+1} alone. In other words, we tested both an unlagged and lagged specification of the price equation as well as with and without the lagged dependent variable. Although there is some a priori preference for the dynamic form, we were concerned that a high loading on a single factor could be attributable to the influence of the lagged dependent variable that might reflect the distributed lagged influence of variables associated with other factors.

Because we found our results generally insensitive to the choice of lag specification, the wage equations are in unlagged form without a lagged dependent variable. However, we tested for single-quarter lags by incorporating lagged as well as concurrent unemployment rates in the explanatory set as well as certain expectational variables that might reflect reaction lags.

Variations in the Sample Period

The sample period for total manufacturing was 1953:1 to 1970:4. Data availability forced us to limit our sample for durables to 1959:1 to 1970:4 and for the industries to 1959:1 to 1971:3.

For total manufacturing, we analyzed the components for 9 subsamples of the period 1953:1 to 1970:4.[h] Not only did we want to test the sensitivity of our results to the particular sample selected, but we were interested in whether the explanation of price level changes is different in different economic circumstances.

In addition to the full sample, we analyzed the total manufacturing data with respect to the following time periods and considerations.

1. *1955:1-1970.* This was to omit the influence of the last years of the Korean War.
2. *1953:1-1960:4 and 1961:1-1970:4.* In this case we were interested in determining if price and wage behavior before the Kennedy administration could be explained by different factors from inflation in the sixties. This separation was based on the hypothesis that economic policy as well as the perception of the causes of inflation changed markedly in the Kennedy era.
3. *Democrats and Republicans.* We also divided the sample into years in which Democrats occupied the White House versus years of Republican administra-

[h]We had insufficient observations for a subsample analysis of the disaggregated series.

tions. If Democrats and Republicans have different philosophies of economic policy, price behavior could be different when these policies are employed for stabilization purposes.

4. *Direction of Change in the Unemployment Rate.* This breakdown was designed to ascertain if price behavior is dissimilar in different phases of the cycle.

5. *Relative Change in Prices and Unemployment.* The sample was divided into quarters for which the wholesale price index and the unemployment rate for manufacturing were moving in the same direction and those in which they were moving in opposite directions. The first group comprised situations in which a cost-push theory of inflation would be most applicable on an a priori basis. The latter group might be expected to exhibit demand-pull characteristics. However, it is important to keep in mind that this interpretation of these samples is somewhat oversimplified because of the possibility of lags in the response of prices to changes in demand.

In the next chapter we shall discuss the results of our analyses of total manufacturing and durables. In Chapter 5 the industry results are presented.

Notes

1. Otto Eckstein and Gary Fromm, "The Price Equation," *The American Economic Review*, 58 (December 1968), pp. 1159-83.

2. George L. Perry, *Unemployment, Money Wage Rates, and Inflation* (Cambridge, Mass.: The M.I.T. Press, 1966).

3. George L. Perry, "Changing Labor Markets and Inflation," *Brookings Papers on Economic Activity* (1970:3), pp. 411-41.

4. Ibid.

5. Otto Eckstein and David Wyss, "Industry Price Equations," *Conference on the Econometrics of Price Determination*, Washington, D.C., 30-31 October 1970.

6. Faith Halfter Ando, *The Cyclical Behavior of Materials Prices in United States Industry*, Unpublished doctoral dissertation, Harvard University, 1966.

7. Eckstein and Wyss, "Industry Price Equations," op. cit.

8. George L. Perry, *Unemployment, Money Wage Rates, and Inflation*, op. cit.

Results for Total Manufacturing and Durables

For both total manufacturing and durables the set of 82 variables was reduced to four principal components that were rotated by the orthogonal varimax criterion to obtain the factor loadings in Tables 4-1, 4-2, 4-3, and 4-4. Although additional components would have contributed significantly to the explained variance of the original set of variables, we could attach no meaningful economic interpretation to them and consequently omitted them from the analysis.

In this chapter we shall discuss the principal components for the manufacturing and durables data. This discussion will be followed by a description of the factor regression equations for the price and wage variables. In addition, we shall evaluate the impact of the policy variables contained in the original explanatory set.

The Factors and Their Interpretation

We have used the principal components of the data set as factors in an analysis of changes in wholesale prices and three wage variables—average weekly earnings (AWE), average hourly earnings (AHE), and (for total manufacturing only) manhour compensation (MHC).[a] For total manufacturing, the four factors explained over 78 percent of the variance in price changes and over 91 percent of the variance in AWE. For durables, they accounted for 95 percent of the variance in the WPI and 93 percent of the variance in AWE in the PCH/4 data transformation. Although the coefficients of multiple determination (R^2) are somewhat lower for the PCH specification (for instance $R^2 = .834$ for durables prices), the four-factor model is clearly powerful for explaining the variance in the dependent variables, particularly in view of the fact that the data is in the form of changes rather than levels.

The rotated factor loadings for all the variables in the total manufacturing set are presented in Tables 4-1 and 4-2 for the full sample period 1953:1 to 1970:4 for the PCH and PCH/4 data transformations. Tables 4-3 and 4-4 are the rotated factor loadings for durable manufacturing for the period 1959:1 to 1970:4 for the PCH and PCH/4 data transformations. For each variable, the percentage of its variance explained by the linear influence of the four factors is provided in the R^2 column. The variance added by each factor and the cumulative variance

---

[a]We shall use the terms "principal components" and "factors" interchangeably in this discussion.

TABLE 4-1
Total Manufacturing

Rotated Factor Loadings for the Full Sample (1953:1-1970:4) with the Wholesale
Price Index Current and Lagged-Percent Change over Four Quarters (F-Ratio in Parentheses)[1]

VARIABLE[2]	Factor 1	Factor 2	Factor 3	Factor 4	R^2
WPI	-.110 (3.98)	.220 (15.88)	.847 (236.00)	.074 (1.79)	.784 (85.90)
corporate tax receipts	.963	.000	-.010	.026	.929
layoff rate	.914	.151	.135	-.072	.882
capacity utilization	.907	.367	-.152	-.031	.944
output	.904	.367	-.087	-.031	.960
GNP/potential GNP	.893	.314	-.243	.074	.960
average weekly earnings	.888	.113	.323	.083	.913
sales	.888	.328	.148	.116	.931
profit/equity	.887	.043	-.184	-.229	.876
accession rate (-1)	.873	.216	.041	.173	.841
money GNP	.861	.313	.166	.239	.923
quit rate	.847	.427	.006	.168	.927
$1/UN^2$	.844	.463	-.097	.117	.950
UN	-.840	-.467	.085	-.134	.949
$1/UN$	.833	.463	-.096	.136	.936
layoff rate (-1)	.833	-.323	.063	-.169	.830
accession rate	.822	-.185	-.085	.099	.727
productivity	.796	-.136	-.198	-.017	.692
$1/UN_A$	.775	.540	-.030	.207	.936
output/previous peak	.768	.097	-.090	-.145	.628
approved capital appropriations	.735	.307	-.048	-.306	.730
unit labor cost	-.703	.073	.531	.322	.885
total employment	.683	.651	.008	.241	.948
real GNP	.564	.328	-.032	-.123	.442
M_1 (-1)	.543	.137	.360	.265	.514
M_2 (-1)	.514	-.019	-.260	.447	.532
direction of unemployment	-.486	.395	.088	.052	.403
debt/GNP	-.486	-.193	-.134	-.119	.305
new orders/sales	.427	-.483	-.149	-.256	.504

VARIABLE[2]	Factor 1	Factor 2	Factor 3	Factor 4	R^2
WPI	-.110	.220	.847	.074	.784
	(3.98)	(15.88)	(236.00)	(1.79)	(85.90)
total employment (-1)	.224	.885	.048	.301	.926
investment in P & E	.096	.873	.221	-.076	.826
$1/UN_A$ (-1)	.364	.839	.016	.300	.927
UN_A (-1)	-.436	-.817	.050	-.217	.908
$1/UN^2$ (-1)	.443	.816	-.063	.201	.906
$1/UN$ (-1)	.432	.812	-.063	.226	.900
Federal Reserve discount rate (-1)	-.039	.797	.340	-.049	.754
expected investment in P & E	.506	.779	.270	.008	.681
quit rate (-1)	.442	.776	.065	.239	.920
backlog of capital appropriations	.521	.728	.175	-.242	.814
4-6 month paper rate	.522	.693	.354	-.004	.878
3-6 month paper rate	.358	.670	.327	-.019	.860
percent of labor force ages 16-19	.092	.659	-.023	.050	.565
standard unit labor cost	.303	.639	-.430	.098	.611
unfilled orders/sales	.372	.606	-.100	.330	.578
(liabilities - internal funds)/assets	.388	.596	.241	.425	.728
percent of labor force black	.079	.572	-.104	-.333	.599
labor force participation rate	.247	.419	-.185	-.248	.277
stock price index (+1)		-.408	-.310	-.428	.507
WPI (-1)	-.244	.120	.818	.127	.759
manhour compensation	-.034	-.085	.804	.173	.685
average hourly earnings	.304	.167	.780	.274	.800
iron and steel prices	.017	.164	.768	-.224	.667
bond yield	-.223	.305	.713	.304	.743
$1/UN_{AL}$ (-1)	-.103	.285	.708	.338	.707
$1/UN_{AL}$	-.186	.257	.703	.393	.750
CPI_{AL}	-.264	-.046	.677	.477	.731

TABLE 4-1 (continued)

VARIABLE[2]	Factor 1	Factor 2	Factor 3	Factor 4]	R^2
WPI	-.110 (3.98)	.220 (15.88)	.847 (236.00)	.074 (1.79)	.784 (85.90)
$1/UN_L(-1)$	-.008	.333	.636	.523	.790
materials cost	.120	.261	.623	-.178	.503
$UN_L(-1)$	.010	-.546	-.596	-.406	.818
$1/UN_L$	.277	.267	.584	.563	.805
guidelines	.115	.189	-.554	-.050	.358
UN_L	-.351	-.463	-.549	-.423	.818
political dummy	.170	.120	-.532	.503	.580
government purchases	.118	.162	-.011	.892	.836
government purchases (deflated)	.125	.183	-.196	.875	.854
government purchases/national income	-.408	-.063	-.037	.808	.825
corporate tax rate	-.034	-.132	.384	.658	.598
percent of labor force female	-.063	.215	.037	.587	.396
defense purchases/government expenditures	.204	.386	-.040	.549	.493
lagged political dummy	.246	.290	-.264	.544	.509
personal tax receipts	.441	.354	.276	.500	.645
personal tax rate	.276	.241	.220	.419	.358
variance added	.363	.144	.083	.070	
cumulative variance explained	.363	.507	.590	.660	

[1]Boxes indicate the factor to which the variable has been assigned.

[2]Variables are unassigned (but included in the components analysis) if there is no factor loading above |.39|. The unassigned variables are cash flow, OASI, indirect tax rate, defense purchases/government purchases, full employment surplus, (ULC-SULC), inventory investment (+1), inventory disequilibrium.

TABLE 4-2
Total Manufacturing

Rotated Factor Loadings for the Full Sample (1953:1-1970:4) with the
Wholesale Price Index Current and Lagged-Quarterly Percent Change (F-Ratio in Parentheses)[1]

VARIABLE[2]	Factor 1	Factor 2	Factor 3	Factor 4	R^2
WPI	-.058 (0.72)	.208 (9.31)	.789 (134.00)	-.024 (0.12)	.670 (48.05)
capacity utilization	.911	.286	-.044	-.114	.926
output	.904	.336	-.010	-.096	.940
GNP/potential GNP	.886	.316	-.139	.062	.907
money GNP	.872	.285	.154	.117	.879
corporate tax receipts	.871	.066	.043	-.090	.774
sales	.862	.264	.140	-.001	.831
layoff rate	-.831	.179	.066	-.083	.734
average weekly earnings	.788	.048	.249	.162	.711
1/UN	.764	.448	.002	.025	.785
1/UN²	.736	.529	-.030	.005	.822
UN	-.736	-.528	.027	-.007	.822
unit labor cost	-.730	.012	.207	.345	.741
accession rate (-1)	.701	.279	.028	.171	.599
output/previous peak	.679	.020	.049	-.084	.471
1/UN$_A$	.670	.607	-.023	.111	.830
accession rate	.596	-.163	-.087	.159	.415
profit/equity	.589	-.046	-.017	-.096	.358
direction of unemployment	-.578	.196	.055	.087	.383
productivity	.566	-.063	-.124	-.064	.344
approved capital appropriations	.450	.323	-.074	-.109	.324
real GNP	.434	.294	-.072	-.122	.295
(ULC-SULC)	.428	-.217	-.013	-.056	.234
M_1 (-1)	.417	.177	.268	.296	.365

TABLE 4-2 (continued)

VARIABLE[2]	Factor 1	Factor 2	Factor 3	Factor 4	R^2
WPI	-.058 (0.72)	.208 (9.31)	.789 (134.00)	-.024 (0.12)	.670 (48.05)
M_2 (-1)	.415	-.048	-.142	.427	.377
$1/UN_A$	.098	.872	-.017	.283	.850
$1/UN^2$ (-1)	.018	.866	-.079	.244	.828
UN (-1)	-.108	-.866	-.077	-.251	.831
1/UN (-1)	.163	.829	-.067	.201	.759
investment in P & E	.045	.727	.255	-.150	.604
backlog of capital appropriations	.305	.709	.118	-.085	.616
4-6 month paper rate	.391	.626	.329	.024	.654
Federal Reserve discount rate (-1)	-.203	.620	.246	-.074	.492
3-6 month paper rate	.414	.609	.309	-.058	.641
total employment	.580	.601	.038	.036	.699
standard unit labor cost	-.018	.592	-.344	-.120	.483
expected investment in P & E	.004	.573	.211	-.149	.395
percent of labor force ages 16-19	.132	.503	.004	.063	.274
unfilled orders/sales	-.021	.475	.046	.328	.336
layoff rate (-1)	-.425	-.437	.171	-.147	.423
$1/UN_{AL}$	.169	.309	.784	.175	.769
$1/UN_{AL}$ (-1)	.398	.098	.777	.103	.782
$1/UN_L$ (-1)	.344	.174	.768	.309	.833
$1/UN_L$	.060	.354	.759	.345	.824
UN_L (-1)	-.435	-.247	.722	-.276	.849
UN_L	-.128	.515	.708	-.290	.867
manhour compensation	.159	-.146	.677	.036	.506
CPI	-.269	-.102	.659	.307	.611
WPI(-1)	-.245	.039	.639	.077	.475
bond yield	.383	.289	.560	.062	.549
average hourly earnings	.404	.030	.542	.248	.519

VARIABLE[2]	Factor 1	Factor 2	Factor 3	Factor 4	R^2
WPI	-.058 (0.72)	.208 (9.31)	.789 (134.00)	-.024 (0.12)	.670 (48.05)
guidelines	.059	.192	-.502	.075	.298
iron & steel prices	.064	.166	.495	-.171	.306
material costs	.142	.223	.411	-.081	.245
government purchases	.079	.214	-.017	.728	.582
government purchases (deflated)	.077	.261	-.150	.693	.577
government purchases/national income	-.476	-.017	-.066	.663	.670
political dummy	.247	.142	-.363	.491	.454
lagged political dummy	.041	.288	-.138	.468	.323
(liabilities-internal funds)/assets	.186	.384	.271	.423	.435
personal tax rate	.070	.155	.098	.422	.217
variance added	.242	.107	.062	.051	
cumulative variance explained	.242	.349	.412	.463	

[1] Boxes indicate the factor to which the variable has been assigned.

[2] Variables are unassigned (but included in the components analysis) if there is no factor loading above |.39|. The unassigned variables are percent of labor force black, percent of labor force female, quit rate, labor force participation rate, cash flow, new orders/sales, unborrowed reserves, OASI, corporate tax rate, personal tax receipts, defense purchases/government purchases, defense purchases/government expenditures, full employment surplus, debt/GNP, inventory investment (+1), stock price index (+1), inventory disequilibrium, quit rate (-1).

TABLE 4-3
Durable Manufacturing

Rotated Factor Loadings for the Full Sample (1959: 1-1970:4) with the Wholesale
Price Index Current and Lagged-Percent Change over Four Quarters (F-ratio in Parenthesis)[1]

VARIABLE[2]	Factor 1	Factor 2	Factor 3	Factor 4	R^2
WPI	-.009 (0.10)	-.054 (4.04)	.973 (1290.48)	-.033 (1.49)	.951 (432.04)
profit/equity	.952	.074	-.141	-.004	.933
capacity utilization	.930	-.196	-.208	-.069	.952
corporate tax receipts	.928	-.049	.051	.124	.882
sales	.914	-.209	.142	.064	.903
output	.908	-.293	-.104	.177	.952
inventory/sales	-.891	-.187	.119	.338	.957
GNP/potential GNP	.873	-.275	-.233	.233	.947
layoff rate	-.872	-.293	.162	-.169	.901
AWE	.872	.126	.379	-.080	.925
quit rate	.868	-.356	.037	.238	.938
accession rate (-1)	.860	-.087	.114	.110	.772
UN	-.851	.399	.161	-.120	.923
approved capital appropriations	.778	-.193	.049	-.089	.659
productivity	.790	.345	-.132	.340	.877
money GNP	.774	-.253	.402	.292	.922
ULC	-.781	-.394	.266	-.264	.924
accession rate	.756	.164	-.012	.214	.648
1/UNA	.756	-.519	-.105	.289	.935
layoff rate (-1)	-.733	.217	.072	-.183	.623
output/previous peak	.729	.144	-.185	-.186	.621
labor force participation rate	.708	-.544	-.062	.370	.938
total employment	.689	-.605	.010	.350	.962
3-6 month paper rate	.649	-.491	.347	-.163	.809
4-6 month paper rate	.607	-.546	.393	-.131	.838
direction of unemployment	-.584	-.192	.194	-.253	.479
stock/price index	.574	.293	-.245	.021	.476
M_2 (-1)	.572	.034	.113	.515	.607
(ULC-SULC)	-.417	.164	-.187	.006	.236

VARIABLE[2]	Factor 1	Factor 2	Factor 3	Factor 4	R^2
WPI	-.009 (0.10)	-.054 (4.04)	.973 (1290.48)	-.033 (1.49)	.951 (432.04)
investment in P & E	.004	-.926	.014	-.017	.861
total employment (-1)	.156	-.888	.027	.379	.958
expected investment in P & E	-.132	-.838	.051	.180	.755
$1/UN_A$ (-1)	.301	-.829	-.070	.309	.878
discount rate (-1)	.054	-.798	.237	-.197	.735
UN (-1)	-.436	-.772	.151	-.152	.832
quit rate (-1)	.504	-.771	.071	.248	.915
backlog of capital appropriations	.404	-.707	.097	-.067	.676
percent of labor force 16-19	.413	-.617	-.005	.049	.630
percent of labor force black	.423	-.596	-.222	-.209	.628
new orders/sales	-.437	-.532	-.149	-.019	.496
real GNP	.474	-.526	.078	-.155	.532
WPI (-1)	-.132	-.158	.943	-.080	.938
CPI	-.378	.038	.886	-.022	.930
AHE	-.162	.254	.882	-.068	.873
bond yield	.125	-.123	.826	.043	.714
steel price index	-.124	.156	.819	-.359	.840
$1/UN_{AL}$ (-1)	-.153	-.236	.810	.419	.910
M_1 (-1)	.415	-.082	.768	.172	.798
$1/UN_{AL}$	.052	-.236	.765	.506	.900
(liabilities-internal funds)/assets	.183	.574	-.632	-.235	.818
UN_L (-1)	.095	.506	-.621	-.411	.819
UN_L	-.253	.421	-.589	-.457	.798
guidelines	.196	-.106	-.540	-.146	.363
government purchases	.075	.170	.009	.904	.852
OASI	.158	.110	-.229	.897	.892
defense/government expenditures	.190	-.226	-.063	.805	.740
SULC	-.086	.189	-.016	-.780	.652

TABLE 4-3 (continued)

VARIABLE[2]	Factor 1	Factor 2	Factor 3	Factor 4	R^2
WPI	-.009 (0.10)	-.054 (4.04)	.973 (1290.48)	-.033 (1.49)	.951 (432.04)
lagged political dummy	.214	.051	.186	.692	.561
political dummy	.134	.125	-.421	.666	.654
percent of labor force female	-.135	-.371	.201	.659	.630
defense/government purchases	-.125	-.234	.310	.560	.480
unfilled orders/sales	-.189	-.350	.025	.536	.446
indirect tax rate	-.364	.179	-.048	-.532	.450
unborrowed reserves	.175	.111	-.470	.479	.493
government purchases (deflated)	.211	-.258	.346	.477	.458
personal tax rate	.102	-.241	.242	.414	.298
variance added	.322	.101	.171	.088	
cumulative variance explained	.322	.423	.594	.682	

[1]Boxes indicate the factor to which the variable has been assigned.

[2]Variables are unassigned (but included in the components analysis) if there is no factor loading above |.39|. The unassigned variables are inventory disequilibrium, inventory investment, corporate tax rate, full employment surplus, debt/GNP, personal tax receipts.

TABLE 4-4
Durable Manufacturing

Rotated Factor Loadings for the Full Sample (1959:1-1970:4) with the Wholesale Price Index Current and Lagged-Quarterly Percent Change (F-ratio in parentheses)[1]

VARIABLE[2]	Factor 1	Factor 2	Factor 3	Factor 4	R^2
WPI	-.068 (1.89)	-.055 (1.24)	.903 (334.02)	-.108 (4.78)	.834 (113.88)
sales	-.953	.055	.121	.093	.934
capacity utilization	-.939	.190	-.149	.044	.941
output	-.938	.192	-.033	.172	.948
inventory/sales	.909	.220	.142	.073	.901
corporate tax receipts	-.904	.006	-.022	.184	.852
productivity	-.898	.136	.046	.149	.849
profit/equity	-.896	-.047	-.121	.176	.851
AWE	-.873	-.107	.235	.040	.830
ULC	.861	-.269	.133	-.196	.869
GNP/potential GNP	-.827	-.306	-.179	.295	.896
UN	.820	-.434	.108	-.112	.885
labor force participation rate	-.761	.511	.018	.238	.897
total employment	-.755	.561	.074	.228	.942
$1/UN_A$	-.704	.566	-.086	.257	.889
layoff rate	.679	.318	.085	-.269	.641
output/previous peak	-.667	.131	-.092	-.051	.474
direction of unemployment	.605	-.110	.091	-.335	.499
inventory investment	-.546	.079	-.018	-.291	.389
unfilled orders/sales	.490	.386	.035	.412	.560
percent labor force 16-19	-.482	.475	.017	-.063	.462
percent labor force black	-.450	.477	-.129	-.150	.442
capital appropriations	-.416	.244	-.036	.205	.276
total employment (-1)	-.269	.854	.090	.124	.826
$1/UN_A$ (-1)	-.263	.838	-.037	.178	.804
UN (-1)	.280	-.808	.120	-.079	.752
investment in P & E	-.321	.673	.125	-.057	.574

TABLE 4-4 (continued)

VARIABLE[2]	Factor 1	Factor 2	Factor 3	Factor 4	R^2
WPI	-.068 (1.89)	-.055 (1.24)	.903 (334.02)	-.108 (4.78)	.834 (113.88)
percent of labor force female	.205	.602	.105	.161	.441
backlog of capital appropriations	-.377	.568	.120	.156	.503
4-6 month paper rate	-.459	.555	.356	-.108	.657
quit rate (-1)	.180	.553	-.019	.011	.338
discount rate (-1)	-.382	.531	.202	-.320	.571
3-6 month paper rate	-.464	.528	.297	-.127	.599
expected investment in P & E	-.107	.488	.185	-.155	.308
real GNP	-.367	.467	.059	-.005	.356
$1/UN_{AL}$ (-1)	.229	.076	.892	.722	.909
CPI	.281	-.169	.890	-.123	.915
$1/UN_{AL}$	.028	.164	.869	.336	.896
WPI $_{AL}$ (-1)	.031	.059	.865	-.240	.811
AHE	-.167	-.415	.759	-.186	.811
UN_L (-1)	-.253	-.267	-.746	-.378	.835
UN_L	.138	-.333	-.737	-.412	.843
steel price index	.133	-.291	.722	-.284	.704
bond yield	-.124	.181	.719	-.110	.577
M_1 (-1)	-.240	.052	.626	.316	.552
(liabilities-internal funds)/assets	.058	-.424	-.602	.099	.556
guidelines dummy	-.099	.083	-.493	.202	.300
SULC	.151	-.156	-.130	-.842	.774
political dummy	-.175	-.028	-.228	.824	.763
lagged political dummy	-.142	.145	.234	.721	.616
government purchases	.038	.051	.053	.681	.470
M_2 (-1)	-.256	-.026	.094	.648	.494
defense/government expenditures	-.071	.393	.002	.550	.463
indirect tax rate	.167	-.176	-.042	-.529	.340

41

VARIABLE[2]	Factor 1	Factor 2	Factor 3	Factor 4	R^2
WPI	-.068 (1.89)	-.055 (1.24)	.903 (334.02)	-.108 (4.78)	.834 (113.88)
variance added	.262	.087	.136	.070	
cumulative variance explained	.262	.349	.485	.555	

[1]Boxes indicate the factor to which the variable has been assigned.

[2]Variables are unassigned (but included in the components analysis) if there is no factor loading above |.39|. The unassigned variables are accession rate, quit rate, layoff rate (-1), inventory disequilibrium, money GNP, new orders/sales, stock price index, unborrowed reserves, OASI, (ULC-SULC), personal tax receipts, corporate tax rate, personal tax rate, defense/government purchases, government purchases (deflated), full employment surplus.

of the variable set explained by the four factors is given in the last two rows of each table.

One of the most interesting findings is the striking degree of factor separation, even for the PCH/4 transformation. In most cases, the variables associate distinctly with a single factor, and variables could be unambiguously assigned to the factor with the dominant loading. For those few variables with two factor loadings of about equal magnitude, such as $M_2(-1)$ for the PCH manufacturing set, assignment is on the basis of a priori expectation as well as consistency with other data transformations. Variables with no loadings above $|.39|$ are unassigned.

Since the factors are mathematical constructs, they must be interpreted in terms of the variables associated with them. Furthermore, in evaluating the relationship between a particular variable and a factor, it must be kept in mind that the signs of the factors are arbitrary. For instance, Factor 2 of the PCH/4 durables set is a negative factor, in the sense that the variables assigned to it all have negative factor loadings. This means the *WPI* (which also has a negative factor loading), is positively associated with the variables on this factor. We shall discuss each factor briefly in turn.

Factor One (F_1) can be interpreted as a general measure of the level of economic activity and labor market conditions. It includes the unlagged labor market variables (and the lagged layoff and accession rates) as well as the product market variables (except investment). It is interesting to note that product market variables are associated with current labor market conditions, indicating that product market conditions influence the labor market without a lag.

F_1 also includes two cost variables, average weekly earnings and unit labor cost. Of the three wage variables, *AWE* is the most likely to be associated with changes in product demand, since it reflects the influence of overtime hours. Unit labor cost has a negative sign, which is opposite from a priori expectation. Apparently this variable is dominated by swings in manhour productivity, which is positively correlated with F_1. Increasing economic activity is associated with rising manhour productivity. Since manhour compensation is unrelated to F_1, this implies falling unit labor costs when economic activity increases.[b]

For PCH/4 durables, some of the financial variables are jointly associated with F_1 and F_2. However, in PCH durables and in all the manufacturing runs (including subsamples), the financial variables are associated with F_2. The industry results also suggest that financial variables are generally associated with the variables in F_2. Because the durable goods industries are more concentrated on the average than total manufacturing, it is possible that changes in credit

---

[b]We shall see, however, that unit labor costs are also (but more weakly) associated with the cost factor, with the correct sign.

conditions are internalized by firms and affect product markets more quickly than in those industries where production decisions are more dispersed.[c]

Factor Two (F_2) includes the employment and unemployment variables lagged one quarter, plant and equipment investment, and the financial variables. Standard unit labor cost for total manufacturing (but not for durables) was also associated with this factor, perhaps because of the lag built in to the averaging process. The labor force composition variables for youth and blacks as well as the labor force participation rate (reflecting the change in the influx of inexperienced workers) also appear on this factor, suggesting that the effect of labor force composition on the wage-price-unemployment relationship may occur with a lag.

The major difference between F_1 and F_2 is the stronger association of the lagged variables and expectational indicators with F_2. This implies that the relationship between F_1 and F_2 is a one-quarter lag, although both can be interpreted as representing demand and labor market conditions.

It is interesting to note that F_2 is a weaker factor for durables than total manufacturing in terms of the explained variance in the original variable set. This may be because the greater diversity of the manufacturing industries relative to durables introduces longer structural lags into the relationship between variables aggregated across firms and industries. The differences between total manufacturing and durables are not very great so that the point should not be overemphasized. However, the industry results presented in Chapter 5 support the hypothesis that lags become less important at higher levels of disaggregation.

Factor Three (F_3) is associated with the price and cost variables and unemployment rate levels. The only wage variable not loading on this factor is average weekly earnings. Thus, the factor is dominated by wages (and the consumer price index which influences wages) and materials costs (including steel).

The negative association of unemployment rate levels with the cost variables implies a Phillips relationship,[d] but the high coefficient on the *CPI* suggests some (but not total) absence of money illusion in wage bargains.[e] What is most interesting, however, is that F_3 is independent of the factors reflecting changes in the level of economic activity. Furthermore, it is the unemployment rates

---

[c]The simultaneity in the relationship between product market activity and the financial variables must also be taken into account in this connection.

[d]This relationship exists even when the unemployment rates are not corrected for changes in the demographic composition of the labor force. Such changes appear to be associated with the level of economic activity, which does not affect the association of variables in F_3.

[e]The statistical interaction between the *CPI* and the unemployment rate levels that causes them to be associated with the same component explains why traditional wage equations are so difficult to specify. Although the collinearity problem could be overcome by using changes in unemployment rates to explain wage changes, our findings indicate that the explanatory power of unemployment rate changes would be very weak, biasing the results in favor of an accelerationist structure.

themselves rather than changes in those rates which are most closely associated with changes in money wages and wholesale and consumer prices.[f]

Unit labor cost is more strongly associated with F_3 for total manufacturing than for durables. However, despite a significant positive association with F_3, ULC is clearly more closely related to product and labor market conditions because of the dominance of the productivity effect. This is interesting in assessing the direction of the relationship between the cost and price variables associated with F_3.[g] We shall return to this point in our discussion of the regression results.

The substantial negative influence of the guidelines suggests that their impact was felt in the price-cost interaction. The negative relationship of F_3 with the political dummies is also interesting.

Associated with *Factor Four* (F_4) are most of the policy variables. These include the various specifications of government purchases and the tax variables (except corporate tax receipts that are highly sensitive to swings in the level of business activity). It also includes the political dummy in lagged and concurrent form (both with positive sign). Money supply with time deposits is also associated with this factor.

Standard unit labor cost is strongly associated with F_4 for durables, but not for total manufacturing. Since this relationship is also present in the industry analyses, it is worthy of some interpretation. If the variables associated with F_4 are less volatile cyclically than others in the set, then it is not surprising that SULC which is a 12-quarter moving average of ULC should be correlated with F_4. For total manufacturing, on the other hand, F_4 is not likely to be much less volatile than the other factors. This is because public policy measures generally reflect reactions to economy-wide changes, of which the manufacturing sector is a substantial component.

In both cases, however, it is interesting to note that the factor reflecting the activities of the public sector is independent of factors associated with activities in the private sector. Perhaps this is due to coincidence of timing together with differences in effectiveness lags. In fact, we found that for subsample periods with more homogeneous economic and political conditions, F_4 collapsed into the other factors, suggesting some consistency in effectiveness lags for such periods.

---

[f]Since unemployment rates are correlated with the level of economic activity, demand *level* would undoubtedly also have been associated with F_3. This implies that the dynamic interaction between wage and price *changes* is influenced by the level, but not the rate of change, of economic activity. Traditional structural models transform all the explanatory variables in the same way as prices and wages are transformed,[1] except for unemployment rates, which are sometimes introduced as levels even when the other variables are expressed as changes.[2]

[g]SULC is negatively related to F_3 in all cases.

Interpretation of Factor Loadings

Initially, we treated the wholesale price index as the variable to be explained by the common factors. However, the explanation of other variables in the set by the factors is also relevant to the model of price determination. Consequently, we shall discuss in some detail the results of the wage equations, that is, the wage variables as linear functions of the factors.

Other variables may also be of interest as dependent variables in a factor regression equation for this data set. The factor loadings in Tables 4-1, 4-2, 4-3, and 4-4 can be interpreted as the factor regression coefficients for the variables. The R^2 is provided for each factor regression equation.

The Price Equation—Total Manufacturing

The four factors accounted for 78.4 percent of the variance in the wholesale price index for PCH/4 and 67.0 percent for the PCH transformation. By far the largest proportion of the variance in the *WPI* was explained by F_3, the cost and unemployment levels factor. For instance, for PCH/4, 71.8 percent of the total variance and 91.6 percent of the explained variance (communality) is attributable to F_3. F_2 accounts for 4.8 percent of the total variance and 6.2 percent of the explained variance and is the only other factor significant at the 95 percent level. F_1 is nearly significant for PCH/4, and has a negative sign, suggesting a weak tendency for compensatory pricing in the short run. However, the overall effect of the level of economic activity on prices is weak and with a lag.

These results suggest that cost-price interaction, dampened by the effect of the unemployment rate, was the most important factor in explaining quarterly changes in wholesale prices for manufacturing in the period 1953:1 to 1970:4. Although less important than the cost factor, F_2 was significant at the 95 percent level with a positive sign. Since F_2 can be interpreted as a lagged demand factor, this may imply that the effect of demand on the *WPI* has a longer lag than the effect of costs. Clearly, however, in percentage terms, the influence of demand, even when lags are accounted for, is considerably weaker than the effect of the cost factor.

The policy factor, F_4, was insignificant for explaining changes in the *WPI*. Perhaps this implies that some aspects of public policy are destabilizing and others are stabilizing and that the two effects nearly cancel each other out. In any event, it should not be inferred that stabilization policy is ineffective. The role of the public sector is generally complementary to the private sector and hence would most likely be destabilizing in the absence of countercyclical action.

Alternative Specifications

The results for the unlagged (*WPI* concurrent) and lagged (*WPI* lead one quarter) specifications both with and without the lagged dependent variable are shown in Tables 4-5 and 4-6. Since the coefficients are not very sensitive to the exclusion of the lagged dependent variable, we conclude that the structural lags are accounted for in the model specification. This suggests that the effect of lags after one or two quarters is not very great, and that the wage-price interaction occurs nearly instantaneously.

In addition to testing for lags by use of the lagged dependent variable, we tried two different undistributed lag patterns for the *WPI* in relation to the remaining set. The effect of leading *WPI* was barely noticeable.

The fact that the unlagged relationship (with concurrent *WPI* as the dependent variable) gives better results in terms of the R^2 than the lagged relationship (with WPI_{+1} as the dependent variable) deserves some comment. First, as noted by Eckstein and Fromm,[3] the wholesale price index is developed from list prices rather than transactions prices. Since in some industries, changes in list prices ratify earlier changes in transactions prices, a lag may be built into the model, even when concurrent values are used.

In addition, it is well known that there is a simultaneity in the relationship between the variables in F_3, particularly the *WPI*, the consumer price index and the wage variables. Consequently, we would expect a higher correlation for the unlagged *WPI*. It is noteworthy, however, that the introduction of a lag does not affect the overwhelming importance of F_3 for the explanation of price level changes.

Finally, the marginal importance of F_2 suggests that some lagged variables are significant determinants of changes in *WPI*. In the lagged specification, F_1 attains a positive sign (but remains insignificant) while the percentage of the variance explained by F_2 declines and becomes insignificant in one case.

Our results strongly support the evidence that costs, dampened by unemployment rates, were the most important factor in explaining quarterly changes in wholesale prices for total manufacturing in the period 1953:1 to 1970:4. The relationship remains invariant to the form of the data, the lag structure selected, or whether the lagged dependent variable is included. F_1 either has a negative sign or is statistically insignificant. F_4, the policy variable, is also insignificant.

Variations in the Sample Period

We examined the components of the full sample for 10 different time periods, in order to test the sensitivity of our results to the particular sample we have selected, and also to investigate whether the explanation of price level changes is different in different economic circumstances. The factor loadings for *WPI*

TABLE 4-5
Total Manufacturing

Factor Loadings for the Wholesale Price Index for Alternative Samples and
Specifications—Percent Change over Four Quarters (F-ratio in Parentheses)[1]

	Factor 1	Factor 2	Factor 3	Factor 4	R^2
1953:1 - 1970:4					
1. Includes WPI_{-1}	-.110 (3.98)	.220 (15.88)	.847 (236.00)	.074 (1.79)	.784 (85.90)
2. Excludes WPI_{-1}	-.145 (5.03)	.331 (26.22)	.758 (137.73)	.057 (0.78)	.708 (56.58)
3. Dependent variable WPI_{+1}; includes WPI	.044 (0.44)	.226 (11.69)	.796 (144.57)	.056 (0.71)	.689 (52.43)
4. Dependent variable WPI_{+1}; excludes WPI	.035 (0.24)	.242 (11.47)	.759 (113.16)	.084 (1.39)	.643 (42.08)
Other samples (all use WPI as dependent variable and include WPI_{-1})					
5. 1955:1 - 1970:4	-.209 (21.10)	.252 (30.70)	.858 (355.94)	-.092 (4.12)	.858 (137.33)
6. 1953:1 - 1960:4	-.198 (7.49)	.443 (37.58)	.110 (2.32)	**	.639 (40.71)
7. 1961:1 - 1970:4	-.132 (18.27)	.169 (29.71)	.941 (924.62)	.032 (1.04)	.932 (324.37)
8. Democratic presidents	.252 (34.30)	*	.702 (265.51)	***	.870 (156.15)
9. Republican presidents	-.174 (13.99)	.168 (13.06)	.888 (362.56)	-.056 (1.44)	.850 (130.33)

TABLE 4-5 (continued)

	Factor 1	Factor 2	Factor 3	Factor 4	R^2
10. Unemployment rate increasing	-.034 (0.44)	*	.889 (300.81)	-.151 (8.72)	.816 (103.48)
11. Unemployment rate decreasing	-.094 (2.03)	.436 (43.70)	.697 (111.63)	.099 (2.25)	.695 (53.17)
12. $\dfrac{dWPI}{dUN} > 0$	.231 (20.48)	*	.866 (287.76)	-.088 (3.00)	.815 (102.79)
13. $\dfrac{dWPI}{dUN} < 0$	-.187 (11.87)	.130 (5.77)	.859 (250.71)	.039 (0.53)	.791 (89.57)

---

[1] F = 4 represents the 95% significance level.

* Factor 2 collapsed into Factor 1 in this sample.

** Factor 4 collapsed into Factor 3 in this sample. WPI loaded on an independent factor with a loading of -.625.

*** In this sample Factor 4 collapsed into Factor 3 but the cost factor split into two components. The square root of the sum of squares of the loadings on these two components is provided as the loading for Factor 3.

TABLE 4-6
Total Manufacturing

Factor Loadings for the Wholesale Price Index for Alternative
Samples and Specifications - Quarterly Percent Change (F-ratio in Parentheses)[1]

	Factor 1	Factor 2	Factor 3	Factor 4	R^2
1953:1-1970:4					
1. Includes WPI_{-1}	-.058 (0.72)	.208 (9.31)	.789 (134.00)	-.024 (0.12)	.670 (48.05)
2. Excludes WPI_{-1}	-.073 (1.10)	.202 (8.51)	.787 (129.36)	-.006 (0.01)	.665 (11.75)
3. Dependent variable WPI_{+1}; includes WPI	.050 (0.36)	.158 (3.64)	.688 (69.27)	.123 (2.20)	.515 (25.13)
4. Dependent variable WPI_{+1}; excludes WPI	.057 (0.50)	.202 (6.18)	.696 (73.77)	-.108 (1.76)	.540 (27.39)
Other samples (all use WPI as dependent variable and include WPI_{-1})					
5. 1955:1 - 1970:4	-.060 (0.80)	.147 (4.84)	.810 (146.49)	.030 (0.21)	.682 (50.76)
6. 1953:1 - 1960:4	.124 (2.33)	.069 (0.72)	.721 (78.48)	-.055 (0.45)	.543 (27.33)
7. 1961:1 - 1970:4	-.257 (23.41)	.182 (11.71)	.822 (238.80)	*	.799 (94.08)
8. Democratic presidents	-.074 (1.08)	.416 (33.75)	.637 (79.01)	-.240 (11.21)	.641 (41.66)
9. Republican presidents	.008 (0.02)	.103 (2.62)	.835 (171.95)	-.109 (2.96)	.720 (59.14)

TABLE 4-6 (continued)

	Factor 1	Factor 2	Factor 3	Factor 4	R^2
10. Unemployment rate increasing	-.028 (0.12)	**	.673 (73.60)	***	.569 (30.80)
11. Unemployment rate decreasing	.134 (3.12)	**	.673 (78.38)	-.033 (0.19)	.595 (34.28)
12. $\dfrac{dWPI}{dUN} > 0$	-.400 (27.78)	.399 (27.57)	.521 (47.08)	.027 (0.12)	.591 (34.20)
13. $\dfrac{dWPI}{dUN} < 0$	.387 (25.47)	-.232 (9.17)	.464 (36.56)	.404 (27.75)	.582 (32.95)

---

[1] F = 4 represents the 95% significance level.

* Factor 4 collapsed into the other factors, associating weakly with Factor 2. The R^2 for all the policy variables were very low for this sample.

** Factor 2 collapsed into Factor 1 in this sample, with output variables loading on a separate component.

*** Factor 4 collapsed into the other factors.

which we obtained for the different sample periods are shown in Tables 4-5 and 4-6.

One of the most interesting results of our subsample analysis was the consistency of the interpretation of our factors.[h] In terms of consistency, our results for PCH were better than for PCH/4, perhaps because the greater percentage variation in the former allowed for more distinct factor separation. (In terms of R^2, PCH/4 was better, which also was to be expected since there is some trend incorporated in this transformation.)

In every sample period, F_3, the cost factor, was the most important for explaining *WPI*. F_2 ranked second, with F_1 insignificant and generally negative. F_4 was usually insignificant. In general, our results for the full sample remained about the same for all of the subsample periods. We shall examine each of these briefly in turn.

1. *1955:1-1970:4.* F_1 gained in significance with a negative sign. F_2 gained marginally. For PCH there was little change in any of the coefficients, with F_2 losing marginally. For both specifications the R^2 for the four factors increased over that for the full sample. In terms of the general relationship between the factors and *WPI* there is not much difference between this period and the full sample.

2. *1953:1-1960:4 vs. 1961:1-1970:4.* For PCH/4, the relationships established for the full sample were reproduced distinctly in the 1961:1 to 1970:4 period, with the highest R^2 for any of the subsamples. Again the cost factor was dominant, explaining over 88 percent of the total variance and 95 percent of the explained variance, with the negative coefficient on F_1 increasing substantially. In 1953:1 to 1960:4, for PCH/4, *WPI* was most highly associated with an independent factor, that is, it was not clearly associated with cost or demand. In the fifties, F_2 was more important than F_3, and had a positive sign. For PCH, however, both periods followed the pattern established in the full sample, with F_3 clearly dominant. However, in the sixties the negative coefficient on F_1 increased and was highly significant.

These results suggest that in the sixties, the structure of the inflationary process changed in such a way that the potential efficacy of aggregate demand measures was weakened. There was a much stronger tendency for compensatory pricing, that is, for short run changes in demand to affect prices and wages negatively. F_3 increased in significance, and within F_3 the *CPI* gained in importance, the factor loading increasing from .68 to .96 in PCH/4.

3. *Democrats vs. Republicans.* For PCH/4 we found the cost factor to dominate in both samples. The demand variables behaved similarly to the full sample in Republican years. F_1 and F_2 collapsed into a single factor in Democratic years reflecting higher serial correlation in the demand variables

---

[h]There was also remarkable consistency in the order in which the principal components were extracted (in terms of the percentage of the total variance of the set explained).

(particularly the unemployment variables). This single factor loading was significant, with a positive sign, but was small (.25) compared with the loading on the cost factor (.70). For the Democrats, the policy variables loaded on the cost factor. The expenditure variables associate positively with costs as do the tax variables (including tax rates), implying that fiscal policy in these years was destabilizing. But the guidelines had a negative association with costs.

For PCH the results for both Republicans and Democrats are consistent with those for the full sample, with a higher R^2 for Republican years. In Democratic years the demand variables of F_2 gain in explanatory power. For Republican years the only significant factor is F_3.

4. *Direction of Change in the Unemployment Rate.* Our original results seem valid in both phases of the cycle. For PCH/4 the loading on F_1 is small with a negative sign. F_3, the cost factor, is more important in the downturn than the upturn, although it still explains most of the variance in *WPI* in both cases. In the upturn, F_2 gains explanatory power, indicating that demand conditions are important, but with a lag. In the downturn, F_1 and F_2 collapse into one, suggesting that reaction lags are not as easy to specify. For instance, the lagged and unlagged unemployment rates both appear on the same factor in the downturn, while there is a distinct separation in the upturn, indicating a higher degree of serial correlation in the unemployment variables in the downswing than in the upswing. In any event, F_1 remains statistically insignificant and with a negative sign even when F_2 collapses into it. Clearly, the interaction of wages and prices retains the bulk of the explanatory power in all phases of the cycle.

For PCH, the results are similar, with the cost factor explaining most of the variance in both phases of the cycle. In both phases, F_1 and F_2 collapsed into a single factor (which remained insignificant).

5. *Relative Change in Prices and Unemployment.* In both cases, the cost factor explained at least 74 percent of the variance in the wholesale price index. For PCH/4, demand factors were insignificant when *WPI* and *UN* moved together. When they moved inversely F_1 took a negative sign. F_2 was significant, explaining 1.7 percent of the variance in *WPI* as compared with 74.0 percent for F_3. Clearly, the structure suggested by the full sample seems invariant to the direction of change of the unemployment rate or its direction of change relative to changes in the wholesale price index.

The Price Equation—Durable Manufacturing

Durable manufacturing is a more homogeneous group of industries than total manufacturing. Product markets are more concentrated and union membership is greater. Many of the products are intermediate goods and hence are sold to firms rather than consumers.

The price equation for alternative specifications and data transformations is shown in Table 4-7. Because some data were not available for early years, the sample is from 1959:1 to 1970:4, and we did not investigate subsamples within the period. Thus, when comparing the durables equation with the results for total manufacturing it may be more appropriate to compare with the period from 1961:1 to 1970:4 for manufacturing.

As with total manufacturing, the results for durables are not significantly affected by lagging the explanatory variables or by the inclusion of the lagged dependent variable. Again, Factor 3 dominates the equation, accounting for 94.7 of the variance in the PCH/4 transformation and 81.5 in PCH, when the lagged dependent variable is included. The coefficients in F_3 are higher than for total

TABLE 4-7
Durable Manufacturing

Factor Loadings for the Wholesale Price Index for
Alternative Specifications and Data Transformations (F-ratio in parentheses)[1]

	Factor 1	Factor 2	Factor 3	Factor 4	R^2
PCH/4					
1. WPI with WPI_{-1}	-.009 (0.10)	.054 (4.04)	.973 (1290.48)	-.033 (1.49)	.951 (432.04)
2. WPI	-.020 (0.47)	.066 (5.00)	.967 (1066.14)	-.054 (3.28)	.942 (358.29)
3. WPI_{+1} with WPI	-.022 (0.68)	.079 (8.78)	.972 (1336.49)	-.042 (2.48)	.953 (449.48)
4. WPI_{+1}	.021 (0.44)	-.058 (3.42)	.965 (934.94)	.005 (0.02)	.934 (312.94)
PCH					
1. WPI with WPI_{-1}	.068 (1.89)	-.055 (1.24)	.903 (334.02)	-.108 (4.78)	.834 (113.88)
2. WPI	.069 (1.80)	-.045 (0.77)	.879 (292.47)	-.208 (16.38)	.823 (103.84)
3. WPI_{+1} with WPI	.087 (3.60)	-.004 (0.01)	.904 (338.61)	-.180 (15.58)	.857 (135.84)
4. WPI_{+1}	.043 (0.72)	-.133 (6.89)	.898 (314.12)	-.045 (0.79)	.828 (107.51)

[1]F = 4 represents the 95% significance level.

manufacturing and so are the coefficients of multiple determination (R^2) for the entire equation. The gains are particularly great for the PCH transformation, where the R^2s increase by about 20 percentage points.

The lagged specifications (with WPI_{+1}, the dependent variable) gain in explanatory power for durables and have slightly higher R^2 than the lagged specification when the lagged dependent variable is included in the explanatory set. For total manufacturing, on the other hand, the unlagged specification was preferred. This suggests that for the more homogeneous industry group, lags are easier to specify. However, we shall see that the unlagged specification again becomes preferred at the industry level.

F_2, the lagged demand factor, is barely significant at the 95 percent level for PCH/4. In the lagged specification it has a negative sign. For PCH, F_2 is generally insignificant but always has a negative sign. This suggests that "stagflation," that is, rising prices in the face of slack levels of economic activity, has characterized price behavior in the durable goods industries in the period since 1959. This is consistent with the model of target return pricing, so often brought forward to explain price behavior in these industries. Firms raise or maintain prices as demand falls in order to attain some target rate of return on their capital. However, it should be kept in mind that the effect of demand, through F_2, is very marginal compared with the overwhelming importance of F_3. Although we observed the tendency for compensatory pricing in total manufacturing, it was always through F_1 only.

F_4, the public policy factor, becomes significant for the PCH transformation and has a negative sign, suggesting that restrictive fiscal measures were associated with price increases in the short run. This does not imply that fiscal policy was destabilizing in the sample period, but only that its short-run impact was the reverse of that suggested by the Keynesian model. It may reflect timing that was stabilizing; that is, when prices increased, restrictive measures were taken.

The effect of monetary policy, on the other hand, was consistent with an aggregate demand model since M_1 (lagged one quarter) entered F_3, the cost factor with a high positive coefficient. This suggests the monetary policy, if properly timed, would have been a potentially powerful anti-inflationary instrument. However, the relationship between M_1 and F_3 might well be spurious, and, consequently, a structural model specifically addressed to the question of the efficacy of monetary policy must be studied before the causality issue can be resolved.

In general, the results for durables were similar to total manufacturing. Four principal components accounted for most of the variance in the wholesale price index, with F_3, the cost factor, dampened by the effect of the unemployment rate level, dominating the explanation. However, a tendency for compensatory pricing was somewhat stronger in durables than for total manufacturing. A lagged specification gained explanatory power for durables, whereas an unlagged model was preferred for total manufacturing.

The Wage Equation–Total Manufacturing

In Chapter 1 we discussed the importance of a model of labor market behavior for explaining price changes. Since it is presumed that prices respond to changes in labor costs, it is important to ascertain whether or not money wages can be stabilized by measures to restrict aggregate demand. Three wage variables are included in the data set for total manufacturing–average weekly earnings, average hourly earnings, and manhour compensation. The relation between each of these variables and the factors was considerably different. When account is taken of overtime, in *AWE*, the level of economic activity becomes more important. On an hourly basis, the cost factor dominates, especially when account is taken of all compensation, including fringes.

AWE, which incorporates the effect of overtime, was most strongly associated with F_1 and secondarily associated with F_3. F_2 and F_4 are insignificant. For PCH/4, F_1 accounts for 78.9 percent of the total and 86.4 percent of the explained variance in *AWE*, and F_3 accounts for 10.4 percent of the total and 11.4 percent of the explained variance.

AHE, which excludes both overtime and fringes, is most highly associated with F_3 for both PCH and PCH/4, with F_1 of secondary importance. The coefficients of F_2 and F_4 are also significant. For PCH/4, F_3 accounts for 60.8 percent of the total and 76.1 percent of the explained variance of *AHE*, and F_1 accounts for 9.2 percent of the total and 11.6 percent of the explained variance.

MHC, which includes all fringe benefits paid by the employer and is the best measure of labor cost from the viewpoint of the firm,[i] is the most strongly associated with F_3 for both PCH and PCH/4. F_1 and F_2 are insignificant in both transformations. For PCH/4, F_3 contributes 64.8 percent to the total and 94.4 percent to the explained variance of *MHC*.

Our results suggest that changes in weekly take-home pay are greatly influenced by changes in the level of economic activity and labor market conditions with little or no lag. The relationship between unemployment rate levels, prices, and production costs, reflected in F_3, is of secondary but minor importance. On the other hand, labor cost from the viewpoint of the firm is insensitive to changes in economic activity or labor market conditions, even when allowance is made for a one- or two-quarter lag.

These results lend support to the view that a cost-push spiral does occur in the absence of rising demand, at least in the short run. The trade-off between money wage changes and unemployment rates varies in its sensitivity to changing demand and labor market conditions, depending on which wage variable is observed. While weekly take-home pay is affected adversely by slack demand, hourly labor costs for the firm are insensitive to it. This suggests that public policy to restrict demand will serve to make workers feel worse off without substantially reducing labor costs for the firm.

[i]It is important to bear in mind that *MHC* represents cost per unit of labor, not per unit of output. We shall return to this point in the summary of our results at the end of this chapter.

The public policy factor, F_4, was significant with a positive coefficient for both *AHE* and *MHC*. Expansionary public policy was associated with rising wages, even when its influence on the level of economic activity, which also inflates wages, is ignored. This suggests that public policy has the predicted Keynesian effect on wages, but that the timing of public policy has been destabilizing. A similar relationship was not present in the price equations.

Because of space limitations, we will report the subsample estimates for the intermediate variable, *AHE*, only.[j] In general, the relative shifts of importance of F_1 and F_3 for *AWE* and *MHC* are maintained in the subsamples.

Tables 4-8 and 4-9 show the regression coefficients (factor loadings) for the *AHE* equation in unlagged form and without the lagged dependent variable. The subsample estimates are similar to those of the full sample, with the 1960s and years of Democratic administrations being more typical. In 1961:1 to 1970:4 and in Democratic years, F_3 clearly dominated the demand factors for explaining changes in *AHE*. In 1953:1 to 1960:4 and in Republican years, the effect of demand conditions is much more important. Business cycle conditions, reflected in the direction of change in the unemployment rate, had no impact on the way the factors affected wage changes.

Although fiscal policy had a net positive impact on wages over the entire period, the coefficient on F_4 was higher in Republican years than any other time, with F_4 dominating the Republican wage equation. In Democratic years, on the other hand, we are unable to identify an independent public policy factor. However, since the fiscal policy variables in Democratic years were positively associated with the cost factor, F_3, we can conclude that fiscal policy in those years also had a positive (destabilizing) impact on wages.

The Wage Equation—Durable Manufacturing

The wage equations for *AHE* and *AWE* for durable manufacturing are shown in Table 4-10. Manhour compensation was not available. Compared with total manufacturing the R^2s were considerably higher for PCH, while for PCH/4 the R^2s were about the same.

Like total manufacturing, F_1 dominated the *AWE* equations and F_3 dominated the explanation of *AHE*. However, for *AHE*, the demand factors, F_1 and F_2, had significant negative coefficients in 3 of 4 cases. For *AWE*, F_2 had significant negative coefficients. We noted, in our discussion of the price equations for durables, the existence of a "stagflation" effect in the durable goods industries. This effect seems to prevail in the labor market as well, since hourly wages rise on the average when demand is falling, even when lags are taken into account. Although weekly earnings have a strong positive association

---

[j]The subsample estimates for the other variables in the subsample periods are available on request from the authors.

TABLE 4-8
Total Manufacturing

Factor Loadings for Average Hourly Earnings for Alternative
Samples – Percent Change over Four Quarters (F-ratio in Parentheses)

	Factor 1	Factor 2	Factor 3	Factor 4	R^2
1. 1953:1 - 1970:4	.304 (32.74)	.167 (9.86)	.778 (214.93)	.274 (26.58)	.800 (94.67)
2. 1955:1 - 1970:4	.154 (13.64)	.151 (13.13)	.910 (474.32)	-.038 (0.82)	.876 (167.19)
3. 1953:1 - 1960:4	.382 (33.38)	.587 (78.79)	.441 (44.53)	**	.698 (53.16)
4. 1961:1 - 1970:4	.261 (77.94)	-.148 (25.08)	.909 (947.28)	.144 (23.86)	.938 (358.05)
5. Democratic presidents	.051 (2.04)	*	.953 (721.33)	***	.912 (241.37)
6. Republican presidents	.377 (53.14)	.372 (51.58)	.395 (131.84)	.430 (68.90)	.815 (101.32)
7. Unemployment rate increasing	.290 (21.14)	*	.791 (157.46)	.100 (2.50)	.722 (60.60)
8. Unemployment rate decreasing	.360 (66.88)	.214 (23.63)	.798 (328.02)	.225 (26.10)	.864 (148.24)
9. $\frac{dWPI}{dUN} > 0$	.456 (51.77)	*	.702 (122.89)	.075 (1.42)	.715 (59.37)
10. $\frac{dWPI}{dUN} < 0$	.357 (52.94)	.052 (1.10)	.811 (273.31)	.321 (42.87)	.829 (114.73)

*Factor 2 collapsed into Factor 1 in this sample.
**Factor 4 collapsed into Factor 3 in this sample. WPI loaded on an independent factor with a loading of -.625.
***In this sample Factor 4 collapsed into Factor 3, but the cost factor split into two components. The square root of the sum of the squares of the loadings on these two components is provided as the loading for Factor 3.

TABLE 4-9
Total Manufacturing

Factor Loadings for Average Hourly Earnings for
Alternative Samples – Quarterly Percent Change (F-ratio in Parentheses)

	Factor 1	Factor 2	Factor 3	Factor 4	R^2
1. 1953:1 - 1970:4	.404 (24.08)	.030 (0.13)	.542 (43.31)	.248 (9.12)	.519 (75.54)
2. 1955:1 - 1970:4	.414 (27.58)	-.055 (0.48)	.581 (54.28)	.212 (7.23)	.558 (29.88)
3. 1953:1 - 1960:4	.508 (28.03)	.197 (4.23)	.223 (5.43)	.134 (1.95)	.365 (13.22)
4. 1961:1 - 1970:4	.221 (9.39)	-.026 (0.13)	.586 (66.35)	*	.632 (40.64)
5. Democratic presidents	.186 (3.76)	-.039 (0.17)	.561 (34.21)	.061 (0.40)	.355 (12.84)
6. Republican presidents	.495 (40.23)	.071 (0.82)	.526 (45.52)	.232 (8.83)	.580 (31.76)
7. Unemployment rate increasing	.022 (0.06)	**	.329 (12.91)	***	.412 (16.35)
8. Unemployment rate decreasing	.342 (19.10)	**	.638 (66.41)	.049 (0.39)	.571 (3.06)
9. $\frac{dWPI}{dUN} > 0$	.168 (3.45)	.307 (11.47)	.540 (35.37)	.021 (0.05)	.415 (16.79)
10. $\frac{dWPI}{dUN} < 0$	.613 (119.75)	-.314 (31.47)	.550 (96.25)	.018 (0.10)	.777 (82.46)

*Factor 4 collapsed into the other factors, associating weakly with Factor 2. The R^2 for all the policy variables were very low for this sample.
**Factor 2 collapsed into Factor 1 in this sample, with output variables loading on a separate component.
***Factor 4 collapsed into the other factors.

TABLE 4-10
Durable Manufacturing

Factor Loadings for Average Hourly Earnings and
Average Weekly Earnings (F-ratio in Parentheses)

	Factor 1	Factor 2	Factor 3	Factor 4	R^2
PCH/4					
AHE	-.162 (14.05)	-.254 (14.54)	.882 (416.53)	-.068 (2.48)	.873 (155.81)
AWE	.872 (689.41)	-.126 (14.39)	.379 (130.23)	-.033 (0.99)	.925 (279.55)
PCH					
AHE	.167 (10.03)	-.415 (61.96)	.795 (227.39)	-.086 (12.45)	.811 (97.26)
AWE	.873 (304.85)	-.107 (4.58)	.246 (24.21)	.040 (0.69)	.830 (110.67)

with changes in economic activity, there is a significant negative impact from lagged demand. Since durable goods industries are characterized by relatively strong unions as well as strong union-management "countervailing power" interaction, these results suggest that unions are able to obtain hourly wage increases when demand is falling to compensate workers for income losses associated with a shorter work week. As demand increases, on the other hand, and weekly income rises, the rate of increase in hourly earnings falls off. Because this phenomenon is cyclical, this would explain the small negative coefficient on the lagged demand factor (F_2) in the AWE equation in the presence of such a large positive coefficient on current demand factor (F_1).

The influence of the public sector, reflected in F_4, is on balance negligible, although the one significant coefficient is negative. With respect to both wages and prices, the influence of the public sector is difficult to assess because the impact of countercyclical timing may be offset by the response of the wage and price variables to the policy measures. Because of the simultaneity inherent in our model, a more detailed a priori specification of the lag structure and the direction of causality is needed to test the efficacy of specific policy instruments. However, our model is capable of assessing the indirect impact of monetary and fiscal policy through the effect of changes in F_1 and F_2 on prices and wages.

Interaction of Wages and Prices—
Total Manufacturing

In view of the dominance of F_3 for explaining changes in the wholesale price index for manufacturing, our analysis will focus on the relationship of the price and wage variables in that component of the data. In addition, we shall consider the way in which the other factors influence the relationship between F_3 and the *WPI*.

The neoclassical theory of price behavior (extrapolated from the model of the profit maximizing firm) suggests that prices will vary directly with changes in marginal unit costs. Changes in marginal costs occur when input prices change and when changes in demand affect factor productivity. Our results indicate that wholesale prices in manufacturing are highly sensitive to changes in input prices, including the cost per unit of labor input, but are relatively unaffected by changes in productivity. Manhour compensation and average hourly earnings are strongly associated with F_3, the factor dominant in explaining price changes, whereas unit labor cost is only weakly related to it. Even when corrected for short-run swings in productivity, standard unit labor cost is not associated with the cost variables that influence prices.

From a theoretical perspective, our results suggest the firms whose actions dominate aggregate price behavior follow markup-pricing practices, raising prices when input prices increase, regardless of expected or actual changes in demand. This type of pricing behavior makes inflation much less sensitive to aggregate demand remedies than the traditional (profit-maximization) model would suggest.

Because of the observed insensitivity of prices to the productivity effect of changing demand conditions, it is likely that the principal anti-inflationary impact of slack demand operates through the labor market. The substantial negative influence of the unemployment rate on F_3 undoubtedly reflects a Phillips-type trade-off between labor market slack and money wage increases.

Although workers' weekly earnings are greatly influenced by demand conditions, manhour compensation is unaffected by the demand factors. This implies that the impact of aggregate demand remedies on employed workers' income is greater than its anti-inflationary impact. Thus, in addition to the inflation-unemployment trade-off traditionally associated with aggregate demand remedies for inflation, the effect on workers' weekly income (unemployment of hours) should also be taken into account.

There is little indication that labor market conditions act on wages with a lag, since association with F_2 was generally weaker than for F_1. However, where demand affected price changes it was through F_2. Since the demand effect is somewhat stronger (and acts faster) in labor markets than in product markets, it is implied that prices are "stickier" than wages in response to changes in demand conditions. When total manhour compensation is used as a measure of wages, however, there is no indication that wages are less "sticky" than prices.

The results for the subperiods were almost always consistent. Where demand factors assumed greater importance for price level changes, for instance in the period 1953:1-1960:4, demand factors also became more important in labor markets. This suggests that there were during the period structural changes that made the inflationary process more or less conducive to aggregate demand remedies, and that these changes were reflected in both product and labor markets.

There is no a priori reason to expect both product and labor markets to move in the same direction with respect to responsiveness of prices to changing demand conditions. If, for instance, wages became more sensitive to changes in demand, the stabilizing impact of a fall in demand would be reflected in F_3 for the price equation, not in the demand factors. However, the tendency we observe for both product and labor markets to vary together in their responsiveness to demand conditions could be attributable to external characteristics of the economic environment. Also, it is consistent with "countervailing power" ideas about the structure of American industry.[4]

The Democratic-Republican breakdown is an interesting exception. In Republican years prices were less responsive to demand than in Democratic years. But Republican years were characterized by a stronger labor market influence on wages and a weaker association with F_3. This may be attributable in part to the fact that Democratic years were generally high-employment years while relatively slack labor markets were often experienced during Republican administrations. It could also be argued that the political environment is generally more favorable to labor in Democratic administrations. Nevertheless, in Republican years, *MHC* remained highly correlated with F_3 and was relatively unaffected by the demand factors.[k] This means that labor costs from the viewpoint of the firm were not as responsive to demand conditions in these years as *AHE*.

Interaction of Wages and
Prices—Durable Manufacturing

Prices were related to the cost factor in durables in much the same way as for total manufacturing. Factor costs rather than cost per unit of output played the major role in explaining changes in the wholesale price index. The impact of unit labor cost was weaker than for total manufacturing, suggesting durables prices are even less affected by short-run swings in productivity.

One major difference between durables and total manufacturing was in the tendency for compensatory pricing. For durables, there is evidence of a weak

[k]The factor loadings in *MHC* for the Republican sample for PCH/4 are

$$a_1 = -.033$$
$$a_2 = -.019$$
$$a_3 = .792$$
$$a_4 = .223$$

but significant negative impact of demand in both the product and labor markets. The effect is strongest from F_2, suggesting that where compensatory pricing occurs it is with a lag. For total manufacturing, on the other hand, there is no evidence of compensatory pricing in the wage equations. In the price equations, negative coefficients were associated with F_1, implying that where there is compensatory pricing, it occurs without a lag.

For durables, prices and wages both tended to move inversely with the factors reflecting changes in economic activity when the cost-price interaction effect was held constant. This suggests a model in which, on both sides of the market, firms and unions attempt to regain losses associated with falling demand by raising prices and negotiating higher hourly wage rates. On the other hand, when demand is increasing rapidly and wages and prices are rising in the Phillipsian relationship of F_3, there is less pressure for additional wage and price increases.

For total manufacturing, on the other hand, compensatory pricing seems to have occurred on the product side of the market only and was subject to a shorter lag than for durables. Whether this implies that the durable goods sector was more likely than total manufacturing to produce inflation during periods of slack demand is uncertain. But compensatory pricing in the labor market suggests that workers in the durables industries are less likely to be susceptible to money illusion in their wage negotiations. That is, if wage bargains are sensitive to changes in take-home pay associated with reduced hours, they are also likely to be sensitive to sustained periods of inflation which erode the purchasing power of the money wage. It is interesting to note, in this connection, that the consumer price index has a substantially higher loading on Factor 3 for durables (.886) than for total manufacturing (.677).[1] This implies that the *CPI* has a stronger positive influence on the interaction between wages and prices for durables than for total manufacturing,[m] that is, that past inflation has a greater effect on money wage increases. This is evidence that aggregate demand remedies were weaker in the durables sector than in total manufacturing, or, alternatively, that the unemployment cost of price stability was potentially greater there.

Secular Trends in the Inflationary
Process for Total Manufacturing

Recent experience with inflation in the United States has led some economists to suggest that structural changes have occurred in the way the inflationary

[1]Using the Kendall formula to estimate the regression coefficient of the *CPI* on average hourly earnings, that is,

$$b_{ij} = a_{ik}a_{kj}$$

where b_{ij} is a regression coefficient, and a_{ik} and a_{kj} are factor loadings, we find that for durables b_{ij} = .781 and for total manufacturing b_{ij} = .520.

[m]This finding is even more significant when account is taken of the closer identification between the *CPI* and the *WPI* for total manufacturing than between the *CPI* and the *WPI* for durables.

process is transmitted. Our results support that hypothesis. In the period
1961:1-1970:4, price behavior for total manufacturing was more like that for
the durables industries than for total manufacturing in the full sample. Table
4-11 shows the factor loadings relevant to an analysis of the major channels
through which the inflationary process is transmitted.

The short-run (unlagged) impact of demand on the *WPI* was significant and
negative, indicating that firms raise prices in the short run to compensate for
losses associated with falling demand. There is a significant and positive
coefficient on F_2, suggesting that with a lag the effect of falling demand is
deflationary and the two effects may cancel each other out. However, if
compensatory pricing produces stagflation in the short run, the effect will be felt
in F_3, the interaction between wages and prices, and will stimulate further
inflation, particularly where money illusion is not present.

Even in this later period, there is no evidence of compensatory pricing in the
labor market. However, there is a marked increase in the factor loading on the
CPI (from .667 to .959) for F_3 as well as an increase in the importance of F_3 for
explaining wage changes.[n]

The evidence of both compensatory pricing in the product market and an
increase in the impact of past inflation on wages implies that aggregate demand
remedies were potentially weaker in the 1960s than in the 1950s for the
manufacturing sector as a whole. Comparable results are not available for the
durable goods industries; however, it is likely that similar structural shifts occurred
there.[o]

TABLE 4-11
Total Manufacturing

Selected Factor Loadings for 1961:1 - 1970:4
Percent Change over Four Quarters

Variable	Factor 1	Factor 2	Factor 3	Factor 4
WPI	-.132	.169	.941	.032
AHE	.261	-.148	.909	.144
CPI	-.194	-.156	.959	.057
AWE	.815	.086	.466	-.032

[n]The implicit Kendall estimate for b_{ij} is .872, compared with .520 for the full manufacturing sample.
[o]Since the durables sample begins in 1959:1, one could argue that the structure represented
by our durables results is more comparable to the manufacturing structure of the 1960s. If
this is the case, we could no longer conclude that aggregate demand remedies were weaker in
the durable goods industries or that the cost of price stability in terms of unemployment

The Policy Variables

Tables 4-12 and 4-13 show the factor pattern for the 19 policy variables in the PCH/4 data transformations. Corporate tax receipts were strongly associated with F_1 as would be expected, since corporate profits are linked to swings in activity in the manufacturing and durable goods industries. Personal tax receipts are weakly associated with F_1 for total manufacturing but not for durables. This indicates that personal incomes are not as strongly related to conditions in the manufacturing sector as corporate incomes.

Both money supply variables are associated with F_1 for manufacturing, and M_2 is related to F_1 for durables. The greater transactions requirements for total manufacturing may explain this discrepancy. The strong positive association of M_1 with F_3 for durables is very interesting and cannot be explained by transactions requirements. For both total manufacturing and durables, M_2 is also associated with the fiscal policy factor, F_4, suggesting that the money supply including time deposits has been more closely coordinated (in terms of timing) with changes in fiscal policy than has M_1 (which excludes time deposits).

The Federal Reserve discount rate appears on F_2 with a positive sign.[p] Although weakly associated with F_3, the major impact of the discount rate seems to be on the demand rather than on the cost side.

Associated with F_3 is the guidelines dummy and the political dummy. Both appear with a negative sign, indicating that the impact of the guidelines as well as of the Democratic administrations has been through the cost factor. This may partly explain why costs explained a smaller proportion of the change in prices in Democratic years than in Republican years.

The bulk of the fiscal policy variables were associated with an independent factor, F_4. As we mentioned earlier, it is likely that this reflects a coincidence in timing with variable effectiveness lags for the variables reflecting conditions in the private sector. In many of the subsample periods, F_4 collapsed into the other factors, indicating some consistency in effectiveness lags for shorter periods.

F_4 was insignificant in the full sample for total manufacturing and in 7 of the 9 subsamples. Where significant, it had a negative effect, indicating that where fiscal policy was effective its short-run impact on prices was the reverse of that suggested by the Keynesian model. Alternatively, the negative coefficient could reflect timing that was designed for stabilization purposes. F_4 was significant in the PCH specification of durables, again with a negative impact.

Despite the marginal importance of F_4 for explaining price changes, we cannot conclude that public policy was ineffective. We were unable to distinguish between autonomous fiscal actions and those induced by swings in private

---

was potentially greater than for total manufacturing. But in any case, our results suggest that Keynesian remedies for inflation were potentially less effective in the 1960s than in the period following the Korean War.

PF_2 is a negative factor in the durables analysis.

TABLE 4-12
Total Manufacturing

Factor Loadings for the Policy Variables in
the Full Sample – Percent Change over Four Quarters[1]

	Factor 1	Factor 2	Factor 3	Factor 4
WPI	-.110 (3.98)	.220 (15.88)	.847 (236.00)	.074 (1.79)
corporate tax receipts	.963	.000	-.010	.026
M^1 (-1)	.543	.137	.360	.265
M^2 (-1)	.514	-.019	-.260	-.447
debt/GNP	-.486	-.193	-.134	-.119
Federal Reserve discount rate (-1)	-.023	.797	.340	-.049
wage-price guidelines	.115	.189	-.554	-.050
political dummy (=1 in Democratic administrations)	.170	.120	-.532	.503
government purchases	.118	.162	-.011	.892
government purchases (deflated)	.125	.183	-.196	.875
government spending/national income	-.408	-.627	-.037	.808
corporate tax rate	-.034	-.132	.384	.658
defense/government expenditure	.204	.386	-.040	.549
lagged political dummy[2]	.246	.290	-.264	.544
personal tax receipts	.441	.354	.276	.500
personal tax rate	.276	.241	.220	.419
unassigned variables				
defense/government purchases	-.020	.074	.292	.009
full employment surplus	-.126	.252	.100	.107
indirect tax rate	-.081	.005	.233	-.169
OASI	.158	-.103	.200	-.050

[1]Boxes indicate the factor to which the variable has been assigned.

[2]This dummy was lagged one year to reflect the lag in the effect of changing public policy on the economy.

TABLE 4-13
Durable Manufacturing

Factor Loadings for the Policy Variables
-Percent Change over Four Quarters[1]

	Factor 1	Factor 2	Factor 3	Factor 4
WPI	-.009 (0.10)	-.054 (4.04)	.973 (1290.48)	-.033 (1.49)
corporate tax receipts	.928	.049	.051	.124
M_2 (-1)	.572	.034	.113	.515
Federal Reserve discount rate (-1)	.054	-.798	.237	-.197
M_1 (-1)	.415	-.082	.768	.172
wage-price guidelines	.196	-.106	-.540	-.146
government purchases	.075	.170	.009	.904
OASI	.158	.110	-.229	.897
defense/government expenditures	.190	-.226	-.063	.805
political dummy (=1 in Democratic administrations)	.134	.125	-.421	.666
defense/government purchases	-.125	-.234	.310	.560
indirect tax rate	-.364	.179	-.048	-.532
government purchases (deflated)	.211	-.258	.346	.477
personal tax rate	.102	-.241	.242	.414
unassigned variables				
corporate tax rate	.055	.036	.095	.283
full employment surplus	-.183	-.007	-.261	-.024
personal tax receipts	-.003	.131	.289	-.306
debt/GNP	-.337	.167	-.113	-.178

[1]Boxes indicate the factor to which the variable has been assigned.

business activity. Furthermore, we had no clear evidence of how fiscal policy was actually timed.

Finally, it is interesting to note the impact of tax rates on F_3. For total manufacturing, corporate, personal, and indirect tax rates all have a positive, significant association with F_3. For durables, this is true of the personal tax rate. This suggests that changes in tax rates behave as costs and have an adverse effect on the trade-off between price stability and unemployment.

Relation to the Theoretical Models

Our results suggest that the inflationary process in manufacturing industries during 1953:1-1970:4 was best described in terms of an interaction between factor costs and prices which was dampened to some extent by the level of the unemployment rate. Changes in demand in product and labor markets as well as changes in the level of economic activity had only a negligible effect on this relationship.

The importance of demand conditions for explaining movements in prices and wages is a measure of the sensitivity of the inflationary process to Keynesian policy remedies. We concluded that the relevant cost variables in the pricing mechanism were factor costs rather than factor costs per unit of output, so that the impact of changes in demand on productivity did not influence prices. Furthermore, there is evidence that short-run changes in demand affected prices inversely, particularly in the durable goods industries and for total manufacturing in the 1960s. In sum, prices were either unaffected by demand or had a perverse relationship to it. Where demand affected prices positively it was with a lag.

Wages for total manufacturing were affected positively by demand, although the cost-price interaction factor dominated the wage equations. For durables, wage changes were inversely related to demand, suggesting compensatory wage-setting. Although the level of unemployment rates dampened the interaction of wages and prices, the process of moving to a higher unemployment rate (by reducing aggregate demand) had a potential inflationary impact. In other words, to move along the Phillips curve would cause the curve to shift outward as firms and unions attempted to recoup losses in total income associated with falling demand by raising prices and negotiating higher hourly wages.

Another gauge of the potential sensitivity of the inflationary process to aggregate demand remedies is the importance of the *CPI* in wage determination. Assuming that the consumer price index serves as a proxy for price expectations, the closer the coefficient on *CPI* is to unity the more complete is the loss of money illusion. Within the Phillips relationship reflected in F_3, the *CPI* is more important in the wage-price interaction for durables than for total manufacturing over the entire sample period.

Our subsample analysis suggests that in the sixties, the structure of the inflationary process changed for total manufacturing in the direction of the durable goods model. There is more evidence of compensatory pricing and F_3 increased in significance. Furthermore, within F_3, the *CPI* gained in importance. This suggests that structural changes in the manufacturing sector since 1960 weakened the potential efficacy of aggregate demand remedies for inflation.

In general, our results suggest that Keynesian remedies taken by themselves were potentially weak anti-inflationary policy instruments in the manufacturing sector during the period since the Korean War. In Chapter 5 we shall examine the results of our industry analysis to ascertain whether the potential impact of Keynesian remedies varies between industries as well as to examine differences in price and wage behavior.

Notes

1. For example see Otto Eckstein and Gary Fromm, "The Price Equation," *The American Economic Review*, 58 (December 1968), 1159-83.

2. For example, see George L. Perry, *Unemployment, Money Wage Rates, and Inflation* (Cambridge, Mass.: The M.I.T. Press, 1966), and A.W. Phillips, "The Relation Between Unemployment and the Rate of Change of Money Wage Rates in the United Kingdom, 1861-1957," *Economica*, 25 (November 1958), pp. 283-99.

3. Op. cit., p. 1167.

4. For a discussion of this theory, see John K. Galbraith, *American Capitalism: The Concept of Countervailing Power* (Boston: Houghton Mifflin Company, 1962).

The Industry Results

We have seen that there are some differences in the way the inflationary process is transmitted between durable manufacturing industries and the total manufacturing sector. This suggests that the structure of the market and type of product will affect the behavior of prices and wages. In this chapter we examine the results of an industry analysis for the manufacturing sector. By disaggregating at the two-digit Standard Industrial Classification (SIC) level of compilation, we have a more refined view of the relationship between price behavior and market structure. In addition, disaggregation allows us to identify lags that may have been obscured in the relationships between aggregate variables.

In addition to evaluating the relation of market structure to pricing, the industry analysis is designed to shed some light on the microeconomics of the inflationary process. Furthermore, it will be of interest to see how the inflationary process is transmitted throughout the economy, particularly where important linkages can be identified between basic and secondary industries. This approach is relevant for designing industry-specific anti-inflation measures. Since the results of our analysis of the total manufacturing sector suggest that Keynesian (aggregate demand) remedies are potentially weak anti-inflation instruments and that trends in the structure of the U.S. economy are in the direction of weakening their potential impact still further, the use of industry-specific remedies is likely to become an important policy alternative in the future. Consequently, analysis of inflation at the industry level will provide a basis for policy discussion.

Choice of Industry Classification

The SIC was chosen principally for statistical convenience. It is important to bear in mind, however, that each "industry" defined by the SIC includes a variety of products and represents a conglomeration of market structures. Consequently, assigning some product classification (basic, nonbasic, durable, homogeneous, and so on) or concentration ratio to one of the SIC industries may be misleading and reduce the statistical significance of some important structural parameters.

Our ability to generalize from our results is also weakened by the unavailability of unemployment rates for 6 of the 19 industries.[a] For these industries we

[a]Unemployment rates were unavailable for tobacco, paper, petroleum, rubber and plastics, leather, and instruments.

used the economy-wide unemployment rate in the potential explanatory set. For only one industry, printing and publishing, were we unable to construct a wholesale price index.

Interpreting the Results

Because of the large number of variables encompassed in this 19-industry study, we have tried to present our results in an economical fashion. This necessitated making certain categorizations that others might find arbitrary. However, we felt that the dangers associated with prejudging the conclusions were outweighted by facilitating the presentation and interpretation.

We found that industry price behavior could be classified into four major groups, each of which is treated separately. Assignment is on the basis of price behavior rather than of wage behavior since the wage equations were much more homogeneous across industries than were the price equations.

The statistical methodology is the same as for total manufacturing and durables. The sample period is 1959:1-1971:3. For each industry four principal components are rotated. Although in some cases the fourth component is superfluous in the sense of lacking a meaningful economic interpretation, we decided to examine a uniform number of components across industries. This procedure facilitated the industry cross-section analysis we later performed on the components. The rotated factor loadings for the percent change over four quarters (PCH/4) and quarterly percent change (PCH) data transformations are listed in Appendix B in the numerical order of the SIC.

There are four specifications for each price equation, a lagged and unlagged form (WPI lead one quarter and WPI concurrent) and both including the excluding the lagged dependent variable. The eight price equations (four for each of the two data transformations) for each industry are arranged by our industry categories in the body of this chapter.

General Remarks about the Factors

There was a striking degree of uniformity in the economic interpretation of the factors across industries. Factor 1, the unlagged demand factor, and Factor 3, the cost and unemployment levels factor, were nearly identical to those for total manufacturing and durables and were the most homogeneous between industries.

F_1 included indicators of economy-wide changes in product and labor market demand as well as industry-specific indicators. The level of the economy-wide unemployment rate was associated with industry-specific unemployment rate levels on F_3. This suggests that strong product market linkages and labor market spillover effects are present for the industries in the manufacturing sector, and that these occur with lags of less than one quarter.

Factor 2 included the financial variables and lagged labor market variables as well as the expectational variables such as anticipated investment in plant and equipment. However, many of the public policy variables were also associated with F_2. In some cases, a separate (fourth) public policy factor could not be clearly identified (although those variables which did associate with F_4 were generally public policy variables). Personal taxes and deflated government purchases were consistently associated with F_2, suggesting that the timing of the impact of these fiscal instruments at the industry level is more closely associated with changing credit conditions than for the manufacturing aggregates.

F_4 included the public policy variables (except direct taxes and deflated government purchases). The political dummies (which equal one in Democratic presidential administrations) were positively associated with F_4. Standard unit labor cost appeared on this factor for most industries, perhaps reflecting a smaller amount of cyclical variation in F_4 than in the other factors.

The impact of the wage-price guidelines was significant in nearly every industry. In all cases it worked through the wage-price interaction represented by F_3 with a negative coefficient ranging between $-.45$ and $-.60$.[b]

The preference for the PCH/4 transformation over PCH was much greater in the industry analyses than for total manufacturing and durables. Although the cumulative variance explained by the four principal components in the PCH transformation was not lower than for the manufacturing aggregates, there were substantially more unassigned variables. For PCH/4 the number of unassigned variables was not greater than for the manufacturing aggregates. This implies that the disaggregated model is no more difficult to specify provided the effect of quarterly cyclical variation is smoothed. Furthermore, it should be noted that the results for PCH were always consistent with those for PCH/4 except for the difficulty in assigning some variables.

The Price Equations

In Chapter 4 we discussed an interpretation of the factor regression equations in terms of alternative theories of price behavior. In the competitive pricing model, prices vary with changes in demand and supply. An increase in demand will cause prices to rise, other things equal. The positive impact of demand on price will be greatest the higher the level of capacity utilization. Supply price depends on unit factor costs, which change with factor prices and productivity. Prices will vary directly with unit factor costs, other things equal.

Although there are many models of oligopoly pricing available, most of them

[b]The only industry for which the guidelines dummy was insignificant, textiles, had an insignificant coefficent on F_3 in the price equation.

recognize that uncertainty about the reactions of other market participants produces behavior inconsistent with short-run profit maximization. One characteristic of oligopoly behavior is said to be mark-up pricing. That is, prices respond to changes in factor costs rather than factor cost per unit of output. This is because changes in wages and important materials prices generally occur industry-wide, and firms, being more certain of their rivals' reactions to cost changes that affect them all, are more likely to raise prices than when firm-specific productivity changes occur. Furthermore, because of the fear that price increases will not be followed industry-wide, firms change prices less frequently than in competitive markets and are presumed to base prices on a long-run measure of cost that is unrelated to short-run swings in productivity.

Another model of oligopoly pricing suggests that changes in demand may have a negative impact on prices. Firms may raise prices when demand falls in order to compensate for losses in sales associated with falling output. This type of behavior is more likely to occur in industries with institutionalized price leadership, where product demand is fairly inelastic and where management is sales-oriented rather than profit-oriented.

A negative response of prices to changes in demand might also reflect the effect of productivity change on unit labor costs, since productivity is highly correlated with demand variables. However, this type of response is most likely to occur in the more competitive industries and so the behavioral model associated with a negative relationship between prices and demand can be deduced from a priori considerations.

Types of Price Behavior

Group I. The dominant form of price behavior followed the pattern of the durable goods aggregation. Seven industries—food, stone, clay and glass, fabricated metals, non-electrical and electrical machinery, transportation, and furniture—all fell into this category. All except food are durable goods industries and all but two durable goods industries—primary metals and instruments—are included in the group. This suggests that pricing behavior within the durables sector is sufficiently homogeneous to make it an appropriate unit for aggregation in price studies.

The regression coefficients for the various specifications of the industry price equations are shown in Tables 5-1 through 5-7. The factor loadings for the full set of variables are found in Appendix B.

For these industries the price equation is dominated by the cost factor, F_3. Where demand is significant, the impact is negative. The effect of F_1 (unlagged demand) and F_2 (lagged demand) is about the same for most of these industries. However the unlagged specification is markedly preferred for all cases except food.

TABLE 5-1
Industry 20   Food

Factor Loadings for WPI for Alternative Specifications
and Data Transformations (F-ratio in parentheses)[1]

	Factor 1	Factor 2	Factor 3	Factor 4	R^2
PCH/4					
1. WPI with WPI_{-1}	-.227 (5.93)	.087 (0.86)	.563 (36.46)	.293 (9.88)	.461 (17.67)
2. WPI	-.212 (4.60)	.058 (0.35)	.540 (29.84)	.253 (6.54)	.404 (13.78)
3. WPI_{+1} with WPI	.009 (0.01)	.419 (15.82)	.319 (9.18)	.185 (3.07)	.312 (9.36)
4. WPI_{+1}	.023 (0.05)	.415 (14.71)	.293 (7.32)	.165 (2.33)	.286 (8.13)
PCH					
1. WPI with WPI_{-1}	.065 (0.29)ˑ	.014 (0.01)	.277 (5.18)	.024 (0.04)	.081 (1.81)
2. WPI	.055 (0.19)	.015 (0.01)	.283 (5.34)	.027 (0.05)	.084 (1.85)
3. WPI_{+1} with WPI	.254 (5.05)	.284 (6.33)	.218 (3.73)	.131 (1.35)	.210 (5.48)
4. WPI_{+1}	.261 (5.29)	.278 (6.00)	.226 (3.95)	.130 (1.30)	.214 (5.54)

[1] F = 4 represents the 95% significance level.

The food industry is the least representative of this group and has the lowest R^2 for the equation as a whole. For the other industries the R^2s are in the .85-.95 range in the PCH/4 transformation.

With the exception of food (whose classification in this group is somewhat arbitrary because of the relatively small coefficient for F_3), the principal common characteristic of these industries is the durable nature of the product and the primary market level.[c] There is considerable variation in concentration ratios,[d] from 5.2 for furniture to 68.6 for transportation.

[c] A substantial part of transportation is secondary market level.

[d] The concentration ratio is the percent of total sales attributable to the four largest firms in 1962:4.

TABLE 5-2
Industry 25 Furniture

Factor Loadings for WPI for Alternative Specifications
and Data Transformations (F-ratio in parentheses)[1]

	Factor 1	Factor 2	Factor 3	Factor 4	R^2
PCH/4					
1. WPI with WPI_{-1}	-.161 (15.76)	-.213 (27.59)	.907 (500.37)	-.093 (5.76)	.903 (183.08)
2. WPI	-.174 (15.13)	-.239 (28.56)	.883 (389.84)	-.130 (8.45)	.884 (147.33)
3. WPI_{+1} with WPI	-.256 (7.24)	-.195 (4.20)	.596 (39.24)	-.089 (0.88)	.466 (17.16)
4. WPI_{+1}	-.258 (7.14)	-.185 (3.67)	.595 (37.95)	-.068 (0.50)	.459 (16.40)
PCH					
1. WPI with WPI_{-1}	.121 (3.20)	-.166 (6.02)	.780 (132.94)	-.281 (17.25)	.730 (53.17)
2. WPI	.127 (3.20)	-.181 (6.51)	.750 (111.72)	-.309 (18.96)	.708 (46.87)
3. WPI_{+1} with WPI	-.078 (0.38)	.136 (1.15)	.139 (1.20)	-.081 (0.41)	.050 (1.04)
4. WPI_{+1}	-.078 (0.37)	.134 (1.10)	.142 (1.32)	-.078 (0.37)	.050 (1.02)

[1] F = 4 represents the 95% significance level.

The results for this group suggest a model of pricing behavior in which factor prices play the major role. In all cases materials costs and average hourly earnings are highly associated with F_3, which in turn explains most of the variance in the *WPI*. Thus, the practice of mark-up pricing seems to predominate in these industries, even where the concentration ratio is low and a competitive mechanism would be most likely to operate.

Changes in demand explain a much smaller proportion of price changes, but where the effect is significant it is generally negative. Furthermore, the effect is fairly evenly distributed between an immediate (unlagged) impact through F_1 and a one-quarter lag through F_2. The insensitivity of the coefficients to the

TABLE 5-3
Industry 32   Stone, Clay and Glass

Factor Loadings for WPI for Alternative Specifications
and Data Transformations (F-ratio in parentheses)[1]

	Factor 1	Factor 2	Factor 3	Factor 4	R^2
PCH/4					
1. WPI with WPI_{-1}	.229 (65.28)	-.390 (189.34)	.802 (800.72)	-.320 (127.47)	.951 (394.63)
2. WPI	.285 (81.22)	-.444 (197.13)	.666 (443.55)	-.467 (218.08)	.940 (313.33)
3. WPI_{+1} with WPI	-.108 (0.87)	-.020 (0.03)	.406 (12.26)	-.061 (0.28)	.180 (4.46)
4. WPI_{+1}	-.009 (0.01)	-.098 (0.71)	.413 (12.58)	-.082 (0.50)	.187 (4.60)
PCH					
1. WPI with WPI_{-1}	.155 (4.92)	-.450 (75.32)	.772 (221.67)	-.156 (9.05)	.836 (103.65)
2. WPI	.127 (4.77)	-.529 (82.71)	.679 (136.26)	-.197 (11.47)	.797 (78.52)
3. WPI_{+1} with WPI	-.136 (1.26)	-.015 (0.02)	.013 (0.01)	-.298 (6.07)	.108 (2.46)
4. WPI_{+1}	-.142 (1.33)	.027 (0.05)	.026 (0.04)	-.262 (4.53)	.090 (1.98)

[1]F = 4 represents the 95% significance level.

exclusion of the lagged dependent variable suggests that the lags are accounted for in F_2 and are not transmitted through the other factors.

It is not clear from the results whether the negative effect of demand reflects compensatory pricing or a response to productivity changes affecting unit labor cost. In either case, however, measures to reduce demand in these industries would have had an inflationary impact and would have worsened the trade-off between inflation and unemployment in the sample period.

The Wage Equation. For all industries in this group, changes in average hourly earnings (*AHE*) are explained predominantly by F_3, the cost-price interaction

TABLE 5-4
Industry 34   Fabricated Metals

Factor Loadings for WPI for Alternative Specifications
and Data Transformations (F-ratio in parentheses)[1]

	Factor 1	Factor 2	Factor 3	Factor 4	R^2
PCH/4					
1. WPI with WPI$_{-1}$	-.338 (77.43)	-.274 (50.88)	.833 (470.30)	.164 (18.22)	.910 (205.59)
2. WPI	-.381 (81.39)	-.323 (58.50)	.776 (337.66)	.202 (22.88)	.893 (166.91)
3. WPI$_{+1}$ with WPI	-.171 (2.60)	-.442 (17.42)	.220 (4.32)	.206 (3.78)	.316 (9.39)
4. WPI$_{+1}$	-.181 (2.39)	-.221 (3.57)	.426 (13.24)	.227 (3.76)	.315 (7.66)
PCH					
1. WPI with WPI$_{-1}$	-.041 (0.27)	.020 (0.07)	.607 (59.93)	-.505 (41.48)	.625 (33.88)
2. WPI	-.045 (0.28)	.013 (0.02)	.505 (35.75)	-.561 (44.11)	.572 (26.72)
3. WPI$_{+1}$ with WPI	.056 (1.20)	-.006 (0.00)	.158 (1.57)	-.048 (0.14)	.030 (0.63)
4. WPI$_{+1}$	.062 (0.24)	-.191 (2.28)	.008 (0.00)	-.025 (0.04)	.041 (0.86)

[1]F = 4 represents the 95% significance level.

factor dampened by unemployment levels. The coefficient for the consumer price index on F_3 is high in all cases, ranging from .754 for transportation to .897 for non-electrical machinery.

The impact of demand on the relationship between wages and unemployment levels varies among industries, with a negative effect predominant. Four industries—food; fabricated metals; electrical equipment; and stone, clay, and glass—exhibit a negative relationship between demand and wage changes. In two—furniture and transportation—demand is insignificant, and in non-electrical machinery demand has a positive effect on wage changes.

TABLE 5-5
Industry 35 Machinery, except electrical

Factor Loadings for WPI for Alternative Specifications
and Data Transformations (F-ratio in parentheses)[1]

	Factor 1	Factor 2	Factor 3	Factor 4	R^2
PCH/4					
1. WPI with WPI_{-1}	-.207 (21.42)	-.165 (13.61)	.893 (398.72)	.084 (3.53)	.874 (145.66)
2. WPI	-.232 (23.01)	-.179 (13.70)	.872 (325.12)	.091 (3.54)	.855 (121.86)
3. WPI_{+1} with WPI	-.069 (0.43)	-.516 (23.86)	.107 (1.03)	.121 (1.31)	.297 (8.88)
4. WPI_{+1}	-.069 (0.42)	-.516 (23.51)	.108 (1.03)	.126 (1.40)	.298 (8.77)
PCH					
1. WPI with WPI_{-1}	-.182 (5.08)	-.092 (1.30)	.688 (72.55)	.271 (11.25)	.589 (30.09)
2. WPI	-.232 (7.91)	-.115 (1.94)	.616 (55.74)	.36? (19.25)	.578 (28.30)
3. WPI_{+1} with WPI	-.191 (3.08)	-.057 (0.27)	.290 (7.11)	.361 (11.02)	.255 (7.19)
4. WPI_{+1}	-.138 (1.59)	-.055 (0.25)	.361 (10.88)	.326 (8.88)	.258 (7.19)

[1]F = 4 represents the 95% significance level.

With the exception of the food industry, changes in average weekly earnings were associated with the unlagged demand factor.[e] This suggests that workers felt the pinch of reduced demand through reductions in *AWE* although hourly earnings (a better measure of labor cost from the firm's perspective) were not reduced. As for the aggregate durables results, this may explain why changes in demand had a negative impact on hourly wages. Workers negotiate compensatory wage increases to offset the losses in weekly earnings associated with reduced demand, and these wage increases have a substantial feedback on prices through the cost-price interaction factor.

[e]For electrical equipment, the lagged demand factor was more important.

TABLE 5-6
Industry 36 Electrical Equipment

Factor Loadings for WPI for Alternative Specifications
and Data Transformations (F-ratio in parentheses)[1]

	Factor 1	Factor 2	Factor 3	Factor 4	R^2
PCH/4					
1. WPI with WPI_{-1}	-.208 (10.73)	-.243 (14.64)	.789 (154.40)	-.147 (5.35)	.746 (61.67)
2. WPI	-.239 (11.46)	-.264 (13.98)	.730 (106.92)	-.180 (6.50)	.691 (46.21)
3. WPI_{+1} with WPI	-.034 (0.14)	-.085 (0.89)	.689 (58.18)	-.055 (0.37)	.486 (19.85)
4. WPI_{+1}	-.052 (0.31)	-.063 (0.46)	.672 (52.23)	-.077 (0.69)	.464 (17.89)
PCH					
1. WPI with WPI_{-1}	-.062 (0.43)	-.117 (1.52)	.642 (45.71)	-.035 (0.14)	.432 (15.97)
2. WPI	-.121 (1.55)	-.139 (2.04)	.465 (22.83)	-.405 (17.32)	.413 (14.54)
3. WPI_{+1} with WPI	-.072 (0.38)	-.005 (0.00)	.355 (9.15)	-.016 (0.02)	.132 (3.19)
4. WPI_{+1}	-.070 (0.35)	-.013 (0.01)	.361 (9.34)	-.003 (6.45)	.135 (3.23)

[1]F = 4 represents the 95% significance level.

For the industries in this group there is evidence that Keynesian measures to stabilize prices would have had a short-run inflationary effect in both the labor and product markets. Higher unemployment rates will dampen the inflationary impact in the long run, but in most cases the positive coefficients on the *CPI* in F_3 is larger than the negative coefficients on the unemployment rate variables, suggesting that the unemployment cost of price stability was high for these industries.

The Policy Variables. The impact of fiscal policy through F_4 varied between the industries. For fabricated metals and food, there was a significant positive

TABLE 5-7
Industry 37 Transportation

Factor Loadings for WPI for Alternative Specifications
and Data Transformations (F-ratio in parentheses)[1]

	Factor 1	Factor 2	Factor 3	Factor 4	R^2
PCH/4					
1. WPI with WPI$_{-1}$	-.043 (0.77)	-.189 (17.17)	.910 (398.24)	-.060 (1.73)	.869 (139.30)
2. WPI	-.112 (5.15)	-.417 (71.39)	.806 (266.73)	-.117 (5.62)	.849 (116.19)
3. WPI$_{+1}$ with WPI	-.215 (3.80)	-.049 (0.20)	.429 (15.11)	-.029 (0.07)	.233 (6.38)
4. WPI$_{+1}$	-.163 (2.16)	-.110 (0.98)	.445 (16.09)	-.010 (0.83)	.237 (6.42)
PCH					
1. WPI with WPI$_{-1}$	-.150 (1.84)	-.138 (1.56)	.435 (15.50)	.010 (0.01)	.231 (6.31)
2. WPI	-.131 (1.36)	-.113 (1.01)	.431 (14.69)	.010 (0.01)	.216 (5.69)
3. WPI$_{+1}$ with WPI	-.024 (0.04)	-.024 (0.04)	.276 (5.29)	.121 (1.02)	.092 (2.13)
4. WPI$_{+1}$	-.026 (0.05)	-.021 (0.03)	.311 (6.69)	.072 (0.36)	.103 (2.37)

[1] $F = 4$ represents the 95% significance level.

coefficient for F_4 in the price equation; for furniture, stone, glass, and clay, and electrical equipment there was a significant negative coefficient; and for non-electrical machinery and transportation F_4 was insignificant.

While M_2 (lagged one quarter) was typically associated with F_1 or F_2, M_1 (lagged one quarter) was associated with F_3 with a high positive coefficient. As for the durables aggregate, this suggests that monetary policy if appropriately timed would have been potentially stabilizing. Although the timing of the impact of M_1 on prices appeared to be more directly associated with F_3 than the effect of fiscal policy, the positive coefficient suggests an overall destabilizing effect from M_1.

In all cases, the effect of the wage-price guidelines was stabilizing. This variable consistently appeared on the cost factor with a negative sign.

Group II. Price behavior in the second group of industries was completely dominated by the cost-price interaction of F_3, with the demand factors insignificant or very weak. Included in this group are tobacco, paper, rubber, and primary metals. All four have relatively high concentration ratios, so the market structure can be designated as oligopolistic. All have a high proportion of the labor force unionized, from 44.5 percent for paper to 78.7 for primary metals. The nature of the products is much less homogeneous across industries than for Group I.

The regression coefficients for the various specifications of the price equations for Group II industries are shown in Tables 5-8 through 5-11. The factor loadings for the full set of variables are found in Appendix B.

These results suggest a strong tendency for mark-up pricing, with factor prices playing the predominant role in the price equations. Productivity swings reflected in the demand factors are insignificant or are cancelled out by other effects. Unlike for the Group I industries, there is no evidence of compensatory pricing.

The Wage Equations. For rubber and primary metals the positive impact of the unlagged demand factor on *AHE* was as great as the impact of F_3. This suggests that the Phillips trade-off in these industries is greatly affected by the rate of change of business activity, with the trade-off improving in periods of slack demand. For both of these industries *AWE* depends principally on the unlagged demand factor.

The combined wage and price equations for these two industries imply a type of pricing behavior which would be more sensitive to Keynesian remedies than for the industries previously examined. Since labor costs were responsive to reductions in aggregate demand and since price changes were strongly associated with changes in factor costs, Keynesian measures would have been potentially stabilizing.

For tobacco and paper, on the other hand, there was a significant negative relationship between F_2 and *AHE*, suggesting a model of compensatory wage behavior similar to the Group I industries. For tobacco, *AWE* was less sensitive to changes in demand than for the other industries in this group.

The potential effect of Keynesian remedies on industries in this group was mixed. Since changes in factor prices were the only significant determinant of price changes,[f] it is particularly important to examine wage behavior for these industries (as well as price behavior in supplier industries) to assess the anti-inflationary impact of aggregate demand remedies.

---

[f]The effect of demand was felt, however, through the unemployment rate levels associated with F_3.

81

TABLE 5-8
Industry 21   Tobacco

Factor Loadings for WPI for Alternative Specifications
and Data Transformations (F-ratio in Parentheses)[1]

	Factor 1	Factor 2	Factor 3	Factor 4	R^2
PCH/4					
1. WPI with WPI_{-1}	.079 (0.71)	.028 (0.09)	.743 (62.49)	-.131 (1.93)	.576 (21.73)
2. WPI	.113 (1.23)	.022 (0.05)	.686 (45.23)	-.164 (2.59)	.511 (16.37)
3. WPI_{+1} with WPI	.125 (1.68)	.679 (49.50)	.294 (9.27)	-.008 (0.01)	.553 (19.79)
4. WPI_{+1}	.022 (0.05)	.679 (45.42)	.227 (5.08)	-.096 (0.91)	.523 (17.17)
PCH					
1. WPI with WPI_{-1}	.208 (2.69)	.034 (0.06)	.433 (11.71)	-.022 (0.02)	.232 (4.82)
2. WPI	.205 (2.48)	.011 (0.01)	.401 (9.47)	-.021 (0.03)	.203 (3.98)
3. WPI_{+1} with WPI	.098 (0.47)	.161 (1.31)	-.048 (0.12)	-.098 (0.47)	.047 (0.79)
4. WPI_{+1}	.117 (0.68)	.205 (2.11)	-.053 (0.13)	-.076 (0.28)	.064 (1.15)

[1]F = 4 represents the 95% significance level.

The Policy Variables. Changes in fiscal policy reflected in F_4 were insignificant in all price equations except primary metals. For primary metals, F_4 had a significant negative coefficient in the regression on *WPI*. This suggests that the timing of fiscal policy variables was neutral with respect to price changes in these industries.

M_1 (lagged one quarter) was consistently associated with F_3 with a positive coefficient. Wage-price guidelines were stabilizing in all cases, appearing on F_3 with a negative sign.

TABLE 5-9
Industry 26   Paper

Factor Loadings for WPI for Alternative Specifications
and Data Transformations (F-ratio in parentheses)[1]

	Factor 1	Factor 2	Factor 3	Factor 4	R^2
PCH/4					
1. WPI with WPI$_{-1}$	-.008 (0.02)	.124 (2.78)	.832 (124.98)	-.056 (0.57)	.712 (42.85)
2. WPI	-.034 (0.17)	.146 (3.21)	.798 (95.80)	-.054 (0.44)	.661 (33.14)
3. WPI$_{+1}$ with WPI	.051 (0.28)	-.477 (24.90)	.542 (32.15)	-.019 (0.04)	.525 (19.15)
4. WPI$_{+1}$	.030 (0.09)	-.525 (29.04)	.489 (25.19)	-.028 (0.08)	.516 (18.12)
PCH					
1. WPI with WPI$_{-1}$	.013 (0.01)	.182 (2.58)	.527 (21.65)	.151 (1.78)	.333 (8.65)
2. WPI	.076 (0.33)	.102 (0.59)	.284 (4.60)	.087 (0.43)	.165 (1.99)
3. WPI$_{+1}$ with WPI	.212 (4.07)	.141 (1.80)	.040 (0.14)	.599 (32.50)	.426 (12.86)
4. WPI$_{+1}$	.155 (2.10)	.137 (1.64)	.134 (1.57)	.597 (31.17)	.417 (17.15)

[1]F = 4 represents the 95% significance level.

Group III. In this group, although the cost factor was significant, price changes were predominantly explained by the negative influence of demand. The two industries in this group—chemicals and petroleum—are highly concentrated with an oligopolistic market structure. Petroleum has a high proportion of union workers (64.8 percent), whereas unionization in chemicals is relatively low (37.7 percent). Both industries encompass a variety of product lines, but the representative product is intermediate market level—neither basic nor household-oriented.

The regression coefficients for the various specifications of the price equa-

TABLE 5-10
Industry 30 Rubber and Plastics

Factor Loadings for WPI for Alternative Specifications
and Data Transformations (F-ratio in parentheses)[1]

	Factor 1	Factor 2	Factor 3	Factor 4	R^2
PCH/4					
1. WPI with WPI_{-1}	-.040 (0.31)	.053 (0.55)	.852 (141.90)	-.057 (0.64)	.734 (47.82)
2. WPI	-.058 (0.56)	.048 (0.38)	.826 (112.97)	-.061 (0.62)	.692 (38.19)
3. WPI_{+1} with WPI	.194 (6.63)	-.173 (5.28)	.797 (111.96)	-.058 (0.59)	.705 (41.42)
4. WPI_{+1}	.186 (5.24)	-.200 (6.05)	.765 (88.56)	-.054 (0.44)	.663 (33.44)
PCH					
1. WPI with WPI_{-1}	-.009 (0.01)	-.025 (0.06)	.634 (35.91)	.123 (1.35)	.418 (12.44)
2. WPI	-.023 (0.04)	-.167 (1.97)	.419 (12.41)	.273 (5.27)	.279 (6.58)
3. WPI_{+1} with WPI	-.064 (0.29)	-.015 (0.02)	.512 (18.72)	.079 (0.45)	.272 (6.48)
4. WPI_{+1}	-.196 (2.42)	-.189 (2.25)	.337 (7.15)	.047 (0.14)	.190 (3.99)

[1]F = 4 represents the 95% significance level.

tions for Group III industries are shown in Tables 5-12 and 5-13. The factor loadings for the full set of variables are found in Appendix B.

Since factor costs play a relatively smaller role in the price equations for these industries, one is tempted to reject the model of mark-up pricing in favor of the model of competitive profit maximization. However, when the full factor matrix is examined, it seems likely that the negative impact of demand in these industries was not predominantly due to the effect of productivity swings on unit labor cost. For petroleum, both unit labor cost and standard unit labor cost

TABLE 5-11
Industry 33 Primary Metals

Factor Loadings for WPI for Alternative Specifications
and Data Transformations (F-ratio in parentheses)[1]

	Factor 1	Factor 2	Factor 3	Factor 4	R^2
PCH/4					
1. WPI with WPI_{-1}	.070 (0.89)	.178 (5.76)	.748 (101.72)	-.251 (11.45)	.659 (39.93)
2. WPI	.057 (0.44)	.226 (6.97)	.674 (61.99)	-.210 (6.02)	.553 (25.15)
3. WPI_{+1} with WPI	.150 (2.05)	.308 (8.62)	.290 (7.65)	-.342 (10.63)	.318 (9.64)
4. WPI_{+1}	.155 (1.15)	.264 (6.22)	.246 (5.40)	-.404 (14.57)	.317 (9.44)
PCH					
1. WPI with WPI_{-1}	.100 (1.07)	.046 (0.23)	.616 (40.58)	.137 (2.00)	.411 (14.65)
2. WPI	.097 (0.90)	.056 (0.30)	.565 (30.63)	.150 (2.16)	.354 (11.32)
3. WPI_{+1} with WPI	.275 (5.80)	.249 (4.75)	.187 (2.68)	-.076 (0.44)	.178 (4.55)
4. WPI_{+1}	.291 (6.46)	.196 (2.93)	.243 (4.50)	-.068 (0.35)	.187 (4.75)

[1] F = 4 represents the 95% significance level.

were associated with F_3.[g] For chemicals, *ULC* was negatively associated with F_1, but it was positively related to F_2. Since the negative impact of changes in F_2 on chemicals prices was nearly as great as those in F_1, the total negative effect of demand changes on the *WPI* cannot be attributed to productivity swings.

In view of the oligopolistic market structure one is inclined toward the view that the negative impact of demand reflects compensatory pricing in these

[g]This was a surprising result in view of the fact that ULC was not related to F_3 in those industry groups where F_3 dominated the price equation.

TABLE 5-12
Industry 28 Chemicals

Factor Loadings for WPI for Alternative Specifications
and Data Transformations (F-ratio in parentheses)[1]

	Factor 1	Factor 2	Factor 3	Factor 4	R^2
PCH/4					
1. WPI with WPI_{-1}	-.418 (27.63)	-.372 (21.88)	.350 (19.37)	-.416 (27.37)	.608 (32.05)
2. WPI	-.427 (25.50)	-.333 (15.51)	.324 (14.68)	-.407 (23.17)	.564 (26.30)
3. WPI_{+1} with WPI	-.373 (20.53)	.000 (0.00)	.367 (19.88)	-.553 (45.14)	.580 (28.53)
4. WPI_{+1}	-.374 (17.88)	-.009 (0.01)	.371 (17.60)	-.495 (31.33)	.523 (22.29)
PCH					
1. WPI with WPI_{-1}	-.238 (6.03)	-.314 (10.50)	.414 (18.25)	-.302 (9.72)	.418 (14.84)
2. WPI	-.253 (6.54)	-.310 (9.82)	.407 (16.92)	-.278 (7.90)	.403 (13.72)
3. WPI_{+1} with WPI	-.204 (3.38)	-.078 (0.49)	.434 (15.28)	-.017 (0.02)	.236 (6.38)
4. WPI_{+1}	-.206 (3.34)	-.073 (0.42)	.419 (13.80)	-.025 (0.05)	.224 (5.87)

[1]F = 4 represents the 95% significance level.

industries. The inflationary impact of slack demand occurred through F_2, suggesting stagflation was sustained over a longer period than for Group I industries.

The Wage Equations. For petroleum both *AWE* and *AHE* were dominated by the Phillips relationship of F_3, with a high coefficient (.880) on the *CPI*. The demand factors had only a small, but negative, impact on the relationship between wage changes and unemployment rates.

For chemicals, on the other hand, changes in *AWE* and *AHE* were negatively

TABLE 5-13
Industry 29 Petroleum

Factor Loadings for WPI for Alternative Specifications
and Data Transformations (F-ratio in parentheses)[1]

	Factor 1	Factor 2	Factor 3	Factor 4	R^2
PCH/4					
1. WPI with WPI_{-1}	.254 (12.36)	-.605 (70.17)	.534 (54.67)	-.135 (3.49)	.734 (46.90)
2. WPI	.268 (11.22)	-.574 (51.28)	.503 (39.53)	-.158 (3.90)	.680 (35.41)
3. WPI_{+1} with WPI	-.311 (8.29)	.080 (0.55)	.498 (21.75)	-.234 (4.69)	.405 (11.57)
4. WPI_{+1}	-.242 (4.42)	.062 (0.29)	.466 (16.37)	-.239 (4.31)	.337 (8.47)
PCH^*					
1. WPI with WPI_{-1}	.057 (0.36)	-.408 (18.61)	.452 (22.84)		.544 (20.28)
2. WPI	.233 (5.69)	-.337 (11.90)	.428 (19.20)		.523 (18.27)
3. WPI_{+1} with WPI	-.018 (0.02)	-.009 (0.00)	.087 (0.41)		.048 (0.86)
4. WPI_{+1}	-.171 (1.56)	-.022 (0.03)	.090 (0.43)		.062 (1.10)

*No Factor 4 on this specification.

[1]F = 4 represents the 95% significance level.

related to F_4 as was standard unit labor cost. This may reflect a spurious relationship associated with the timing of union contracts, but it does suggest that wages in this industry have been considerably more stable than other costs. This is the only industry for which a clear Phillips relationship between wage changes and unemployment rates was not evident.

Because of the weaker feedback of wage changes into price changes, labor market conditions are not as crucial to the inflationary process as in Groups I and II. However, the results suggest that Keynesian remedies would have been even less effective in these industries than in those exhibiting pure mark-up pricing.

The Policy Variables. For chemicals the fiscal policy variables associated with F_4 had a substantial negative impact. This was undoubtedly due in part to the effect of the wage variables that appeared on F_4 with large negative coefficients. For petroleum, F_4 was insignificant.

M_1 (lagged one quarter) was positively associated with F_3, although the coefficient was smaller for petroleum than for other industries. Wage-price guidelines had the usual stabilizing relationship to F_3, with a particularly large coefficient ($-.720$) for petroleum.

Group IV. Price changes in this last group of industries were predominantly explained by the positive influence of the unlagged demand factor, F_1. The industries in this group—textiles, lumber and wood, and leather—have competitive market structures with low union representation in the labor force. Textiles and leather employ a high percentage of women workers relative to other industries. In all cases, within each industry classification, the products are relatively homogeneous.

The regression coefficients for the various specifications of the price equations for Group IV industries are shown in Tables 5-14 through 5-16. The factor loadings for the full set of variables are found in Appendix B.

For these industries, factor costs play a much smaller role than demand with an insignificant influence in textiles and the strongest effect in leather. Although in a competitive model, price is affected by both demand and supply conditions, these results suggest that shifts in demand have dominated cost changes for explaining price behavior in Group IV industries in the sample period.

Since the coefficient on the demand factor is positive, the impact appears to be through the demand function rather than through the productivity effect on unit labor costs—since rising prices were associated with falling unit labor cost over the period.

Since both textiles and lumber and wood are primary products, it is interesting to note how they behaved as material costs. The *WPI* for textiles was used as the materials cost for apparel and the *WPI* for lumber and wood was the materials cost for paper and for furniture. In both cases, the materials cost variable was associated with the unlagged demand factor rather than the cost factor. These were the only indexes of materials cost not associated with F_3. Because of the predominance of F_3 for explaining price changes in Groups I, II, and III, it is suggested that the responsiveness of textiles and lumber and wood prices to demand conditions had in user industries a secondary impact that reduced the influence of the cost-push spiral and was favorable to the efficacy of aggregate demand measures.

88

TABLE 5-14
Industry 22   Textiles

Factor Loadings for WPI for Alternative Specifications
and Data Transformations (F-ratio in parentheses)[1]

	Factor 1	Factor 2	Factor 3	Factor 4	R^2
PCH/4					
1. WPI with WPI_{-1}	.402	.608	.128	-.225	.598
	(24.92)	(57.01)	(2.53)	(7.79)	(30.74)
2. WPI	.423	.551	.145	-.203	.544
	(23.93)	(40.61)	(2.80)	(5.13)	(24.25)
3. WPI_{+1} with WPI	.718	.315	.123	-.212	.675
	(98.34)	(18.92)	(2.89)	(8.56)	(42.92)
4. WPI_{+1}	.721	.273	.118	-.189	.644
	(89.07)	(12.77)	(2.39)	(6.11)	(36.78)
PCH					
1. WPI with WPI_{-1}	.491	.303	.053	-.255	.401
	(24.95)	(9.49)	(0.28)	(6.72)	(13.83)
2. WPI	.502	.225	.054	-.175	.336
	(23.15)	(4.64)	(0.27)	(2.80)	(10.28)
3. WPI_{+1} with WPI	.501	.249	.059	-.141	.484
	(30.15)	(7.45)	(0.42)	(2.39)	(19.37)
4. WPI_{+1}	.657	.128	.056	-.177	.482
	(50.83)	(1.93)	(0.37)	(3.69)	(18.92)

[1] F = 4 represents the 95% significance level.

The Wage Equations. Wage behavior in Group IV was not significantly different from that of the other groups. Average weekly earnings were strongly influenced by unlagged demand (F_1) with the effect being somewhat weaker in leather. Average hourly earnings were explained by changes in F_3, the cost-unemployment rate factor.

For textiles, the interpretation of F_3 is different from the other groups. It is dominated by the unemployment variables and the coefficient on the *CPI* in the PCH/4 transformation is relatively low (.563). This suggests that money wages in textiles are more sensitive to labor market conditions than in the other industries and that the trade-off between unemployment and price stability is more favorable. The failure of materials costs to achieve a sufficiently high factor loading for assignment is also interesting, in view of the contention that U.S.

TABLE 5-15
Industry 24   Lumber & Wood

Factor Loadings for WPI for Alternative Specifications
and Data Transformations (F-ratio in parentheses)[1]

	Factor 1	Factor 2	Factor 3	Factor 4	R^2
PCH/4					
1. WPI with WPI_{-1}	.757 (111.21)	.163 (5.16)	.310 (18.65)	-.015 (0.04)	.696 (45.02)
2. WPI	.749 (98.60)	.143 (3.59)	.297 (15.50)	-.002 (0.00)	.670 (39.25)
3. WPI_{+1} with WPI	.562 (29.72)	.062 (0.36)	.203 (3.88)	-.109 (1.12)	.373 (11.69)
4. WPI_{+1}	.548 (27.21)	.069 (0.43)	.208 (3.92)	-.111 (1.12)	.360 (10.87)
PCH					
1. WPI with WPI_{-1}	.504 (32.93)	.510 (33.72)	.130 (2.19)	-.119 (1.84)	.545 (23.55)
2. WPI	.548 (36.66)	.448 (24.50)	.136 (2.26)	-.077 (0.72)	.525 (21.36)
3. WPI_{+1} with WPI	.126 (0.99)	.201 (2.53)	.022 (0.03)	-.017 (0.02)	.057 (1.19)
4. WPI_{+1}	.129 (1.02)	.184 (2.07)	.026 (0.04)	-.012 (0.01)	.052 (1.06)

[1]F = 4 represents the 95% significance level.

foreign trade policy, having raised cotton prices in the U.S. market relative to those abroad, has made the U.S. textile industry less competitive.

Because costs have very little impact on prices in this industry group, labor market behavior was not as important in the inflationary mechanism as in Groups I and II. Group IV industries were the only group for which Keynesian measures would have had a significant anti-inflationary impact in the sample period. For all the industries, changes in aggregate demand (reflected in *GNP*) were strongly associated with the industry-specific demand factor without a lag.

To the extent that hourly wages were not responsive to these measures,

TABLE 5-16
Industry 31 Leather

Factor Loadings for WPI for Alternative Specifications
and Data Transformations (F-ratio in parentheses)[1]

	Factor 1	Factor 2	Factor 3	Factor 4	R^2
PCH/4					
1. WPI with WPI_{-1}	.658 (90.75)	.032 (0.21)	.473 (46.89)	-.336 (23.66)	.771 (53.86)
2. WPI	.673 (75.48)	.089 (1.32)	.440 (32.26)	-.254 (10.75)	.718 (39.88)
3. WPI_{+1} with WPI	.540 (23.28)	.257 (5.28)	.203 (3.29)	-.020 (0.03)	.399 (10.62)
4. WPI_{+1}	.518 (20.47)	.283 (6.11)	.189 (2.73)	-.008 (0.00)	.384 (9.77)
PCH					
1. WPI with WPI_{-1}	.548 (26.69)	.132 (1.55)	.267 (6.34)	-.267 (6.34)	.460 (13.62)
2. WPI	.538 (23.13)	.137 (1.50)	.216 (3.73)	-.238 (4.53)	.412 (10.97)
3. WPI_{+1} with WPI	.349 (6.88)	.047 (0.12)	.142 (1.14)	-.076 (0.33)	.150 (2.82)
4. WPI_{+1}	.356 (6.96)	.075 (0.31)	.099 (0.54)	-.044 (0.11)	.144 (2.64)

[1]F = 4 represents the 95% significance level.

aggregate demand remedies would have resulted in a profit squeeze. For all three industries, profit/equity had a high positive association with F_1. Furthermore, these industries had among the lowest average profit/equity ratios of all the manufacturing industries in the sample period. Given the highly competitive market structure, measures to restrict demand would have been likely to drive some producers out of business. Thus, even though aggregate demand measures are not industry-specific, the impact is felt differently in different industries, with respect to profits as well as prices. This is important to bear in mind when assessing the neutrality of Keynesian remedies on resource allocation vis-à-vis other measures such as wage-price guidelines or moral suasion.

The Policy Variables. Since changes in *GNP* affected prices through F_1, fiscal and monetary measures had a potential stabilizing effect. However, the fiscal policy factor, F_4, had a weak negative association with price changes in textiles and leather and was insignificant for lumber and wood. This may reflect effectiveness lags, since prices in these industries are highly volatile.

M_1 (-1) was associated with F_3 in all cases, but the association with price changes was not as great as for the other industry groups, since F_3 was less important than the demand factors for explaining price changes. The same is true of the guidelines, which had a negative association with F_3. However, to the extent the guidelines moderated wage increases (*AHE* was largely influenced by F_3), they could potentially mitigate the profit squeeze associated with restrictive fiscal measures for these industries.

Unassigned Industries

Three industries—printing and publishing, apparel, and instruments—were unassigned. For printing and publishing a *WPI* was not available. For the other two industries, we could not obtain satisfactory price equations.[h] The regression coefficients for the price equations for apparel and instruments are shown in Tables 5-17 and 5-18. The factor loadings for the full variables sets are found in Appendix B.

The wage equations for these industries all followed the normal pattern.[i] For all these industries, F_3 explained most of the variance in *AHE* while *AWE* was dominated by short-run changes in demand, through F_1. Among the three industries, wages in instruments were least affected by changing demand conditions. The impact of F_4 was weak or insignificant in all cases.

**Relation of Market Structure
to Price Behavior**

The industry groups based on ex post analyses of price behavior did not correspond to an ex ante categorization based on market structure, although there was clearly some relationship between the market structure, nature of the product, and price equations. Group I industries had similar types of products, whereas Groups II and IV were more homogeneous with respect to market structure. Although there was not a one-to-one correspondence between market structure and price behavior, it did seem that prices in the more competitive

---

[h]Other researchers have excluded instruments from their analyses due to "inadequate price data." Thus the series we used for the *WPI* may not have been a reliable indicator of actual price movements. See Eckstein and Wyss, "Industry Price Equations," op. cit., p. 137.

[i]This confirms the reliability of most of the data and suggests that the problem was with the price variables.

TABLE 5-17
Industry 23 Apparel

Factor Loadings for WPI for Alternative Specifications
and Data Transformations (F-ratio in parentheses)[1]

	Factor 1	Factor 2	Factor 3	Factor 4	R^2
PCH/4					
1. WPI with WPI_{-1}	-.171 (1.84)	-.116 (0.85)	-.069 (0.30)	-.011 (0.01)	.048 (1.01)
2. WPI	-.170 (1.79)	-.119 (0.88)	-.073 (0.33)	-.012 (0.01)	.049 (1.01)
3. WPI_{+1} with WPI	-.224 (3.22)	-.044 (0.12)	-.065 (0.27)	-.097 (0.60)	.066 (1.41)
4. WPI_{+1}	-.225 (3.20)	-.043 (0.12)	-.067 (0.29)	-.096 (0.58)	.066 (1.39)
PCH					
1. WPI with WPI_{-1}	-.006 (0.00)	.003 (0.00)	.014 (0.01)	.121 (0.89)	.015 (0.30)
2. WPI	-.056 (0.19)	.006 (0.00)	.021 (0.03)	0.14 (0.01)	.004 (0.08)
3. WPI_{+1} with WPI	.202 (2.58)	-.033 (0.07)	.059 (0.22)	.080 (0.41)	.052 (1.10)
4. WPI_{+1}	.202 (2.54)	-.033 (0.07)	.058 (0.21)	.081 (0.41)	.052 (1.08)

[1]$F = 4$ represents the 95% significance level.

industries had a stronger positive relationship to changing demand conditions and that compensatory pricing was characteristic of oligopolistic market structures.

To test the hypothesis that price behavior is related to market structure, we regressed several variables reflecting market structure and product characteristics on the factor regression coefficients across industries. This gave us eighteen observations for the factor regression coefficients for F_1, F_2, and F_3.[j]

In each equation the coefficients a_1, a_2, and a_3 on factors F_1, F_2, and F_3,

[j]We omitted analysis of F_4 because it was so frequently insignificant.

TABLE 5-18
Industry 38 Instruments

Factor Loadings for WPI for Alternative Specifications
and Data Transformations (F-ratio in parentheses)[1]

	Factor 1	Factor 2	Factor 3	Factor 4	R^2
PCH/4					
1. WPI with WPI_{-1}	-.453 (15.14)	-.007 (0.00)	-.239 (4.22)	.271 (5.42)	.336 (8.27)
2. WPI	-.411 (10.91)	-.003 (0.00)	-.205 (2.71)	.213 (2.93)	.257 (5.53)
3. WPI_{+1} with WPI	-.450 (13.99)	-.126 (1.10)	-.113 (0.88)	.246 (4.18)	.291 (6.70)
4. WPI_{+1}	-.408 (10.24)	-.060 (0.22)	-.100 (0.62)	.199 (2.44)	.220 (4.51)
PCH					
1. WPI with WPI_{-1}	-.032 (0.06)	-.210 (2.49)	-.281 (4.46)	.090 (0.46)	.132 (2.48)
2. WPI	-.030 (0.05)	-.206 (2.31)	-.262 (3.74)	.090 (0.44)	.120 (2.18)
3. WPI_{+1} with WPI	-.086 (0.38)	-.039 (0.08)	-.207 (2.22)	.031 (0.05)	.053 (0.91)
4. WPI_{+1}	-.082 (0.34)	-.034 (0.06)	-.190 (1.81)	.030 (0.05)	.045 (0.75)

[1]F = 4 represents the 95% significance level.

respectively, from the regression on *WPI* [k] were the dependent variables. Four explanatory variables were included:

1. *Profit/equity*. This variable was selected as a performance criterion as well as a measure of market power. It is an average of quarterly profit/equity over the full sample period.

2. *Concentration ratio*. The concentration ratio is the percent of total

[k]Parameter estimates from the equations for PCH /4, unlagged specification with the lagged dependent variable included, were used in all cases.

industry sales attributable to the four largest firms in 1962:4. This is another measure of market power with high concentration ratios suggesting oligopolistic patterns of behavior.

3. *Market level.* This scaled variable assigned numbers 1, 2, 3 to basic, intermediate, and final categories, respectively. The assignment was based on a priori considerations from an evaluation of the commodities produced by each industry group.

4. *Union-firm interaction.* Price behavior could be affected by the strength of bilateral monopoly in wage negotiations. We introduced a dummy variable equal to one where the percent of the labor force unionized was above 50 percent and where, at the same time, the concentration ratio for the industry was above 48 percent and zero otherwise. Unionization was derived from estimates by Leonard W. Weiss.[1]

The data used in the regressions are shown in Table 5-19 and the regression coefficients for the three equations are in Table 5-20. The variables reflecting differences in market structure had a significant relationship to the variation in the way demand affects price changes. However, market structure (as measured by the variables we chose) does not explain interindustry differences in the coefficient on the cost-price interaction. This lack of significance in Equation 3 could be due to the unavailability of unemployment rates for six industries—instruments, tobacco, paper, petroleum, rubber, and leather. Unemployment rates were a substantial component of F_3 for those industries for which it was available and, consequently, must have had an impact on the way F_3 affected the *WPI*, that is, on the size of a_3. That there is considerable variation among the industries lacking unemployment data with respect to the explanatory variables may explain why we could find no systematic variation with a_3.

In the equation for a_1, there was a significant negative coefficient for profits/equity. The mean value of a_1 was near zero (.010) with a standard deviation of .342. This means that for industries with relatively high profit/equity, changing demand conditions had a negative relationship with price changes in the short run. For industries with low profit/equity, changing demand was positively associated with price changes. This implies that the short-run impact of Keynesian remedies for inflation is more likely both to produce price increases in industries with high profit/equity and to be stabilizing in less profitable industries. Our results suggest, however, that the short-run impact of demand on prices is related to the profit rate of the industry rather than to the market structure of nature of the product.[1]

When allowance is made for a one-quarter lag, all the structural variables become significant in explaining interindustry differences in the impact of demand on prices. In the equation for a_2, the impact of profit/equity is negative,

[1]Of course, profitability is undoubtedly related to market structure and the nature of the product.

TABLE 5-19

Explanatory Variables for Cross-section
Analysis of Price Behavior

Industry	Profit/ Equity	Concentration Ratio	Market Level	Unioni- zation
transportation	13.31	68.6	2	59.67
electrical equipment	11.13	34.4	1	52.00
non-electrical machinery	10.83	20.6	1	45.60
fabricated metals	9.75	14.7	1	52.45
stone, clay, and glass	9.35	18.1	1	44.03
furniture	9.84	5.2	3	29.00
lumber and wood	8.74	21.2	1	20.48
instruments	14.60	37.9	2	37.30
food	10.07	21.8	3	44.71
tobacco	14.06	70.9	3	53.00
textiles	7.35	22.0	2	30.85
apparel	10.30	4.9	3	55.00
paper	8.66	20.7	2	44.51
chemicals	13.10	35.3	1	37.70
petroleum	11.16	50.3	1	64.82
rubber	10.15	48.1	2	53.88
leather	9.20	26.7	2	37.99
primary metals	8.38	35.6	1	78.72

Source: 1. Profit/equity – Bureau of Economics, Federal Trade Commission.
Average of quarterly values, 1959:1 – 1971:3.

2. Concentration ratio – Bureau of Economics, Federal Trade Commission.
1962:4.

3. Unionization – Leonard W. Weiss, Appendix to "Concentration and
Labor Earnings," American Economic Review, 56 (March 1966),
pp. 96–117.

suggesting that even with a lag, compensatory pricing persists in the more highly profitable industries.[m]

With profit/equity constant, there is less tendency for compensatory pricing among the more highly concentrated industries. The simple correlation between the profit rate and concentration ratio is .637. Thus, the common observation that the more concentrated industries raise prices when demand falls may be related to the high profit rates in these industries rather than to the nature of oligopoly behavior, per se. The positive coefficient for the concentration ratio suggests that the reaction of prices to aggregate demand remedies was somewhat

[m]The mean value of a_2 is $-.072$ with a standard deviation of .27, which implies that compensatory pricing is even greater with a lag than in the very short run.

TABLE 5-20

Cross-section Regressions on the Factor Loadings
for F_1, F_2, and F_3 (F-ratios in parentheses)*

Dependent Variables	Profit/ Equity	Concentration Ratio	Market Level	Union-Firm Interaction
a_1	-15.331* (11.27)	1.148 (2.14)	0.010 (0.01)	-0.019 (0.00)
a_2	-11.902* (14.95)	1.730* (10.69)	0.204* (11.06)	-0.555* (8.03)
a_3	- 5.101 (0.76)	-0.045 (0.00)	-0.85 (0.54)	0.383 (1.06)

*Significant at the 95% level.

more stabilizing in the more concentrated industries. This may reflect the differential impact of moral suasion which is generally assumed to be most effective in the highly concentrated industries, where offenders can be more easily singled out.[2]

The impact of demand was more likely to be positive in consumer goods industries, while compensatory pricing characterized basic industries. This was consistent with a priori expectation. Among other reasons, demand is generally less elastic in basic and intermediate industries than in the consumer goods sector.

The union-firm interaction variable had a negative relationship with inter-industry variations in F_2. Where strong unions interact with firms in highly concentrated industries there is more likely to be compensatory pricing than in industries without such interaction. The simple correlation of this variable with the concentration ratio is .809, suggesting that the observed tendency for compensatory pricing in concentrated industries may be attributable to bilateral monopoly elements (as well as high profit rates) rather than to product market concentration per se.

We have already commented on the failure of the market structure variables to explain interindustry variations in a_3, the impact of the cost-unemployment factor, F_3, on price behavior. It is likely that the exclusion of unemployment variables in certain industries affected the relationship between F_3 and prices. Alternatively, we could interpret the results to mean that interindustry variations in F_3 were unrelated to the market structure variables in our equation.

General Observations

We found that four general types of pricing behavior could be identified for the nineteen manufacturing industries. Except for Group IV, factor prices seem to be the relevant cost variable rather than unit factor cost. This suggests that mark-up pricing is the (statistically) predominant form of behavior, even in the more competitive industries.

The influence of demand was more variable among the industry groups. Changes in the level of demand had a predominantly negative impact on prices, however, suggesting that the overall short-run effect of reducing aggregate demand is inflationary. Although the lags in the adjustment of price changes to changes in the factors seem to be short, there is no evidence that the tendency toward compensatory pricing is reduced in the second quarter, since the coefficients on F_2 most often remain negative.

To the extent that unemployment rates are increased by aggregate demand measures, the wage-price spiral will be dampened. However, the short-run price increases associated with falling demand will be transmitted into further price increases through the impact of the *CPI* on wages and prices in F_3. The accelerationist hypothesis that the loss of money illusion increases with the length of the inflationary period was not directly tested in our study. However, even when the length of the price rise is ignored, the coefficient on the *CPI* in the wage equations was quite high, the Kendall coefficients being on the order of 0.6 to 0.7.

Because demand changes affected prices differently in various industries, aggregate demand remedies would potentially have affected industry prices differently and hence would have influenced the structure of relative prices. Measures to reduce money *GNP*, for example, would have caused prices in Group III to rise relative to Groups I and II and prices in Group IV to fall relative to these groups. There would also have been a differential impact on profits, with high profit industries gaining and low profit industries experiencing a squeeze.

The impact on relative profits is partly due to differences in price behavior and partly to the relative homogeneity of wage behavior across industry groups. Hourly earnings were much less affected by demand changes than were prices. Perhaps this reflected differences in timing, with union contracts tending to stabilize wage changes in the face of short-run changes in demand conditions. In addition, spillover effects in the labor markets could serve as buffers to the impact of changes in industry-specific conditions. In most cases, the level of the economy-wide unemployment rate was associated with the industry-specific unemployment rates where those were available.

Thus, the industry analysis of price behavior suggests that Keynesian remedies for inflation potentially not only had a perverse impact on but also were not neutral with respect to relative prices or profits across manufacturing industries.

This is an important consideration when they are weighted against price controls and other less-conventional anti-inflation policy instruments.

The Policy Variables

We have suggested that the potential short-run impact of monetary and fiscal policy can be gauged by the responsiveness of prices to F_1 and F_2. As changes occur in the level of unemployment the effect is also felt through F_3. However, the fiscal policy variables (except for direct taxes) were associated with an independent factor, F_4, reflecting some coincidence of timing with variable effectiveness lags.

In most cases, F_4 had a significant negative association with price changes. This could imply that fiscal policy was timed in such a way as to be stabilizing (restrictive measures being associated with rising prices), or it could reflect a short-run perverse response of prices to fiscal remedies (rising prices being associated with restrictive measures). There is no noticeable gain in significance of F_4 in the lagged specifications; however, we have previously noted that lags tend to be short in the industry analyses.

As for durables, the personal tax variables were associated with F_2, suggesting they have a lagged impact on demand. Changes in the tax rate were positively related to F_2, while changes in tax receipts had a negative association with F_2. There was no systematic relationship between the tax rate variables and F_3 such as we saw in the durables and manufacturing analyses. This is probably because the tax variables are aggregated over the entire economy and changes in these effective aggregate tax rates have a weaker industry-specific impact on costs and prices than they have for the manufacturing aggregates.

Corporate tax receipts were positively associated with changes in F_1, as expected. The corporate tax rate had a weaker, negative association with F_1 or was unassigned.[n]

Monetary policy had an interesting, mixed effect, M_1 (-1), money supply excluding time deposits, lagged one quarter, was nearly always associated with F_3, the cost-price interaction factor. Since F_3 dominated the explanation of price changes in most industries, monetary policy, it is suggested, could have been a potentially powerful anti-inflationary device although it was timed in such a way as to be destabilizing. However, the relationship could also be attributable to endogenous effects of price changes on M_1 (-1). Consequently, policy conclusions should be based on a study to determine direction of causality rather than on an analysis of association such as we have made.

M_2 (-1) money supply including deposits, lagged one quarter is usually associated with F_1 or F_4 or both. This suggests that M_2 (-1) is the monetary

[n]That is, it had no factor loading above | .39 |.

variable most often coordinated (in terms of timing) with fiscal measures, although swings in M_2 (-1) are also strongly induced by current changes in demand through F_1. It is interesting to note that the effect of demand on M_2 (-1) is usually greater than on M_1 (-1), since M_1 (-1) is less often associated with either of the demand factors.

The Federal Reserve discount rate, lagged one quarter, nearly always associated with the other interest rate variables on F_2. The positive coefficient suggests that credit policy has been timed so as to be stabilizing, while the association with F_2 implies it acted as a demand inhibitor rather than as a cost variable at the industry level.

In nearly all cases the wage-price guidelines dummy had a strong negative impact on F_3. As for durables and total manufacturing this impact suggests that the guidelines imposed during 1962:1 through 1966:4 significantly dampened the interaction between wages, prices, and other costs.

It is interesting to note that the macroeconomic policy variables, as well as such economy-wide aggregates as GNP and the overall unemployment rate, associated with industry-specific economic conditions in much the same way as with the manufacturing aggregates. For instance, changes in GNP were nearly always associated with changing demand conditions at the industry level without a lag, and the overall unemployment rate was associated with industry unemployment rates. This undoubtedly reflects input-output linkages in product markets and spillover effects in labor markets, which apparently occur with very short lags.

However, even though changes in macroeconomic policy variables have a similar impact on product demand and labor market conditions for the various industries within the manufacturing sector, their impact on industry prices is much more variable because of interindustry differences in the way changing demand conditions affected prices. Thus, the effect of fiscal and monetary policy on relative industry prices and profits is much less "neutral" than the interindustry impact on demand and unemployment.[o] On the other hand, the effect of wage-price guidelines was more evenly distributed across-the-board, since except for the industries in Group IV, measures that dampened the cost-price interaction had a substantial anti-inflationary impact.

Notes

1. Leonard W. Weiss, Appendix to "Concentration and Labor Earnings," *American Economic Review*, 56 (March 1966), pp. 96-117, Table A-2.

2. See J.T. Romans, "Moral Suasion as an Instrument of Economic Policy," *The American Economic Review*, 56 (December 1966), pp. 1220-25.

---

[o]Of course, monetary policy is notably nonneutral in its impact on demand and unemployment. The construction and automobile industries are usually hardest hit by restrictive credit policies.

Summary and Conclusions

Our stated objective for this study was to examine the channels through which the inflationary process has been transmitted in the U.S. manufacturing sector in order to assess the potential impact of anti-inflation policy. Although our methodology did not test specific structural hypotheses about price behavior, it shed some light on the interrelationships between variables most commonly used in empirical studies of inflation.

We analyzed aggregate data for total manufacturing and durables manufacturing industries, since these are the indicators on which policy recommendations are often based. The analysis at the two-digit level of the SIC investigated the microeconomic underpinnings of the inflationary process and allowed us to assess the industry-specific impact of alternative measures.

Methodological Considerations

It is important to bear in mind that factor analysis is a measure of association, and inferences of causality should only be made with great caution. This was particularly noticeable in assessing the impact of the policy variables on prices and wages. We noted that the relationships obtained were more likely to be related to coincidental timing rather than to impact. Thus, in gauging the effectiveness of restrictive fiscal policy, for instance, we assumed fiscal measures would operate through reducing aggregate demand and, consequently, examined the effect of falling demand rather than the policy variables themselves on prices.

We attempted to account for lags in the relationship between the variables other than policy instruments by lagging the explanatory set and by including the lagged dependent variable. In addition, one factor incorporated lagged variables so that a two-quarter lag was obtained. However, in most cases, the unlagged specification was preferred and the results were not affected significantly if the lagged dependent variable was excluded. This is consistent with most other studies in which lags between prices, wages, and product and labor market conditions have been found to be short. When lags are short a statistical model of association between variables is appropriate for examining structural relationships.

On the other hand, timing difficulties and longer impact lags make it more difficult to interpret the relationship of the policy variables to prices and wages.

101

The problem is also complicated by the inability to separate induced from discretionary policy changes. Consequently, we assume that Keynesian-type remedies have their principal impact through changing demand and credit conditions and evaluate their potential effect in terms of the relationship between demand and credit conditions on the inflationary process. Similarly, we assume that wage-price controls dampen increases in factor costs and (depending on how the controls are structured) of consumer prices; therefore we evaluate the potential effect of controls by the relationship of these variables to the inflationary process.

Description of the Inflationary Process

We found that the predominant form of price behavior in the manufacturing sector in the sample period[a] was a strong interaction between changes in prices, changes in factor costs, and unemployment levels. Price changes were associated with changing factor costs rather than with factor costs per unit of output, suggesting a mark-up pricing model not affected by swings in productivity. The association of unemployment rate levels with these variables suggests a Phillips relationship in the labor market[b] with a substantial positive coefficient on the consumer price index; this, in turn, implies some (but not total) absence of money illusion.

Although the unemployment levels dampened the inflationary effect of costs, through F_3, the actual inflation-unemployment trade-off was affected by changes in the level of economic activity. Throughout the manufacturing sector, there was a weak but perverse response to changing demand conditions which served to worsen the inflation-unemployment trade-off when demand fell and to improve it when demand increased. Because this response was greatest in the durables industries and in the more highly concentrated markets, we attributed it to compensatory pricing rather than to a response to productivity changes.

Although the short-run inflationary influence of falling demand was independent of the Phillips relationship in F_3, it would have been felt in F_3 (although with some lag) through the effect on the *CPI* and materials costs. It would also affect prices in other industries without significant negative coefficients for F_1 and F_2 owing to product market linkages affecting materials costs and the *CPI*.

Although our methodology provided no direct test of the accelerationist

[a]It is important to bear in mind that the sample periods are different. The industry studies contain three observations from 1971, and both the industry studies and durables start later than total manufacturing. The later the sample, the greater is the bias toward stagflationary behavior due to the influence of the post-1968 experience.

[b]In most cases, average hourly earnings and manhour compensation were the only wage variables associated with unemployment levels. Average weekly earnings were tied to changing demand and labor market conditions.

model (since we could not allow for the effect of the length of the inflationary period on the coefficient for the *CPI*), the implications of our results are much the same. As demand is reduced through restrictive monetary and fiscal measures, there is a short-run inflationary impact that is transmitted into a higher rate of inflation through F_3. However, unlike the accelerationist view, our results suggest that the inflationary process is dampened in the longer run since higher unemployment rates are established. But the unemployment rate required to reduce the inflation rate to a given level is higher than before, since the Phillips curve shifts rightward as a result of the restrictive measures.

From a policy perspective, our results suggest that Keynesian policy remedies have in the manufacturing sector a potential short-run inflationary effect that worsens the long-run trade-off between inflation and unemployment. The potential detrimental influence of the loss of money illusion in wage bargains is also evident. These findings are consistent with recent experience. Stabilization policy has relied most heavily on Keynesian remedies during a period in which inflationary expectations had been allowed to develop as a result of a sustained period of inflation and a wartime psychology associated with the Vietnam conflict.

Our results indicate, on the other hand, that wage-price controls would have a potentially stabilizing impact. Not only does the guidelines dummy have a consistent negative relationship with F_3 in all our samples, but the predominance of the cost-price interaction over demand factors for explaining price changes suggests that direct intervention in the cost-price spiral would be more powerful than traditional Keynesian remedies.

We noted earlier that there have been two basic approaches to wage-price controls in the U.S. experience. The guidelines of the 1960s emphasized moderating increases in unit labor costs by allowing wage increases only to the extent productivity increased. Pressure was put directly on labor unions to hold down wage increases and on firms to prevent prices from rising. Price controls in the Nixon administration, on the other hand, focused on eliminating inflationary expectations which accelerate wage increases in addition to direct pressure on unions and firms. Thus, it was hoped that both direct and indirect pressure would stabilize wages and prices.

Short-run productivity changes seem to have had little, if any, effect on prices in the manufacturing sector, so that the guidelines work principally by mitigating the rise in factor costs. Although distributive considerations favor tying wage increases to estimated productivity gains, the observation that price increases may be related to wage changes rather than to unit labor costs must be considered if the potential effect of a particular guideline on prices is to be assessed. Suppose, for instance, wages are allowed to rise by 3 percent in anticipation of a 3 percent increase in labor productivity. Although there would be no increase in unit labor cost (and the competitive model would predict no price increase), prices might rise in response to the increased factor cost. This suggests that prices cannot be allowed to "float" in response to wage controls, but must also be controlled or, at least, some moral suasion applied if price increases (and an increase in the profit share) are to be prevented by this type of policy.

Price policy designed to eliminate inflationary expectations is also likely to be effective in the manufacturing sector, in view of the importance of the *CPI* in the wage-price interaction. The importance of the *CPI* not being reduced at the industry-level suggests that the influence was not simply simultaneity in the relationship between the *WPI* for manufacturing and the *CPI*, but was an important structural factor in wage determination.

Although the strong association of prices and factor costs and the Phillips trade-off between wage changes and unemployment rates was prevalent in most industries, there was considerable interindustry variation in the influence of changing demand conditions on that relationship. This implies that aggregate demand measures affect the industries differently with respect to price changes, profits, and the inflation-employment trade-off.

On the other hand, wage behavior among industries was more homogeneous. This implies that Keynesian measures have a more uniform impact across the board in labor markets than in product markets. This effect, however, accentuates differences in the profit squeeze among industries associated with differences in the responsiveness of industry prices to aggregate demand pressures.

Wage-price controls are often criticized because they are not equally effective (or enforceable) across industries. However, we saw that industries are much more homogeneous both with respect to the effect of changing factor costs on prices as well as to the effect of the *CPI* on wages. Thus, although differences in enforceability cannot be overlooked, a policy of wage-price controls, if properly administered, could have a more uniform impact across manufacturing industries than could the supposedly more neutral Keynesian measures.

If there is an industry-specific bias inherent in the enforceability and impact of wage price controls, it is likely to favor the more competitive industries. This is because moral suasion is more difficult to apply in these industries where offenders are harder to identify and because factor costs play a weaker role in price determination. On the other hand, we have suggested that the industry-specific bias of Keynesian measures is unfavorable to the more competitive industries.

If the short-run inflationary effect of Keynesian measures can be reduced or eliminated by direct price controls, there is no reason to reject fiscal and monetary policy as important stabilization instruments. In fact, by improving the trade-off between inflation and unemployment, controls would presumably make Keynesian measures more effective. Our results simply suggest that these measures taken alone had the potential to produce undesirable results given the structure of wage and price determination in the sample period. This conclusion is consistent with the observed inability of monetary and fiscal measures to reduce the inflation rate in the manufacturing sector in the period since 1971.

Relation to Other Studies

We have already mentioned A.W. Phillips' 1958 study, which represented one of the first attempts to analyze the relationship between macroeconomic conditions and the inflationary process.[1] Using annual data for the period 1861-1957 in the United Kingdom, Phillips found a long run trade-off between the level of aggregate unemployment and the rate of change of aggregate money wages. He found the functional form of the relationship to be nonlinear and to be highly stable over the entire period. Although he noted that price changes affected the relationship between wage changes and unemployment, particularly when price changes were extreme, the effect of past inflation was not introduced into the analysis in a systematic way. Furthermore, Phillips omits consideration of other variables that might have had an effect on the process of wage determination.

Our study shows that in U.S. manufacturing industries there has existed a trade-off between money wage changes and unemployment, but that this trade-off is not stable with respect to changing levels of economic activity nor with respect to changes in consumer prices. Consequently, it suggests that Phillips model was not complete, since it omitted important structural factors in the wage-determination process.

A later analysis, by Richard Lipsey,[2] using essentially the same sample[c] incorporated both price changes and changes in the unemployment rate into the basic Phillips relation between wage change and unemployment levels. Lipsey found the importance of the price variable for explaining wage change increasing in later years. Furthermore, the rate of change of unemployment was not clearly related to wage change, the effect changing from negative to positive in different periods. These results are consistent with our findings.

One of the first econometric macroeconomic studies of wage determination in the U.S. economy was by George Perry in 1966.[3] His quarterly data for the U.S. manufacturing sector covered the period 1947:1-1960:4. Perry found that the impact of changes in the *CPI* increased in importance after 1953 and that living costs were more important for explaining wage changes in the durable goods industries than in the nondurables. This was one of the first studies to suggest that the structure of wage determination may be changing over time and that wage behavior is different in different industries.

Since the principal concern of these macroeconomic wage studies was the impact on the inflationary process, some economists attempted to develop more complete, multi-equation models in which wages were included in the price equation. However, the inclusion of the consumer price index in the wage

[c]Lipsey used annual data for the U.K. for the period 1862-1957.

equation raised the question of bias. The same objection could be raised to our results, particularly for the manufacturing aggregates where the *WPI* and *CPI* are most closely identified. Because of the simultaneity in wage-price determination, it is necessary to consider the possibility that there is an upward bias in the loadings of the *WPI* and the wage variables on F_3.

However, other studies have shown remarkably little bias. Klein and Ball[4] estimated a four-equation model for the United Kingdom with wages and prices as endogenous variables. The parameter-estimates using limited information-maximum likelihood were nearly identical with the ordinary least squares estimates, indicating little bias from ignoring simultaneity. Gordon[5] suggests that there may actually be a downward bias on the regression coefficient for the *CPI* in traditional wage equations. Thus, there is no evidence from other studies that the dominance of F_3 in our wage and price equations was due to an upward bias because of the simultaneity of wage and price determination. Furthermore, the overwhelming importance of F_3 for explaining price and wage behavior characterized our industry studies where there was no definitional relationship between the *WPI* and *CPI*.

A study by Eckstein and Fromm[6] of quarterly price changes in total manufacturing and durable manufacturing industries for the period 1954:1-1965:4 was one of the first to test hypotheses about the microeconomic foundations of aggregate price behavior. Because our samples for total manufacturing nearly coincide, their results are the most comparable to ours. Eckstein and Fromm found that costs played the dominant role in their price equations with materials costs and labor costs variables highly significant. In fact, they conclude that the coefficients on the cost variables were unrealistically large but provide no theoretical explanation of this result. Demand variables were significant, but accounted for a much smaller part of the variance in price changes than in costs, with the effect of demand being weaker for durables industries than for nondurables. Standard unit labor cost, which eliminates short-run swings in productivity, was generally preferred to unit labor costs, particularly for durables. Furthermore, they found evidence of compensatory, target return, pricing behavior in the durables industries.

In general, the results of the Eckstein and Fromm study are consistent with our findings. Although mark-up pricing seemed to prevail in both the durables and nondurables industries and costs were generally more important for explaining price changes than the demand variables, there was evidence that where changes in demand influence prices the effect was negative in the more highly concentrated durable goods industries and positive in the more competitive nondurables sector.

Robert Gordon has experimented with a variable coefficient on a price expectations variable in economy-wide wage equations.[7] The price expectations variable is a distributed lag of past changes in the *CPI*. He concluded that the elasticity of wage change with respect to price expectations increases with the rate of inflation, reaching unity at an inflation rate of about 7 percent.[d] This suggests that a complete model of the inflationary process, particularly for short-run policy planning, should take into account the instability of certain important structural parameters.

The only analysis of price behavior at the two-digit level of the SIC which we found comparable to ours was a study by Eckstein and Wyss for the period 1954:1 through 1969:2.[8] Price equations were estimated by ordinary least squares for each industry. Like our study, they found lags to be short. Where costs were important, they entered as factor costs, that is wage rates and materials costs, rather than as unit factor costs. This was consistent with our finding and suggests that mark-up pricing characterizes nearly all manufacturing industries, even the more competitive ones. Their finding that the effect of the guideposts of the early 1960s on prices was through the cost variables was the same as ours.

There were several interesting differences between the Eckstein and Wyss results and our own. Unlike the earlier Eckstein and Fromm study, Eckstein and Wyss found prices in the more competitive industries to be less sensitive to the demand variables and more highly influenced by costs than the oligopolistic industries. However, the emphasis on capacity utilization as a demand variable could explain this result. The competitive industries would be expected to adjust prices more frequently to changes in demand than oligopolies, which tend to adjust output levels. This suggests that for oligopolies, changes in capacity utilization are more indicative of responses to changing demand conditions than for competitive industries, for which this variable is a poor indicator. Eckstein and Wyss did, however, find evidence of compensatory pricing in the most highly concentrated industries, which was consistent with our findings.

Eckstein and Wyss were better able to categorize price behavior strictly in terms of market concentration than we were. Perhaps their use of capacity utilization as one of only two demand variables explains this result, since the influence of this variable is likely to be sensitive to market concentration. In our study, the capacity variables were only a small part of the demand components so that the relationship between the effect of demand on prices was related to market structure in a different way, with product classification playing a larger role in price behavior. Clearly, the interpretation of capacity utilization as a pure demand variable is questionable (since it reflects a reaction to changes in demand which represents an alternative to price changes) and, consequently, the implications of the Eckstein and Wyss model, both for the theory of the firm as well as in a policy perspective, are somewhat different from our own.

Another finding of Eckstein and Wyss that seems to differ from our results,

[d]Gordon estimates that to keep the unemployment rate at 4.2 percent, given the current rate at which inflationary expectations develop, inflation would reach 14.7 percent by 1986 in the absence of price controls.

may actually be consistent with them. We found substantial labor market and product market linkages within the manufacturing sector. Furthermore, swings in industry demand were associated with changes in aggregate demand, reflected in *GNP* and economy-wide unemployment rates. Industry prices responded differently to aggregate demand measures, however, because of interindustry differences in price behavior. Eckstein and Wyss, examining only the relationship between industry prices and macroeconomic conditions, conclude macroeconomic variables are not very important in industry price equations. This may mean simply that demand variables (other than capacity utilization) are not very important for most industries. In any event, the conclusion supports our view that aggregate demand remedies are not likely to be very effective anti-inflation instruments.

It is important to keep in mind that the methodology used in all the studies cited is different from our own. In all cases, some form of regression analysis was applied to a small set of variables which were selected to avoid multicollinearity. Consequently, our results are not strictly comparable. However, it is legitimate to compare the interpretation of our results with those of other researchers.

Our findings are not inconsistent with the rather universal view that the so-called Phillips curve, which has had such an important influence on policy decisions, is affected by, among other things, the ongoing rate of inflation and changes in the level of economic activity. It is now generally accepted that the higher the rate of inflation, the greater will be the unemployment rate associated with any reduction in the rate of wage change when aggregate demand remedies are used alone. However, our conclusion that restrictive demand measures will have an additional inflationary impact because of the tendency for compensatory pricing, particularly in durable manufacturing, will be more controversial since it has not been systematically considered in the literature cited.

Since there have been fewer industry studies of price behavior than there are aggregate models, it is more difficult to place our industry results into perspective. However, there are some interesting differences between our findings and those of Eckstein and Wyss that merit consideration.

Policy Conclusions and Recommendations

Because of the unconventional methodology used in this study, some readers will undoubtedly reject it as a structural model of the inflationary process. Nevertheless, our results unquestionably support the view that the U.S. economy cannot continue to rely solely on aggregate demand measures to produce price stability, at least within the manufacturing sector.

Admittedly, the alternatives are not clear, although our results point in the direction of increased use of wage-price guidelines or controls. Although experience with wage-price guidelines and price controls has not been conclusive, we have less evidence that they will not work than we do for Keynesian policies.

Of three major arguments in favor of Keynesian remedies and opposed to price controls, two were directly addressed in our study and one we will reject out of hand. The latter is the contention that the major problem with price controls is administrative, not theoretical. Administrative costs and problems associated with Keynesian stabilization policy have been far from negligible and it is likely that a cost-effectiveness study would show a policy of price controls to be at least competitive on that score.

A second reason why Americans cling so tightly to Keynesian policy instruments and remain skeptical of price controls is the belief that aggregate demand remedies are neutral whereas price controls interfere with the market mechanism. In addition to a number of sound theoretical arguments that refute that contention,[9] our results suggest that the industry-specific impact on prices of Keynesian remedies may be even more variable than price controls, even when allowance is made for inequities in enforcement.

Perhaps the most comforting aspect of Keynesian policies and the most disquieting aspect of price controls is the belief that the former are based on a consistent theoretical model of price and income determination. Price controls have an intuitive appeal, but the mechanism through which they operate is viewed as less sophisticated and their impact is less certain. However, our results suggest that the Keynesian model is not applicable to price behavior in all, or even most, manufacturing industries, and that, therefore, the impact of aggregate demand measures on prices is no more certain. In fact, it appears that the effect of cost changes on prices is much more uniform across manufacturing industries than the influence changes in aggregate demand and that, consequently, the effect of controlling cost increases would be much easier to assess.

But just because the prevailing policy model seems to have become unreliable, this does not excuse shoddy model building and ad hoc policy planning by proponents of a different view. We clearly need a more careful investigation of the channels through which the inflationary process is transmitted, with particular emphasis on the relation between production costs and prices, in order to assess the potential efficacy of wage-price controls. Hopefully, this study will be viewed as a step in that direction.

Notes

1. A.W. Phillips, "The Relation Between Unemployment and the Rate of Change of Money Wage Rates in the United Kingdom, 1861-1957," *Economica*, 25 (November 1958), pp. 283-99.

2. Richard G. Lipsey, "The Relation Between Unemployment and the Rate of Change of Money Wage Rates in the United Kingdom, 1862-1957: A Further Analysis," *Economica*, 27 (February 1960), pp. 1-31.

3. George L. Perry, *Unemployment, Money Wage Rates and Inflation* (Cambridge, Mass.: The M.I.T. Press, 1966).

4. L.R. Klein and R.J. Ball, "Some Econometrics of the Determination of Absolute Prices and Wages," *The Economic Journal*, 69 (September 1959), pp. 465-82.

5. Robert J. Gordon, "Inflation in Recession and Recovery," *Brookings Papers on Economic Activity* (1971:1), pp. 105-58.

6. Otto Eckstein and Gary Fromm, "The Price Equation," *The American Economic Review*, 58 (December 1968), pp. 1159-83.

7. Robert J. Gordon, "Wage-Price Controls and the Shifting Phillips Curve," *Brookings Papers on Economic Activity* (1972:2), pp. 385-421.

8. Otto Eckstein and David Wyss, "Industry Price Equations," *Conference on the Econometrics of Price Determination*, Washington, D.C., 30-31 October 1970.

9. For a discussion of the theoretical issues see Nancy S. Barrett, *The Theory of Macroeconomic Policy* (Englewood Cliffs, N.J.: Prentice-Hall, Inc., 1972) and Paul A. Samuelson, "Wage-Price Guideposts and the Need for Informal Controls in a Mixed Economy," in *Full Employment Guideposts, and Economic Stability: Rational Debate Seminars*, Washington, D.C., 1967.

Appendixes

Appendix A: Sources of Data[a]

I. *Labor Market Variables*   *Source*

UN	unemployment rate[1,2,3]	BLS
UN_A	unemployment rate (civilian)	BLS
	direction of unemployment[1,2]	
	equals 1 when the unemployment rate	
	increased from the previous quarter	
	and zero when it decreased	
$UN\uparrow$	direction of unemployment[3]	
	equals 1 when the unemployment rate	
	increased for three successive quarters	
	(zero otherwise)	
$UN\downarrow$	direction of unemployment[3]	
	equals 1 when the unemployment rate	
	decreased for three successive quarters	
	(zero otherwise)	
	total employment[1,2,3]	BLS
	percent negro and nonwhite (civilian labor force)	BLS
	percent 16 to 19 years old (civilian labor force)	BLS
	percent women[2,3]	BLS
	layoff rate[1,2,3]	BLS
	accession rate[1,2,3]	BLS
	quit rate[1,2,3]	BLS
	labor force participation rate (civilian labor force)	BLS
AHE	average hourly earnings[1,2,3]	BLS
AWE	average weekly earnings[1,2,3]	BLS
MHC	manhour compensation	BLS

II. *Demand Variables*

GNP	gross national product (current)	OBE

[a]Some variables were not available for durables and the industries. Others are economy-wide observations. Superscripts mean the variable was available for

    1. manufacturing
    2. durable manufacturing
    3. industry

Where there is no superscript, the variable is economy-wide.

GNP	gross national product (deflated)	OBE
	output[1,2,3]	FRB
	output per manhour[1,2,3]	BLS
	sales[1,2,3]	CB
	new orders/sales[1,2,3]	CB
	unfilled orders/sales[1,2,3]	CB
	capacity utilization[1]	ERP
	GNP/potential GNP (deflated)	OBE
	output/previous peak output[1,2,3]	FRB
	P & E investment (deflated)[1,2,3]	OBE
	expected P & E investment—next quarter (deflated)[1,2,3]	OBE
	approved capital appropriations[1]	NICB
	backlog of capital appropriations[1]	NICB
	inventory stock/sales[1,2,3]	NICB
	inventory investment[1,2,3]	CB
	inventory disequilibrium[1,2]	CB, E & F
	ratio of inventory stock to sales minus a 12-quarter moving average of that ratio	
	index of 425 industrial stock prices	S & P
	national income	OBE
	stock price index[3]	S & P

III. *Financial Variables*

	cash flow[1,2,3] (retained earnings plus depreciation and inventory valuation adjustment)	FTC
	profit rate[1,2,3] (profit after tax to equity)	FTC
	liabilities minus cash flow/assets[1,2,3]	FTC
	Federal Reserve discount rate (NY)	FRB
	unborrowed reserves of Federal Reserve member banks	FRB
	Moody's corporate bond yield (industrials)	MIS
	rate on 3-to-6-month finance company paper	FRB
	rate on 4-to-6-month prime commercial paper	FRB

IV. *Price and Cost Variables*

WPI	wholesale price index[1,2,3]	BLS
	wholesale price index (iron and steel)	BLS
	materials costs[1,2,3]	E & W, FA, OBE

CPI	consumer price index	BLS
ULC	unit labor cost[1,2,3]	CB
$SULC$	standard unit labor cost[1,2,3] a 12-quarter moving average of ULC	
	index of output price	E and W

V. *Policy Variables*

	federal government purchases of goods and services, current and constant dollars	OBE
	federal government purchases for national defense	OBE
	federal government expenditures	OBE
	federal debt to GNP	ERP
	full employment budget surplus	FRB (St. Louis)
	corporate tax rate	
	personal tax rate	
	indirect tax rate	
	personal tax receipts	OBE
	corporate profit tax accruals	OBE
M_1	money supply (excluding time deposits)	
M_2	money supply (including time deposits)	FRB
	political dummy, equals 1 in Democratic and zero in Republican administrations	
	guidelines dummy, equals 1 during 1962:1-1966:4 and zero all other times	GP
$OASI$	old-age, survivors, disability, and health insurance benefits	OBE

Key to Sources

BLS	Bureau of Labor Statistics
CB	Census Bureau
E & F	Otto Eckstein and Gary Fromm, "The Price Equation," *The American Economic Review*, 58 (December 1968), pp. 1159-83.
E & W	Otto Eckstein and David Wyss, "Industry Price Equations," *Conference on the Econometrics of Price Determination*, Washington, D.C., 30-31 October 1970.
ERP	Economic Report of the President
FA	Faith Halfter Ando, *The Cyclical Behavior of Materials Prices in United States Industry*, unpublished doctoral dissertation, Harvard University, 1966

FRB	Board of Governors of the Federal Reserve System
(St. Louis)	Federal Reserve Bank of St. Louis
FTC	Federal Trade Commission
GP	George L. Perry, *Unemployment, Money Wage Rates, and Inflation* (Cambridge, Mass.: The M.I.T. Press, 1966)
MIS	Moody's Investor Service
NICB	National Industrial Conference Board
OBE	Office of Business Economics
S & P	Standard and Poor's

Appendix B: Rotated Factor Loadings for the Industry Variables

TABLE B-1
Industry 20 Food

Rotated Factor Loadings for 1959:1-1971:3 with the Wholesale Price Index
Current and Lagged - Percent Change over Four Quarters (F-ratio in Parentheses)[1]

VARIABLE[2]	Factor 1	Factor 2	Factor 3	Factor 4	R^2
WPI	-.227	-.087	.563	-.293	.461
	(5.93)	(0.86)	(36.46)	(9.88)	(17.76)
1/UN_A	.921	-.072	.003	-.163	.880
1/UN²	.828	-.006	-.058	-.091	.697
UN	-.828	.003	.059	.094	.697
UN ↑	-.769	.176	-.030	.057	.626
real GNP	.767	.152	.053	.139	.633
4-6 month paper rate	.756	-.257	.211	.215	.719
3-6 month paper rate	.746	-.186	.154	.221	.663
1/UN² (-1)	.730	-.212	.058	-.056	.585
UN (-1)	-.729	.209	-.058	.058	.582
money GNP	.641	.354	.455	-.181	.776
ULC	-.636	.217	.257	.514	.782
discount rate (-1)	.613	-.246	-.128	.518	.721
total employment	.575	-.427	.432	-.037	.701
lagged political dummy	.547	-.000	.299	-.482	.621
quit rate	.534	-.112	.289	-.176	.418
output	.459	.041	.365	-.064	.349
debt/GNP	-.428	.189	.132	.209	-.280
percent of labor force female	.417	.236	.197	.003	.268
GNP/potential GNP	-.089	.889	-.031	-.062	.803
personal tax receipts	-.338	.763	.114	.121	.724
unborrowed reserves	-.185	.745	-.072	-.104	.613
personal tax rate	.478	-.722	.221	.060	.802
government purchases (deflated)	.505	-.710	.264	.012	.829
M1 (-1)	.157	.667	.615	.036	.848
M2 (-1)	.382	.636	.223	-.461	.813

TABLE B-1 (continued)

VARIABLE[2]	Factor 1	Factor 2	Factor 3	Factor 4	R^2
WPI	-.227 (5.93)	-.087 (0.86)	.563 (36.46)	-.293 (9.88)	.461 (17.67)
total employment (-1)	.418	-.550	.398	.089	.644
investment in P & E	.097	-.500	.154	-.056	.283
inventory investment	-.012	.481	-.168	-.161	.286
expected investment in P & E	.021	-.409	.038	-.075	.175
$1/UN_{AL}$ (-1)	.203	-.189	.905	.084	.904
$1/UN_{AL}$	.353	-.119	.874	-.007	.902
UN_L (-1)	-.194	.169	-.835	-.033	.765
$1/UN_L$ (-1)	.166	-.178	.831	-.007	.750
CPI	-.413	.191	.785	.304	.915
$1/UN_L$	.348	-.141	.766	-.013	.728
UN_L	-.391	.143	-.765	-.027	.760
labor force participation rate	.201	-.254	.625	-.337	.610
assets/liabilities - internal funds	.017	.528	-.606	.210	.690
bond yield	.264	.405	.602	.239	.653
materials cost	.035	.046	.567	-.355	.451
WPI (-1)	-.321	-.109	.559	-.340	.543
sales	-.280	-.375	.556	-.497	.776
guidelines	.271	.107	.545	-.292	.468
AWE	-.366	.426	.540	.520	.877
AHE	-.456	.384	.539	.549	.948
defense/government purchases	.086	-.183	.488	-.097	.289
manhour productivity	.328	.029	.481	.048	.342
stock price index	-.153	.050	-.472	.087	.256
corporate tax receipts	.218	.100	.466	.082	.282

VARIABLE[2]	Factor 1	Factor 2	Factor 3	Factor 4	R^2
WPI	-.227	-.087	.563	-.293	.461
	(5.93)	(0.86)	(36.46)	(9.88)	(17.67)
political dummy	.234	-.153	-.129	.744	.648
indirect tax rate	-.421	.083	-.336	.666	.740
SULC	-.510	.351	-.109	.614	.772
cash flow	-.163	.150	.000	-.579	.385
government purchases	.162	-.309	.366	.547	.556
inventory/sales	.128	.110	-.223	.523	.357
government purchases/national income	-.386	-.300	.240	.453	.501
profits/equity	.273	.347	-.114	-.417	.381
corporate tax rate	.015	-.185	.324	.412	.309
variance added	.255	.089	.139	.083	
cumulative variance explained	.255	.344	.483	.566	

[1]Boxes indicate the factor to which the variable has been assigned.

[2]Variables are unassigned (but included in the components analysis) if there is no factor loading above |.39|. The unassigned variables are layoff rate, accession rate, output/previous peak, ULC-SULC, UN↑, UN↓, government expenditures, full employment surplus.

TABLE B-2
Industry 20 Food

Rotated Factor Loadings for 1959:1-1971:3 with the Wholesale Price Index
Current and Lagged - Quarterly Percent Change (F-ratio in Parentheses)[1]

VARIABLE[2]	Factor 1	Factor 2	Factor 3	Factor 4	R^2
WPI	-.065	.014	-.277	.024	.081
	(0.29)	(0.01)	(5.18)	(0.04)	(1.81)
UN	.695	-.003	-.079	-.158	.514
$1/UN^2$	-.694	-.001	.078	.159	.514
debt/GNP	.564	-.026	.027	.004	.319
government purchases/national income	.500	-.136	-.131	.065	.290
$1/UN_A$	-.489	-.488	.151	.255	.565
layoff rate	-.421	.343	-.005	.088	.303
manhour productivity	.419	-.323	-.053	.112	.295
UN↓	-.400	-.033	.007	.205	.203
SULC	.180	.729	-.018	-.256	.630
accession rate	.053	-.651	.111	.001	.439
total employment	.240	-.615	-.071	.004	.441
political dummy	-.184	-.595	-.126	.093	.413
lagged political dummy	-.232	-.593	-.343	-.232	.560
UN↑	.245	.578	.109	-.333	.517
government purchases	.209	-.504	-.187	.076	.338
$1/UN$ (-1)	.042	-.502	-.027	.055	.257
UN (-1)	-.044	.500	.026	-.053	.256
indirect tax rate	.146	.479	.059	-.066	.259
output	.304	-.444	-.013	-.187	.304
$1/UN_{AL}$ (-1)	.072	-.116	-.918	.180	.894
UN_L (-1)	-.144	.220	.899	-.106	.889
$1/UN_L$ (-1)	.201	.263	-.883	.112	.901
$1/UN_{AL}$	-.623	.257	-.882	.240	.907

VARIABLE[2]	Factor 1	Factor 2	Factor 3	Factor 4	R²
WPI	-.065	.014	-.277	.024	.081
	(0.29)	(0.01)	(5.18)	(0.04)	(1.81)
UN$_L$	.203	.246	.845	-.194	.853
1/UN$_L$	-.234	-.224	-.841	.200	.852
CPI	.158	.321	-.819	.022	.800
AWE	.214	.513	.590	-.187	.692
guidelines	-.159	-.240	.522	.044	.357
M$_1$ (-1)	-.145	-.031	-.435	-.282	.291
GNP/potential GNP	.166	.003	-.009	-.902	.842
government purchases (deflated)	.008	-.171	-.070	.901	.846
personal tax rate	.025	-.148	-.055	.891	.820
personal tax receipts	-.030	.127	-.079	-.832	.715
bond yield	.062	.053	-.385	.684	.623
4-6 month paper rate	-.162	-.205	.143	.657	.519
3-6 month paper rate	-.089	-.231	-.087	.622	.455
discount rate (-1)	-.084	-.095	.010	.534	.301
defense/government expenditures	.045	-.369	-.021	-.491	.380
variance added	.065	.099	.140	.072	
cumulative variance explained	.065	.164	.304	.376	

[1] Boxes indicate the factor to which the variable has been assigned.

[2] Variables are unassigned (but included in the components analysis) if there is no factor loading above |.39|. The unassigned variables are WPI, WPI (-1), percent of labor force female, quit rate, total employment (-1), investment in P & E, profit/equity, cash flow, output/previous peak, expected investment in P & E, AHE, ULC, corporate tax rate, (ULC-SULC), inventory investment, stock price index, inventory/sales, materials cost, real GNP, money GNP, unborrowed reserves, defense/government purchases, full employment surplus, M$_2$ (-1), labor force participation rate.

TABLE B-3
Industry 21 Tobacco

Rotated Factor Loadings for 1959:1–1971:3 with the Wholesale Price Index
Current and Lagged – Percent Change over Four Quarters (F-ratio in Parentheses)[1]

VARIABLE[2]	Factor 1	Factor 2	Factor 3	Factor 4	R^2
WPI	.079	-.028	.748	.131	.576
	(0.71)	(0.09)	(62.49)	(1.93)	(21.73)
real GNP	-.742	.172	-.060	-.048	.586
government purchases/national income	.728	.006	.025	-.597	.886
3-6 month paper rate	-.713	-.476	.030	-.122	.750
4-6 month paper rate	-.708	-.531	.060	-.166	.814
money GNP	-.688	.112	.205	-.444	.725
1/UNA	-.672	-.235	-.348	.471	.850
discount rate (-1)	-.602	-.496	.068	.112	.626
corporate tax rate	.567	-.071	.365	-.096	.469
quit rate	-.550	-.143	-.177	-.403	.516
output/previous peak	.526	-.172	.046	.289	.392
percent of labor force female	-.437	.237	.084	.041	.256
GNP/potential GNP	-.151	.912	.045	.071	.863
unborrowed reserves	.046	.868	-.073	-.008	.760
personal tax receipts	.133	.803	.259	.117	.743
government purchases (deflated)	-.174	.784	.022	-.451	.849
personal tax rate	-.127	-.778	.048	-.424	.805
total employment	-.083	-.660	-.204	.033	.485
bond yield	-.225	-.625	.516	-.220	.755
M₂(-1)	-.379	-.482	.053	-.460	.591
total employment (-1)	-.083	-.660	-.204	.033	.485
layoff rate	.011	.451	-.292	-.035	.291
CPI	.050	.093	.958	.079	.936
SULC	.046	.354	.839	.013	.832
1/UN$_{AL}$ (-1)	-.194	-.338	.701	-.471	.865

VARIABLE[2]	Factor 1	Factor 2	Factor 3	Factor 4	R^2
WPI	.079	-.028	.748	.131	.576
	(0.71)	(0.09)	(62.49)	(1.93)	(21.73)
WPI (-1)	.109	.204	.700	.216	.591
sales	-.097	-.034	.686	-.129	.498
ULC	.022	-.416	.676	-.307	.725
AHE	.130	.213	.674	.173	.546
assets/liabilities - internal funds	.208	.214	-.653	.323	.620
M_1 (-1)	-.473	.407	.638	-.145	.817
inventory/sales	.176	.118	-.630	.079	.448
1/UNAL	-.298	-.293	.609	-.577	.850
AWE	.316q	.256	.579	.090	.509
guidelines	-.279	.040	-.560	.104	.404
corporate tax receipts	.375	.029	.482	.200	.414
government purchases	.247	-.137	-.060	-.887	.870
defense/government expenditures	.004	.049	-.133	-.783	.633
indirect tax rate	.304	.014	.025	.681	.557
lagged political dummy	.398	-.139	-.045	-.600	.541
political dummy	.110	-.047	-.456	-.593	.582
labor force participation rate	-.062	-.193	.339	-.580	.492
manhour productivity	.076	-.382	-.380	-.543	.591
defense/government purchases	.101	-.094	.318	-.534	.405
output	.259	-.276	-.307	.457	.446
variance added	.087	.189	.182	.110	
cumulative variance explained	.087	.276	.458	.568	

[1] Boxes indicate the factor to which the variable has been assigned.

[2] Variables are unassigned (but included in the components analysis) if there is no factor loading above $|.39|$. The unassigned variables are accession rate, profit/equity, cash flow, (ULC-SULC), inventory invest-ment, full employment surplus, debt/GNP.

TABLE B-4
Industry 21 Tobacco

Rotated Factor Loadings for 1959:1-1971:3 with the Wholesale Price Index
Current and Lagged - Quarterly Percent Change (F-ratio in Parentheses)[1]

VARIABLE[2]	Factor 1	Factor 2	Factor 3	Factor 4	R^2
WPI	.208	.034	.433	-.022	.232
	(2.69)	(0.06)	(11.71)	(0.02)	(4.82)
corporate tax rate	.730	-.214	.039	.015	.581
output/previous peak	.719	-.300	.192	.085	.650
corporate tax receipts	.715	-.119	.108	-.024	.538
output	.676	-.289	.325	.116	.660
profit/equity	.638	-.054	.048	-.086	.419
sales	.633	.017	.232	-.094	.463
inventory/sales	-.587	-.289	.007	-.042	.430
labor force participation rate	.512	.281	.018	.057	.345
assets/liabilities - internal funds	.456	.172	-.227	-.210	.333
$1/UN_A$	.036	.676	-.150	.281	.559
money GNP	-.109	.632	.138	-.184	.464
lagged political dummy	.125	.575	.199	.241	.445
quit rate	.257	.480	-.114	.024	.310
real GNP	-.057	.476	-.011	.074	.236
political dummy	.104	.464	-.187	.155	.286
AWE	.363	-.461	.207	.200	.427
AHE	-.093	-.410	.369	.128	.329
CPI	.078	-.194	.878	.078	.821
SULC	.045	.080	.838	-.181	.743
$1/UN_{AL}$ (-1)	.192	.032	.742	.237	.645
$1/UN_{AL}$	.205	.219	.703	.303	.676
M_1 (-1)	.006	.396	.602	-.193	.557
ULC	-.375	.111	.560	.041	.468

VARIABLE[2]	Factor 1	Factor 2	Factor 3	Factor 4	R^2
WPI	.208	.034	.433	-.022	.232
	(2.69)	(0.06)	(11.71)	(0.02)	(4.82)
guidelines	.002	.293	-.508	.025	.345
WPI (-1)	.019	.127	.485	.044	.254
manhour productivity	.382	.157	-.404	.116	.347
GNP/potential GNP	.121	.195	.074	-.918	.901
government purchases (deflated)	.026	.074	-.022	.909	.832
personal tax rate	.008	.044	-.029	.893	.801
personal tax receipts	.032	.029	.098	-.874	.775
bond yield	.068	.154	.332	.732	.674
4-6 month paper rate	-.064	.390	.130	.671	.622
3-6 month paper rate	-.123	.386	.103	.637	.580
discount rate (-1)	.036	.237	-.067	.538	.351
defense/government expenditures	.073	.172	.014	-.506	.292
cash flow	.193	.246	.080	-.504	.358
variance added	.097	.076	.093	.130	
cumulative variance explained	.097	.173	.266	.396	

[1]Boxes indicate the factor to which the variable has been assigned.

[2]Variables are unassigned (but included in the components analysis) if there is no factor loading above |.39|. The unassigned variables are total employment, percent of labor force female, layoff rate, accession rate, total employment (-1), (ULC-SULC), inventory investment, unborrowed reserves, indirect tax rate, government purchases, full employment surplus, debt/GNP, government purchases/national income, M_2 (-1).

TABLE B-5
Industry 22 Textiles

Rotated Factor Loadings for 1959:1-1971:3 with the Wholesale Price Index
Current and Lagged - Percent Change over Four Quarters (F-ratio in Parentheses)[1]

VARIABLE[2]	Factor 1	Factor 2	Factor 3	Factor 4	R^2
WPI	-.402	.608	.128	-.225	.598
	(24.92)	(57.01)	(2.53)	(7.79)	(30.74)
profit/equity	-.911	.242	-.167	-.020	.918
output	-.894	.289	.073	.179	.920
sales	-.854	.323	.075	-.125	.855
AWE	-.831	.204	.228	-.275	.859
layoff rate	-.827	.019	-.039	-.149	.708
corporate tax receipts	-.823	.467	-.069	-.066	.906
productivity	-.796	.370	.204	.276	.887
inventory/sales	-.784	-.169	.054	.244	.707
output/previous peak	-.764	-.203	.010	.142	.646
M_2 (-1)	-.735	-.279	.371	-.003	.755
money GNP	-.718	.267	.532	-.078	.876
stock price index	-.715	.070	-.273	.071	.595
ULC	.712	-.284	.077	-.511	.855
accession rate	-.708	.061	.193	.421	.720
corporate tax rate	.687	.152	.139	-.033	.515
total employment	-.666	.474	.510	.094	.937
quit rate	-.627	.440	.199	.193	.664
$1/UN_A$	-.607	.565	.213	.417	.907
UN	.553	-.226	-.23	-.306	.451
$1/UN^2$	-.551	-.224	-.020	.304	.447
GNP/potential GNP	-.502	-.450	-.154	-.494	.723
UN↑	.473	.054	.159	-.146	.273
cash flow	-.431	-.060	.057	.034	.194
percent of labor force female	-.410	-.225	.202	-.11	.259

VARIABLE[2]	Factor 1	Factor 2	Factor 3	Factor 4	R^2
WPI	-.402 (24.92)	.608 (57.01)	.128 (2.53)	-.225 (7.79)	.598 (30.74)
discount rate (-1)	-.077	.868	.112	-.097	.768
4-6 month paper rate	-.293	.825	.258	.073	.839
3-6 month paper rate	-.357	.802	.197	.038	.811
WPI (-1)	.024	.710	.146	-.097	.535
total employment (-1)	-.324	.638	.569	.092	.844
expected investment in P&E	-.093	.613	-.360	.215	.560
government purchases/national income	.373	-.611	.396	.468	.888
investment in P&E	-.258	.594	-.313	.099	.528
government purchases (deflated)	.139	.589	.437	.518	.826
personal tax rate	.191	.583	.385	.515	.790
real GNP	-.331	.573	.117	-.003	.451
unborrowed reserves	-.356	-.570	-.146	-.303	.564
assets/liabilities - internal funds	-.069	-.449	-.054	-.083	.216
$1/UN_{AL}$	-.024	.238	.942	-.048	.947
$1/UN_{AL}$ (-1)	.178	.225	.923	-.128	.951
$1/UN_L$ (-1)	-.018	.012	.904	.091	.827
UN_L (-1)	-.016	-.030	-.868	-.080	.760
$1/UN_L$	-.175	-.038	.867	.138	.803
UN_L	.193	.012	.837	-.109	.749
AHE	-.327	.228	.681	-.400	.782
labor force participation rate	.150	.104	.620	.176	.448
bond yield	.108	.501	.599	-.077	.628
lagged political dummy	-.291	.072	.567	.441	.606
defense/government purchases	-.072	-.047	.507	.068	.269
indirect tax rate	.305	-.038	-.451	-.413	.469
defense/government expenditures	-.256	.146	.449	.428	.472

130

TABLE B-5 (continued)

VARIABLE[2]	Factor 1	Factor 2	Factor 3	Factor 4	R^2
WPI	-.402	.608	.128	-.225	.598
	(24.92)	(57.01)	(2.53)	(7.79)	(30.74)
SULC	.138	.151	.222	-.846	.807
political dummy	-.298	-.266	.191	.762	.776
CPI	.329	-.113	.563	-.710	.943
government purchases	-.059	-.246	.619	.630	.844
M_1 (-1)	-.508	-.065	.531	-.610	.917
personal tax receipts	-.206	-.545	-.049	-.603	.705
UN (-1)	.271	-.394	-.050	-.441	.426
$1/UN^2$ (-1)	-.269	.392	.053	.441	.423
variance added	.279	.11	.151	.089	
cumulative variance explained	.279	.390	.541	.630	

[1] Boxes indicate the factor to which the variable has been assigned.

[2] Variables are unassigned (but included in the components analysis) if there is no factor loading above $|.39|$. The unassigned variables are (ULC-SULC), inventory investment, materials cost, UN↓, full employment surplus, debt/GNP, guidelines.

TABLE B-6
Industry 22 Textiles

Rotated Factor Loadings for 1959:1-1971:3 with the Wholesale Price Index
Current and Lagged – Quarterly Percent Change (F-ratio in Parentheses)[1]

VARIABLE[2]	Factor 1	Factor 2	Factor 3	Factor 4	R^2
WPI	.491	-.303	.053	-.255	.401
	(24.95)	(9.49)	(0.28)	(6.27)	(13.83)
output	.885	.099	-.117	.060	.810
cash flow	.831	.111	-.204	-.014	.745
profit/equity	.828	.157	-.213	-.013	.756
corporate tax receipts	.811	.049	.144	-.035	.682
total employment	.790	-.240	.311	-.067	.788
productivity	.782	-.185	.021	.207	.689
sales	.756	.030	-.020	-.105	.584
money GNP	.703	.082	.163	.065	.531
output/previous peak	.678	.082	-.115	.004	.480
1/UNA	.665	-.457	-.046	.209	.697
AWE	.629	-.169	.114	-.202	.478
ULC	-.629	.191	.195	-.297	.558
M_1 (-1)	.549	.200	.458	-.360	.681
government purchases/national income	.542	.093	.299	.448	.593
accession rate	.528	-.101	.008	.208	.332
total employment (-1)	.481	-.477	.325	.056	.567
layoff rate	-.480	-.103	.046	-.030	.244
quit rate	.467	-.163	.082	.040	.253
M_2 (-1)	.461	-.008	.213	.046	.260
corporate tax rate	-.442	-.074	.143	.032	.222
government purchases (deflated)	-.094	-.873	.133	.198	.828
personal tax rate	-.119	-.860	.103	.186	.799
GNP/potential GNP	.357	-.823	-.032	-.118	.820
personal tax receipts	.157	.789	.028	.191	.685
4-6 month paper rate	.328	-.734	.203	-.065	.692

TABLE B-6 (continued)

VARIABLE[2]	Factor 1	Factor 2	Factor 3	Factor 4	R^2
WPI	.491 (24.95)	-.303 (9.49)	.053 (0.28)	-.255 (6.72)	.401 (13.83)
3-6 month paper rate	.358	-.691	.160	-.065	.635
bond yield	.053	-.673	.394	-.166	.638
discount rate (-1)	.225	-.651	-.063	-.127	.494
defense/government expenditures	.140	-.486	.124	-.235	.326
WPI (-1)	.031	-.480	.071	-.080	.243
$1/UN_{AL}$ (-1)	-.207	-.119	.905	-.051	.879
$1/UN_{AL}$	-.026	-.232	.902	.019	.868
$1/UN_L$ (-1)	-.054	-.082	.899	.301	.886
UN_L (-1)	.130	-.048	-.867	-.338	.886
$1/UN_L$	.119	-.217	.850	.147	.806
UN_L	-.067	.237	-.823	-.148	.760
CPI	-.205	.025	.723	-.497	.812
lagged political dummy	.201	-.194	.541	.516	.637
AHE	.334	-.046	.426	-.026	.296
SULC	-.138	.354	.001	-.698	.631
political dummy	.340	-.085	.160	.685	.617
government purchases	-.038	-.051	.405	.589	.515
UN (-1)	-.087	-.059	-.010	-.428	.194
$1/UN^2$ (-1)	.089	-.060	.007	.426	.194
variance added	.167	.083	.135	.061	
cumulative variance explained	.167	.250	.385	.446	

[1]Boxes indicate the factor to which the variable has been assigned.

[2]Variables are unassigned (but included in the components analysis) if there is no factor loading above $|.39|$. The unassigned variables are UN, $1/UN^2$, investment in P & E, expected investment in P & E, assets/liabilities-internal funds, (ULC-SULC), inventory investment, stock price index, inventory/sales, materials cost, UN↑, UN↓, real GNP, unborrowed reserves, indirect tax rate, defense/government purchases, full employment surplus, debt/GNP, guidelines, labor force participation rate.

TABLE B-7
Industry 23 Apparel

Rotated Factor Loadings for 1959:1-1971:3 with the Wholesale Price Index
Current and Lagged - Percent Change over Four Quarters (F-ratio in Parentheses)[1]

VARIABLE[2]	Factor 1	Factor 2	Factor 3	Factor 4	R^2
WPI	.171	-.116	-.069	-.011	.048
	(1.84)	(0.85)	(0.30)	(0.01)	(1.01)
total employment	-.897	.222	-.057	.072	.862
output	-.895	.126	-.265	.029	.888
1/UN	-.886	.284	.095	.234	.929
1/UN²	-.800	.57	.030	.337	.779
UN	-.798	-.164	-.029	-.339	.780
quit rate	-.787	.206	.107	-.150	.696
output/previous peak	-.761	-.126	-.107	.106	.618
money GNP	-.743	-.174	.526	.078	.865
3-6 month paper rate	-.726	.429	.248	-.227	.824
layoff rate	-.708	.386	-.050	-.140	.672
4-6 month paper rate	-.698	.498	.296	-.202	.863
cash flow	-.692	-.192	.030	.096	.526
total employment (-1)	-.690	.465	.000	.013	.692
productivity	-.690	.319	.317	-.018	.678
1/UN² (-1)	-.687	.446	.091	.181	.712
UN (-1)	-.682	-.453	-.090	-.183	.712
corporate tax rate	.623	.123	.081	.065	.414
real GNP	-.608	.227	.188	-.215	.503
ULC	.608	-.377	.540	.188	.838
profit/equity	-.607	-.133	.087	-.036	.395
materials cost	-.597	.045	.208	-.296	.489
accession rate	-.590	.121	-.094	.443	.567
UN↑	.509	-.095	.025	-.408	.435
sales	-.498	-.001	.086	.333	.366
stock price index	-.493	-.267	.359	.194	.481

TABLE B-7 (continued)

VARIABLE[2]	Factor 1	Factor 2	Factor 3	Factor 4	R^2
WPI	.171 (1.84)	-.116 (0.85)	-.069 (0.30)	-.011 (0.01)	.048 (1.01)
GNP/potential GNP	-.169	.842	-.072	-.152	.767
personal tax receipts	.145	.814	.063	.192	.725
personal tax rate	-.202	.776	.242	.258	.768
unborrowed reserves	.001	-.774	-.133	.046	.618
government purchases (deflated)	-.245	.764	.294	.277	.808
M_2 (-1)	-.478	.548	.305	.366	.757
discount rate (-1)	-.465	.535	.208	-.435	.735
inventory/sales	-.049	.476	.078	-.155	.259
assets/liabilities - internal funds	.147	-.423	.020	-.007	.201
$1/UN_{AL}$ (-1)	.018	.251	.943	.073	.958
$1/UN_{AL}$	-.157	.200	.925	.167	.948
UN_L (-1)	.096	-.170	-.906	-.051	.861
$1/UN_L$ (-1)	-.039	.163	.900	.117	.852
UN_L	-.216	-.110	-.884	-.171	.869
$1/UN_L$	-.138	.116	.884	.238	.870
CPI	.418	-.204	.760	.376	.935
M_1 (-1)	-.312	-.553	.678	-.191	.899
bond yield	-.138	.477	.641	-.137	.676
AHE	.241	-.308	.619	.350	.659
SULC	.251	-.408	.588	-.509	.835
labor force participation rate	.003	.348	.520	.248	.453
AWE	-.353	-.428	.481	.355	.665
guidelines	-.301	.017	-.422	.142	.290
defense/government purchases	.008	.149	.415	.238	.252

VARIABLE[2]	Factor 1	Factor 2	Factor 3	Factor 4	R^2
WPI	.171 (1.84)	-.116 (0.85)	-.069 (0.30)	-.011 (0.01)	.048 (1.01)
political dummy	-.190	.032	-.091	.843	.757
government purchases	-.040	.149	.333	.838	.837
government purchases/national income	.540	.008	.160	.751	.881
defense/government expenditures	-.278	.026	.227	.594	.482
indirect tax rate	.362	-.161	-.293	-.504	.497
lagged political dummy	-.379	.135	.419	.497	.585
variance added	.265	.102	.156	.080	
cumulative variance explained	.265	.367	.523	.603	

---

[1]Boxes indicate the factor to which the variable has been assigned.

[2]Variables are unassigned (but included in the components analysis) if there is no factor loading above $|.39|$. The unassigned variables are WPI, percent of labor force female, corporate tax receipts, (ULC–SULC), inventory investment, UN↓, full employment surplus, debt/GNP.

TABLE B-8
Industry 23 Apparel

Rotated Factor Loadings for 1959:1-1971:3 with the Wholesale Price Index
Current and Lagged – Quarterly Percent Change (F-ratio in Parentheses)[1]

VARIABLE[2]	Factor 1	Factor 2	Factor 3	Factor 4	R^2
WPI	-.006	.003	.014	-.121	.015
	(0.00)	(0.00)	(0.01)	(0.89)	(0.30)
total employment	.724	.315	-.206	.158	.691
money GNP	.696	-.024	.132	.171	.532
1/UN$_A$	.624	.496	-.143	.024	.657
output	.580	.252	-.295	.482	.720
layoff rate	-.534	.151	.061	.253	.375
quit rate	.527	.219	.014	.028	.327
AWE	.526	-.093	.179	-.483	.550
cash flow	.498	-.029	-.055	.135	.270
output/previous peak	.483	.093	-.151	.384	.412
political dummy	.413	.300	-.075	-.403	.429
sales	.407	-.106	-.017	-.044	.179
corporate tax rate	-.400	-.067	.104	-.331	.285
government purchases (deflated)	-.153	.880	.082	-.154	.829
personal tax rate	-.189	.862	.058	-.141	.802
personal tax receipts	.273	.822	.057	.142	.774
GNP/potential GNP	.421	-.806	.007	.218	.875
4-6 month paper rate	.246	.719	.156	.189	.637
3-6 month paper rate	.251	.676	.120	.197	.573
bond yield	-.084	.669	.383	.106	.613
UN†	-.305	-.622	.068	.036	.486
discount rate	.173	.592	.013	.64	.408
total employment (-1)	.346	.508	-.139	.178	.429
1/UN$_L$ (-1)	-.043	.196	.931	.096	.917
UN$_L$ (-1)	.040	-.188	-.930	-.072	.908
1/UN$_{AL}$ (-1)	-.117	.164	.930	-.108	.917

VARIABLE[2]	Factor 1	Factor 2	Factor 3	Factor 4	R^2
WPI	-.006	.003	.014	-.121	.015
	(0.00)	(0.00)	(0.01)	(0.89)	(0.30)
$1/UN_{AL}$	.057	.289	.894	-.113	.899
$1/UN_L$	.192	.271	.854	-.196	.879
UN_L	-.206	-.305	-.850	.145	.879
CPI	-.189	-.107	.829	.077	.740
SULC	-.079	-.319	.666	.051	.553
M_1 (-1)	.482	-.187	.483	.186	.535
guidelines	.072	.165	-.416	-.005	.206
lagged political dummy	.265	.389	.411	-.172	.421
ULC	-.191	-.177	.375	-.638	.615
government purchases/national income	-.368	-.004	.103	-.607	.515
productivity	.303	.178	-.249	.601	.547
government purchases	.108	.226	.147	-.530	.366
UN	-.478	-.189	.163	.507	.548
$1/UN^2$	.480	.192	-.163	-.506	.549
UN (-1)	-.171	-.335	-.024	-.437	.333
$1/UN^2$ (-1)	.173	-.337	.025	.437	.335
AHE	.190	-.219	.415	-.429	.441
accession rate	.176	.289	-.181	-.426	.329
variance added	.081	.142	.127	.068	
cumulative variance explained	.081	.223	.350	.418	

[1] Boxes indicate the factor to which the variable has been assigned.

[2] Variables are unassigned (but included in the components analysis) if there is no factor loading above $|.39|$. The unassigned variables are WPI, WPI (-1), percent of labor force female, profit/equity, assets/ liabilities-internal funds, corporate tax receipts, (ULC-SULC), inventory investment, stock price index, inventory/sales, materials cost, UN↓, real GNP, unborrowed reserves, indirect tax rate, defense/government purchases, defense/government expenditures, full employment surplus, debt/GNP, M_2 (-1), labor force participation rate.

TABLE B-9
Industry 24 Lumber and Wood

Rotated Factor Loadings for 1959:1-1971:3 with the Wholesale Price Index
Current and Lagged - Percent Change over Four Quarters (F-ratio in Parentheses)[1]

VARIABLE[2]	Factor 1	Factor 2	Factor 3	Factor 4	R^2
WPI	.757	.163	.310	-.015	.696
	(111.21)	(5.156)	(18.65)	(0.04)	(45.02)
profit/equity	.899	.032	-.161	.141	.855
corporate tax receipts	.888	.214	.039	.098	.846
output	.847	.237	-.151	.054	.800
layoff rate	-.846	-.024	.072	-.157	.747
inventory/sales	-.825	.037	.126	-.228	.750
M2 (-1)	.818	-.038	.195	.326	.814
productivity	.815	.231	-.069	.062	.725
sales	.794	.394	.171	.134	.834
materials cost	.756	.163	.310	-.015	.695
output/previous peak	.750	-.261	-.168	.113	.671
total employment	.703	.624	.039	-.011	.885
AWE	.663	-.008	.365	-.326	.679
M1 (-1)	.660	-.016	.623	-.232	.879
ULC	-.657	-.306	.425	-.275	.782
money GNP	.641	.452	.390	.175	.797
GNP/potential GNP	.606	-.431	-.053	-.247	.617
corporate tax rate	-.557	.042	.191	-.081	.355
assets/liabilities - internal funds	.495	-.329	.067	.239	.415
WPI (-1)	.474	.422	.400	-.026	.563
4-6 month paper rate	.128	.911	.190	-.011	.882
3-6 month paper rate	.198	.892	.130	-.047	.855
total employment (-1)	.320	.823	.105	-.082	.797
discount rate (-1)	-.097	.778	.151	-.292	.723
$1/UN_A$	.363	.770	-.039	.392	.883
quit rate	.526	.696	-.084	.229	.820
real GNP	.250	.693	.069	-.052	.550

139

VARIABLE	factor 1	factor 2	factor 3	factor 4	R
WPI	.757 (111.21)	.163 (5.156)	.310 (18.65)	-.015 (0.04)	.696 (45.02)
government purchases	-.245	.651	.255	.417	.723
$1/UN^2$ (-1)	.153	.647	.047	.322	.548
UN (-1)	-.154	-.645	-.043	-.329	.550
personal tax rate	-.285	.624	.221	.392	.673
personal tax receipts	.420	-.614	.121	-.315	.667
unborrowed reserves	.483	-.559	-.069	-.067	.555
debt/GNP	-.098	-.405	-.111	-.248	.247
$1/UN_{AL}$ (-1)	-.087	.233	.929	.147	.946
$1/UN_{AL}$	.085	.301	.887	.249	.947
UN_L (-1)	-.040	-.257	-.868	-.128	.838
$1/UN_L$ (-1)	.037	.219	.866	.114	.813
UN_L	-.183	-.196	-.824	-.186	.785
$1/UN_L$	.168	.144	.816	.199	.755
CPI	-.073	-.262	.811	-.421	.909
AHE	.313	-.134	.659	-.393	.705
bond yield	-.166	.502	.624	.002	.669
guidelines	.162	.212	-.567	.156	.417
labor force participation rate	-.224	.177	.525	.408	.524
defense/government purchases	-.106	.013	.451	.301	.305
government purchases	.023	-.040	.301	.861	.834
political dummy	.174	.003	-.186	.837	.766
SULC	.046	-.303	.280	-.743	.724
government purchases/national income	-.269	-.534	.218	.672	.857
defense/government expenditures	.162	.059	.213	.656	.505
lagged political dummy	.259	.335	.282	.599	.617
indirect tax rate	-.228	-.290	-.167	-.599	.522
accession rate	.318	.260	-.105	.447	.380
variance added	.267	.160	.120	.083	
cumulative variance explained	.267	.427	.547	.630	

[1] Boxes indicate the factor to which the variable has been assigned.

[2] Variables are unassigned (but included in the components analysis) if there is no factor loading above |.39|. The unassigned variables are UN, $1/UN^2$, percent of labor force female, (ULC-SULC), inventory investment.

TABLE B-10
Industry 24 Lumber and Wood

Rotated Factor Loadings for 1959:1-1971:3 with the Wholesale Price Index
Current and Lagged – Quarterly Percent Change (F-ratio in Parentheses)[1]

VARIABLE[2]	Factor 1	Factor 2	Factor 3	Factor 4	R^2
WPI	.504 (32.93)	-.510 (33.72)	.130 (2.19)	.119 (1.84)	.545 (23.55)
output	.835	-.123	.123	.104	.738
productivity	.769	-.119	.080	.118	.627
profit/equity	.737	-.107	-.121	.089	.578
output/previous peak	.707	.101	-.120	.192	.561
ULC	-.648	.135	.347	-.033	.560
corporate tax receipts	.644	-.320	.002	-.151	.539
layoff rate	-.629	-.019	.063	-.199	.440
sales	.612	-.439	.089	-.044	.578
AWE	.605	-.010	.308	.174	.492
materials cost	.535	-.469	.119	.143	.540
UN (-1)	-.446	-.060	-.101	.148	.235
$1/UN^2$ (-1)	.444	.053	.098	-.146	.231
$1/UN^2$	-.278	-.667	-.080	.093	.537
UN	.281	.662	.077	-.096	.533
total employment (-1)	-.036	.657	.081	-.116	.453
1/UNA	.300	-.537	.095	-.440	.581
total employment	.435	-.517	.052	-.055	.462
M_1 (-1)	.356	-.493	.430	.280	.633
M_2 (-1)	.371	-.485	.010	-.087	.381
government purchases/national income	-.083	.479	.127	-.129	.269
WPI (-1)	.198	-.446	.184	-.202	.312
real GNP	-.010	-.440	.053	-.089	.214
money GNP	.382	-.410	.122	.094	.337

VARIABLE[2]	Factor 1	Factor 2	Factor 3	Factor 4	R[2]
WPI	.504	-.510	.130	.119	.545
	(32.93)	(33.72)	(2.19)	(1.84)	(23.55)
$1/UN_{AL}$ (-1)	-.079	.150	.921	-.132	.894
UN_L (-1)	-.134	-.171	-.912	-.155	.903
$1/UN_L$ (-1)	.157	.214	.909	-.179	.929
$1/UN_{AL}$	.018	.008	.899	-.247	.869
$1/UN_L$	-.039	-.239	.865	-.079	.812
UN_L	.050	.249	-.864	.124	.827
CPI	-.167	.013	.830	.174	.747
AHE	.327	-.030	.517	-.219	.423
guidelines	.098	-.088	-.504	-.239	.328
government purchases (deflated)	-.125	-.127	.154	-.844	.769
personal tax receipts	.160	.025	.015	.824	.707
personal tax rate	-.159	.124	.131	.824	.737
GNP/potential GNP	.299	-.054	-.072	.798	.735
4-6 month paper rate	-.016	-.530	.232	-.593	.688
bond yield	-.141	-.252	.443	-.568	.602
3-6 month paper rate	-.004	-.548	.195	-.550	.640
SULC	-.226	.061	.356	.486	.418
unborrowed reserves	.067	-.287	-.065	.478	.320
discount rate (-1)	-.079	-.313	.127	-.439	.313
lagged political dummy	.272	-.106	.350	-.438	.399
political dummy	.484	-.021	-.143	-.430	.440
variance added	.148	.063	.133	.095	
cumulative variance explained	.148	.211	.344	.439	

[1] Boxes indicate the factor to which the variable has been assigned.

[2] Variables are unassigned (but included in the components analysis) if there is no factor loading above |.39|. The unassigned variables are percent of labor force female, accession rate, quit rate, cash flow, assets/liabilities-internal funds, corporate tax rate, (ULC-SULC), inventory investment, inventory/sales, indirect tax rate, government purchases, defense/government expenditures, full employment surplus, debt/GNP, labor force participation rate.

TABLE B-11
Industry 25 Furniture

Rotated Factor Loadings for 1959:1-1971:3 with the Wholesale Price Index
Current and Lagged – Percent Change over Four Quarters (F-ratio in Parentheses)[1]

VARIABLE[2]	Factor 1	Factor 2	Factor 3	Factor 4	R^2
WPI	.161 (15.76)	-.213 (27.59)	.907 (500.37)	-.093 (5.36)	.607 (183.08)
profit/equity	-.902	.007	-.092	.043	.825
output	.889	.337	-.090	.183	.945
corporate tax receipts	-.879	.056	-.023	.182	.809
total employment	-.863	.428	.098	.172	.968
accession rate	.858	.008	-.061	.304	.832
quit rate	-.819	.376	-.026	.145	.834
sales	.804	.367	-.116	.207	.838
output/previous peak	-.783	.082	-.087	-.014	.628
money GNP	-.780	.150	.462	.182	.883
layoff rate	.773	.158	.038	-.134	.654
productivity	-.759	.491	.041	.311	.936
1/UNA	-.743	.536	-.047	.271	.938
AWE	.731	-.133	.476	-.159	.821
ULC	.728	-.464	.325	-.296	.943
UN	-.725	-.281	.013	-.039	.611
1/UN²	-.679	-.283	-.010	.033	.607
M₂ (-1)	.652	-.374	.263	.347	.791
inventory/sales	-.643	.407	.163	.001	.618
materials cost	-.602	-.164	.390	.061	.596
cash flow	.599	-.016	-.176	.129	.411
corporate tax rate	-.507	-.105	.014	-.135	.388
UN↓	.504	-.120	-.004	-.153	.294
UN↑	-.494	.068	.108	-.086	.278
real GNP		.140	.484	.144	.519

VARIABLE[2]	Factor 1	Factor 2	Factor 3	Factor 4	R^2
WPI	.161 (15.76)	-.213 (27.59)	.907 (500.37)	-.093 (5.26)	.607 (183.08)
government purchases (deflated)	-.007	.772	.068	.423	.779
4-6 month paper rate	-.452	.768	.198	-.050	.836
personal tax receipts	-.139	-.766	.288	.250	.751
personal tax rate	-.032	.759	.030	.395	.734
unborrowed reserves	-.275	-.747	.050	-.084	.644
discount rate (-1)	-.233	.744	.192	-.278	.722
GNP/potential GNP	-.460	-.719	.134	-.247	.807
3-6 month paper rate	-.500	.711	.166	-.095	.791
total employment (-1)	-.566	.671	.124	.180	.818
bond yield	-.076	.589	.575	.090	.691
UN (-1)	.355	-.587	.015	-.139	.490
$1/UN^2$ (-1)	-.349	.586	-.011	.135	.483
AHE	.096	-.056	.957	-.035	.930
WPI (-1)	.194	-.209	.883	-.163	.888
$1/UN_{AL}$	.109	.350	.841	.326	.947
CPI	.338	-.167	.840	-.083	.882
$1/UN_{AL}$	-.092	.343	.811	.399	.943
UN_L (-1)	-.005	-.324	-.772	-.289	.784
UN_L	.282	-.263	-.769	-.280	.818
M_1 (-1)	-.470	-.280	.757	-.097	.883
$1/UN_L$ (-1)	.066	.290	.748	.396	.805
$1/UN_L$	-.170	.221	.735	.418	.793
guidelines	-.265	.078	-.546	.023	.579
government purchases	-.046	.057	.217	.898	.328
political dummy	-.197	.020	-.305	.768	.723
government purchases/national income	.462	-.277	-.037	.759	.868
SULC	.241	-.459	.154	-.707	.793

TABLE B-11 (continued)

VARIABLE[2]	Factor 1	Factor 2	Factor 3	Factor 4	R²
WPI	.161 (15.76)	-.213 (27.59)	.907 (500.37)	-.093 (5.26)	.607 (183.08)
percent of labor force female	-.029	-.069	.367	.671	.591
indirect tax rate	.336	-.151	-.083	-.649	.563
defense/government expenditures	-.292	.039	.144	.648	.527
lagged political dummy	-.356	.258	.200	.588	.579
labor force participation rate	.069	.237	.394	.529	.497
assets/liabilities-internal funds	.190	-.255	.207	-.438	.336
defense/government purchases	.029	.094	.401	.406	.338
variance added	.307	.125	.167	.077	
cumulative variance explained	.307	.432	.599	.676	

[1] Boxes indicate the factor to which the variable has been assigned.

[2] Variables are unassigned (but included in the components analysis) if there is no factor loading above |.39|. The unassigned variables are (ULC-SULC), inventory investment, full employment surplus, debt/GNP.

145

TABLE B-12
Industry 25 Furniture

Rotated Factor Loadings for 1959:1-1971:3 with the Wholesale Price Index
Current and Lagged - Quarterly Percent Change (F-ratio in Parentheses)[1]

VARIABLE[2]	Factor 1	Factor 2	Factor 3	Factor 4	R^2
WPI	.121 (3.20)	.166 (6.02)	.780 (132.94)	-.281 (17.25)	.730 (53.17)
total employment	.829	-.232	.020	.359	.871
output	.818	-.263	-.119	.244	.812
AWE	.697	.074	.203	-.120	.547
$1/UN_A$	.680	-.290	-.079	.414	.723
productivity	.677	-.314	-.074	.394	.718
output/previous peak	.667	-.144	-.088	-.118	.488
profit/equity	.666	.133	-.056	.033	.466
money GNP	.661	.204	.158	.247	.565
accession rate	.636	.116	-.091	.275	.501
sales	.613	-.182	-.102	.302	.510
corporate tax receipts	.606	.055	-.030	.104	.381
ULC	-.600	.279	.329	-.443	.742
layoff rate	-.595	-.062	.077	.046	.366
government purchases/national income	-.569	.013	.117	.308	.433
M_1 (-1)	.533	.221	.524	-.161	.634
$1/UN^2$	.529	-.032	.052	-.037	.285
UN	-.525	.031	.050	.042	.281
quit rate	.521	-.122	-.055	.331	.393
materials costs	.496	.158	.191	-.087	.315
M_2 (-1)	.475	.114	-.035	.060	.243
UN↓	.441	.165	-.060	.129	.242
corporate tax rate	-.412	.095	.014	.054	.182
GNP/potential GNP	.262	.915	.035	-.013	.908
government purchases (deflated)	-.024	-.892	.059	.198	.840
personal tax rate	-.041	-.880	.038	.184	.811

TABLE B-12 (continued)

VARIABLE[2]	Factor 1	Factor 2	Factor 3	Factor 4	R^2
WPI	.121 (3.20)	.166 (6.02)	.780 (132.94)	-.281 (17.25)	.730 (53.17)
personal tax receipts	.092	.856	.092	-.129	.767
bond yield	.120	-.724	.402	-.072	.706
4-6 month paper rate	.428	-.632	.204	-.139	.644
defense/government expenditures	.013	.618	.088	.383	.537
3-6 month paper rate	.444	-.584	.166	.137	.584
discount rate (-1)	.292	-.560	.001	.077	.405
unborrowed reserves	.070	.407	.001	-.088	.178
$1/UN_{AL}$ (-1)	-.262	-.177	.903	.116	.928
$1/UN_{AL}$	-.078	-.242	.886	.240	.907
$1/UN_L$ (-1)	-.288	-.123	.824	.341	.894
UN_L (-1)	.313	.112	-.824	-.316	.890
CPI	-.135	-.054	.819	-.341	.809
UN_L	-.052	.141	.814	-.299	.775
$1/UN_L$	.021	-.140	.811	.304	.771
AHE	.288	.115	.781	-.216	.753
WPI (-1)	-.015	.094	.742	-.253	.623
guidelines	.038	-.055	-.490	.287	.327
SULC	-.081	.294	.114	-.752	.671
lagged political dummy	.063	-.179	.372	.655	.604
political dummy	.163	-.084	-.080	.653	.466
government purchases	-.116	-.032	.192	.612	.426
$1/UN^2$ (-1)	.112	-.006	.025	.540	.305
UN (-1)	-.108	.008	-.026	-.536	.299
total employment (-1)	.423	-.153	.071	.520	.480
indirect tax rate	-.057	.125	-.032	-.459	.230
variance added	.182	.099	.136	.062	
cumulative variance explained	.182	.281	.417	.479	

[1] Boxes indicate the factor to which the variable has been assigned.

[2] Variables are unassigned (but included in the components analysis) if there is no factor loading above $|.39|$. The unassigned variables are percent of labor force female, cash flow, assets/liabilities-internal funds, (ULC-SULC), inventory investment, inventory/sales, UN↑, real GNP, full employment surplus, debt/GNP, labor force participation rate.

TABLE B-13
Industry 26 Paper

Rotated Factor Loadings for 1959:1-1971:3 with the Wholesale Price Index
Current and Lagged – Percent Change over Four Quarters (F-ratio in Parentheses)[1]

VARIABLE[2]	Factor 1	Factor 2	Factor 3	Factor 4	R^2
WPI	.008 (0.02)	-.124 (2.78)	-.832 (124.98)	-.056 (0.57)	.712 (42.85)
output	-.927	-.202	.158	.002	.925
cash flow	-.873	-.269	.150	.188	.893
inventory/sales	.871	.051	-.334	.033	.874
corporate tax receipts	-.865	-.119	.003	.198	.802
productivity	-.864	-.352	.085	-.022	.879
profit/equity	-.839	-.374	.195	.204	.924
layoff rate	.814	-.037	-.194	-.372	.840
sales	-.809	.001	-.212	.075	.705
money GNP	-.786	.012	-.328	.255	.791
1/UN	-.757	-.430	.121	.261	.841
accession rate	-.750	-.309	.219	.409	.872
ULC	.741	.473	-.361	-.074	.909
AWE	-.701	.479	-.350	-.147	.871
materials cost	-.697	.323	-.240	.072	.653
quit rate	-.689	-.494	-.015	.253	.783
output/previous peak	-.663	.379	.253	-.064	.652
3-6 month paper rate	-.676	-.573	-.201	-.130	.842
4-6 month paper rate	-.652	-.635	-.230	-.096	.891
stock price index	-.585	.157	.082	-.134	.392
M2 (-1)	-.565	.466	-.049	.417	.712
real GNP	-.448	-.382	-.111	-.073	.365
total employment (-1)	-.197	-.857	-.238	-.210	.873
personal tax receipts	.051	.819	-.234	-.108	.740
unborrowed reserves	-.063	.799	.077	.023	.648
GNP/potential GNP	-.063	-.799	.077	.023	.648
investment in P & E	.037	-.790	.048	-.019	.628

TABLE B-13 (continued)

VARIABLE[2]	Factor 1	Factor 2	Factor 3	Factor 4	R^2
WPI	.008 (0.02)	-.124 (2.78)	-.032 (124.98)	-.056 (0.57)	.712 (42.85)
government purchases (deflated)	-.252	-.743	-.110	.319	.729
personal tax rate	-.207	-.733	-.091	.287	.671
total employment	-.533	-.728	-.138	.239	.890
discount rate (-1)	-.358	-.633	-.256	-.307	.689
expected investment in P & E	.021	-.610	.129	-.046	.392
corporate tax rate	-.148	.514	-.264	.027	.357
CPI	.187	.241	.874	-.126	.873
WPI (-1)	.262	-.089	-.806	-.044	.729
$1/UN_{AL}$ (-1)	-.110	-.269	-.800	.347	.845
AHE	.037	.465	-.759	-.260	.861
$1/UN_{AL}$	-.290	-.241	-.719	.422	.837
bond yield	-.217	-.518	-.626	.070	.712
M_1 (-1)	-.512	-.454	-.613	-.017	.845
guidelines	-.092	-.110	.583	.024	.361
government purchases	-.085	-.082	-.057	.916	.856
government purchases/national income	-.469	.160	-.023	.780	.854
political dummy	-.130	-.047	.467	.746	.793
SULC	.039	.331	-.450	.747	.872
defense/government expenditures	-.248	-.022	-.083	.714	.579
indirect tax rate	.406	.165	.062	.634	.597
lagged political dummy	-.314	-.226	-.040	.621	.536
assets/liabilities - internal funds	-.042	-.027	.435	.560	.505
labor force participation rate	-.069	-.290	-.463	.519	.573
defense/government purchases	-.052	-.082	-.455	.455	.423
variance added	.301	.149	.130	.095	
cumulative variance explained	.301	.450	.580	.675	

[1]Boxes indicate the factor to which the variable has been assigned.

[2]Variables are unassigned (but included in the components analysis) if there is no factor loading above |.39|. The unassigned variables are percent of labor force female, (ULC-SULC), inventory investment, full employment surplus, debt/GNP.

TABLE B-14
Industry 26 Paper

Rotated Factor Loadings for 1959:1-1971:3 with the Wholesale Price Index
Current and Lagged - Quarterly Percent Change (F-ratio in Parentheses)[1]

VARIABLE[2]	Factor 1	Factor 2	Factor 3	Factor 4	R^2
WPI	.013 (0.01)	-.182 (2.58)	.527 (21.65)	.151 (1.78)	.333 (8.65)
output	.891	.029	-.104	-.030	.807
profit/equity	.834	.064	-.055	.080	.710
productivity	.777	.142	-.134	.015	.642
cash flow	.742	.160	.002	.025	.577
corporate tax receipts	.733	-.107	.151	-.003	.571
ULC	-.703	.207	.378	-.074	.686
money GNP	.697	.118	.134	.075	.524
1/UNA	.669	-.376	-.150	.123	.627
sales	.666	.172	.309	-.154	.592
accession rate	.576	-.104	-.121	.239	.415
layoff rate	-.570	-.048	.004	-.051	.330
total employment	.530	-.406	-.107	.431	.643
output/previous peak	.508	.340	-.034	-.124	.390
AWE	.485	.254	.428	-.211	.528
materials cost	.468	.112	.308	-.113	.339
government purchases (deflated)	-.032	-.857	-.042	.203	.776
personal tax rate	-.074	-.846	-.039	.176	.753
GNP/potential GNP	.245	.830	.117	-.107	.801
personal tax receipts	.144	.797	.133	-.082	.681
bond yield	.090	-.745	.329	.095	.681
4-6 month paper rate	.417	-.733	.202	.038	.754
3-6 month paper rate	.446	-.691	.187	.006	.711
discount rate (-1)	.194	-.654	.001	-.143	.486
total employment (-1)	.209	-.571	-.086	.387	.527
defense/government expenditures	.283	.499	.008	.327	.436
investment in P & E	.018	-.437	-.253	.204	.296

TABLE B-14 (continued)

VARIABLE[2]	Factor 1	Factor 2	Factor 3	Factor 4	R^2
WPI	.013	-.182	.527	.151	.333
	(0.01)	(2.58)	(21.65)	(1.78)	(8.65)
CPI	-.275	-.078	.881	.038	.860
AHE	-.006	.251	.746	-.183	.653
M_1 (-1)	.371	.145	.693	-.106	.650
$1/UN_{AL}$(-1)	-.181	-.194	.648	.564	.808
guidelines	.055	-.039	-.556	.059	.318
WPI (-1)	-.227	-.124	.465	.184	.317
government purchases	.099	.045	-.023	.724	.536
SULC	-.180	.068	.594	-.664	.830
$1/UN_{AL}$	.010	-.281	.608	.612	.824
political dummy	.347	.001	-.349	.611	.616
government purchases/national income	-.436	.153	-.014	.569	.537
variance added	.165	.129	.093	.064	
cumulative variance explained	.165	.294	.387	.451	

---

[1]Boxes indicate the factor to which the variable has been assigned.

[2]Variables are unassigned (but included in the components analysis) if there is no factor loading above |.39|. The unassigned variables are percent of labor force female, quit rate, expected investment in P & E, assets/liabilities—internal funds, corporate tax rate, (ULC–SULC), inventory investment, stock price index, inventory/sales, real GNP, unborrowed reserves, indirect tax rate, defense/government purchases, full employment surplus, debt/GNP, M_2 (-1), labor force participation rate.

TABLE B-15
Industry 27 Printing and Publishing

Rotated Factor Loadings for 1959:1-1971:3
– Percent Change over Four Quarters (F-ratio in Parentheses)[1]

VARIABLE[2]	Factor 1	Factor 2	Factor 3	Factor 4	R^2
AHE	.407 (101.10)	.224 (30.65)	.831 (421.63)	.000 (0.00)	.915 (186.21)
$1/UN_A$	-.899	.014	-.046	-.223	.860
output	-.863	-.159	-.163	-.206	.838
profit/equity	-.801	.037	.142	-.166	.690
productivity	-.796	-.180	-.216	-.248	.774
accession rate	-.794	-.093	-.084	-.288	.728
ULC	.752	.222	.471	.188	.872
quit rate	-.747	-.023	.027	.379	.744
3-6 month paper rate	-.725	-.314	.282	-.145	.724
4-6 month paper rate	-.715	-.377	.307	-.207	.790
$1/UN^2$	-.700	.064	-.050	-.192	.534
UN	.700	-.068	.052	.195	.535
layoff rate	.696	-.040	-.233	.298	.629
real GNP	-.672	-.043	.165	-.006	.489
money GNP	-.648	.394	.362	-.297	.795
cash flow	-.572	-.196	.515	-.077	.636
SULC	.530	.023	.393	.658	.869
indirect tax rate	.531	-.223	.120	.516	.613
discount rate (-1)	-.507	-.461	.294	-.073	.561
lagged political dummy	-.499	.138	-.009	-.467	.486
UN↓	-.496	.152	.022	.015	.269
corporate tax rate	-.469	.028	.013	-.190	.257
debt/GNP	.448	.165	-.183	.194	.299
UN (-1)	.421	.229	.184	.378	.407
$1/UN^2$ (-1)	-.419	-.233	-.182	-.375	.404
guidelines	-.407	.026	-.367	.376	.442

152

TABLE B-15 (continued)

VARIABLE[2]	Factor 1	Factor 2	Factor 3	Factor 4	R^2
AHE	.407 (101.10)	.224 (30.65)	.831 (421.63)	.000 (0.00)	.915 (186.21)
GNP/potential GNP	.050	.843	.183	.318	.848
unborrowed reserves	.187	.801	-.003	.215	.723
personal tax receipts	.360	.763	.221	.182	.794
M_2 (-1)	-.394	.737	.138	-.165	.744
personal tax rate	-.335	-.603	-.024	-.487	.714
government purchases (deflated)	-.383	-.584	-.008	-.519	.756
AWE	-.056	.222	.877	.007	.821
CPI	.492	.063	.760	-.264	.893
inventory/sales	.279	-.033	-.749	-.079	.646
M_1 (-1)	-.131	.540	.734	-.142	.868
sales	-.026	-.005	-.715	.239	.569
corporate tax receipts	-.520	-.119	.658	-.109	.729
assets/liabilities-internal funds	-.402	-.164	.650	-.040	.613
political dummy	-.305	.234	-.641	-.352	.682
materials cost	.048	-.023	.627	.304	.488
full employment surplus	.182	-.169	-.441	-.057	.262
$1/UN_L$ (-1)	-.065	-.134	.095	.834	.727
UN_L (-1)	.156	.247	-.144	.812	.758
government purchases	-.099	.200	-.365	-.796	.817
$1/UN_{AL}$	-.172	-.023	.516	-.777	.900
$1/UN_L$	-.347	-.022	.147	-.769	.734
$1/UN_{AL}$ (-1)	-.007	-.127	.551	-.769	.910
UN_L	.435	.166	-.132	.743	.787
labor force participation rate	-.173	-.003	.115	.724	.567
total employment (-1)	-.141	-.483	-.007	-.688	.727
defense/government purchases	.007	.104	.047	-.670	.462
defense/government expenditures	-.261	.324	-.247	-.644	.649

VARIABLE[2]	Factor 1	Factor 2	Factor 3	Factor 4	R^2
AHE	.407	.224	.831	.000	.915
	(101.10)	(30.65)	(421.63)	(0.00)	(186.21)
government purchases/national income	.462	.184	-.457	-.632	.856
total employment	-.423	-.434	.036	-.629	.800
percent of labor force female	-.108	-.155	-.012	-.578	.370
bond yield	-.158	-.425	.397	-.566	.683
variance added	.300	.082	.137	.110	
cumulative variance explained	.300	.382	.519	.629	

---

[1] Boxes indicate the factor to which the variable has been assigned.

[2] Variables are unassigned (but included in the components analysis) if there is no factor loading above |.39|. The unassigned variables are output/previous peak, new orders/sales, (ULC-SULC), inventory investment, UN↑.

TABLE B-16
Industry 27   Printing and Publishing

Rotated Factor Loadings for 1959:1-1971:3
- Quarterly Percent Change (F-ratio in Parentheses)[1]

VARIABLE[2]	Factor 1	Factor 2	Factor 3	Factor 4	R^2
AHE	.039 (0.44)	-.196 (11.19)	-.870 (220.60)	.071 (1.46)	.801 (77.82)
output	-.739	.206	.283	-.127	.684
$1/UN_A$	-.699	.154	.138	-.215	.578
profit/equity	-.639	-.150	-.074	-.031	.437
productivity	-.630	.237	.323	-.200	.597
government purchases/national income	.564	.334	.141	-.058	.453
money GNP	-.562	.157	-.103	.285	.432
real GNP	-.550	.070	.003	-.014	.308
corporate tax receipts	-.493	-.175	-.271	-.446	.547
cash flow	-.492	-.169	-.228	-.310	.418
$UN\downarrow$	-.485	.182	.088	.051	.279
$1/UN^2$	-.449	-.054	-.049	-.039	.209
UN	.447	.056	.048	-.038	.207
layoff rate	.418	-.165	.050	.106	.216
quit rate	-.413	.361	.114	-.046	.316
corporate tax rate	.411	.127	.068	.010	.189
UN_T (-1)	-.181	-.861	.184	.135	.826
$1/UN_L$ (-1)	.252	.849	-.205	-.097	.836
UN_L	.157	-.800	.188	.165	.726
$1/UN_L$	-.158	.753	-.263	-.126	.677
$1/UN_{AL}$	-.038	.708	-.597	-.211	.903
SULC	.332	-.692	-.414	.166	.787
$1/UN_{AL}$ (-1)	.155	.658	-.635	-.162	.886
lagged political dummy	-.286	.612	.010	-.135	.474
government purchases	.126	.575	.205	-.037	.389
total employment	-.419	.503	.083	-.170	.465

VARIABLE[2]	Factor 1	Factor 2	Factor 3	Factor 4	R^2
AHE	.039 (0.44)	-.196 (11.19)	-.870 (220.60)	.071 (1.46)	.801 (77.82)
total employment (-1)	-.029	.483	-.016	-.221	.283
1/UN2 (-1)	.125	.472	.206	.222	.330
UN (-1)	-.129	-.469	-.207	-.218	.327
CPI	.208	.107	-.870	-.103	.823
AWE	-.282	-.107	-.678	.125	.567
M_1 (-1)	-.319	-.024	-.602	.193	.502
ULC	.550	-.260	-.557	.191	.717
guidelines	-.206	-.126	.537	-.018	.347
political dummy	-.234	.470	.473	-.026	.500
materials cost	-.109	.136	-.464	-.044	.247
GNP/potential GNP	-.146	-.116	-.129	.913	.886
personal tax rate	-.041	.209	.082	-.888	.840
government purchases (deflated)	-.066	.244	.086	-.887	.858
personal tax receipts	-.043	-.105	-.189	.860	.788
bond yield	-.124	.294	-.299	-.695	.674
defense/government expenditures	-.072	.281	.088	.602	.455
4-6 month paper rate	-.401	.221	-.140	-.572	.557
percent of labor force female	-.108	.024	-.072	-.559	.330
3-6 month paper rate	-.406	.183	-.109	-.529	.490
discount rate (-1)	-.328	.144	.001	-.434	.317
accession rate	-.228	.151	.146	-.424	.276
variance added	.166	.100	.094	.075	
cumulative variance explained	.166	.266	.360	.435	

Boxes indicate the factor to which the variable has been assigned.

[1]Boxes indicate the factor to which the variable has been assigned.

[2]Variables are unassigned (but included in the components analysis) if there is no factor loading above |.39|. The unassigned variables are output/previous peak, sales, assets/liabilities-internal funds, (ULC-SULC), inventory investment, inventory/sales, UN↑, unborrowed reserves, indirect tax rate, defense/government purchases, full employment surplus, debt/GNP, M_2 (-1), labor force participation rate.

TABLE B-17
Industry 28 Chemicals

Rotated Factor Loadings for 1959:1-1971:3 with the Wholesale Price Index
Current and Lagged — Percent Change over Four Quarters (F-ratio in Parentheses)[1]

VARIABLE[2]	Factor 1	Factor 2	Factor 3	Factor 4	R^2
WPI	-.418 (27.63)	-.350 (21.88)	.372 (19.37)	-.416 (27.37)	.608 (32.05)
corporate tax receipts	.914	.002	-.071	-.084	.898
profit/equity	.897	.015	.272	.114	.892
output	.883	-.352	-.109	.225	.965
inventory/sales	-.859	-.025	-.234	.081	.800
layoff rate	-.859	.174	.060	-.190	.809
sales	.853	-.066	-.176	.032	.764
productivity	.852	-.337	-.150	.308	.956
cash flow	.846	.069	.052	-.070	.748
ULC	-.765	.385	-.023	-.484	.968
money GNP	.757	-.050	-.465	.045	.794
$1/UN_A$	.715	-.515	-.058	.212	.853
accession rate	.700	-.473	.003	.356	.841
M_2 (-1)	.672	.410	-.286	.318	.802
output/previous peak	.652	.418	.139	.165	.646
stock price index	.608	.298	.429	-.201	.683
(ULC-SULC)	.594	.065	.186	.194	.429
quit rate	.577	-.570	-.132	.197	.715
UN	-.496	.466	.022	-.348	.585
$1/UN^2$	.483	-.472	-.027	.353	.581
real GNP	.480	-.387	-.077	.089	.394
expected investment in P & E	-.421	-.313	.142	.347	.416
personal tax receipts	.075	.827	-.083	-.235	.752
government purchases (deflated)	.079	-.793	-.207	.285	.804
personal tax rate	.036	-.786	-.252	.270	.510
GNP/potential GNP	.333	.777	.069	-.167	.747

157

VARIABLE [2]	Factor 1	Factor 2	Factor 3	Factor 4	R^2
WPI	-.418 (27.63)	-.350 (21.88)	.372 (19.37)	-.416 (27.37)	.608 (32.05)
unborrowed reserves	.168	.775	.101	.024	.640
4-6 month paper rate	.540	-.725	-.232	-.196	.909
discount rate (-1)	.167	-.700	-.136	-.350	.658
total employment	.237	-.684	-.386	.482	.905
3-6 month paper rate	.597	-.663	-.175	-.230	.880
total employment (-1)	-.075	-.650	-.464	.502	.896
UN (-1)	-.239	.637	.051	-.265	.536
$1/UN^2$ (-1)	-.230	-.635	-.055	.269	.532
WPI (-1)	-.395	.527	-.323	-.330	.646
investment in P & E	-.316	-.405	.235	.024	.319
$1/UN_{AL}$ (-1)	-.059	-.260	-.941	.036	.959
$1/UN_{AL}$	.132	-.258	-.925	.120	.954
$1/UN_L$	.057	-.221	-.809	.157	.731
$1/UN_L$ (-1)	-.085	-.225	-.809	.042	.714
UN_L (-1)	.126	.288	.806	-.130	.765
UN_L	-.069	.293	.783	-.241	.762
materials cost	-.084	.344	-.776	.113	.740
CPI	-.304	.266	-.747	-.457	.930
M_1 (-1)	.493	.379	-.636	-.305	.885
bond yield	.091	-.529	-.636	-.197	.732
labor force participation rate	-.081	-.191	-.557	.324	.458
guidelines	.216	-.108	.510	.254	.383
defense/government purchases	-.004	-.055	-.485	.206	.281
political dummy	.201	-.035	.080	.832	.740
AWE	.271	.134	-.385	-.800	.879
AHE	-.130	.316	-.510	-.749	.939
government purchases	.080	-.056	-.396	.788	.788
government purchases/national income	-.425	.246	-.256	.702	.799

TABLE B-18
Industry 28 Chemicals

Rotated Factor Loadings for 1959:1-1971:3 with the Wholesale Price Index
Current and Lagged - Quarterly Percent Change (F-ratio in Parentheses)[1]

VARIABLE[2]	Factor 1	Factor 2	Factor 3	Factor 4	R^2
WPI	.238 (6.03)	-.314 (10.50)	-.414 (18.25)	.302 (9.72)	.418 (14.84)
output	-.840	.336	.091	-.262	.896
corporate tax receipts	-.811	.082	.086	.003	.672
profit/equity	-.783	-.231	.183	.006	.701
productivity	-.752	.266	.075	-.378	.785
money GNP	-.708	-.099	-.071	-.173	.546
sales	-.671	-.027	-.070	-.176	.487
cash flow	-.662	-.247	-.043	-.042	.502
ULC	.631	-.265	-.238	.526	.802
1/UNA	-.594	.355	.140	-.362	.630
M_1 (-1)	-.591	-.100	-.468	.278	.655
output/previous peak	-.568	-.018	.125	.069	.344
government purchases/national income	.551	-.123	-.113	-.338	.446
M_2 (-1)	-.503	.074	-.081	-.052	.268
inventory/sales	.453	.025	-.039	-.059	.211
layoff rate	.469	-.287	-.093	.064	.315
accession rate	-.450	.325	.149	-.272	.405
government purchases (deflated)	.123	.806	-.095	-.322	.777
personal tax rate	.151	.801	-.071	-.284	.750
GNP/potential GNP	-.336	-.782	.073	.179	.762
personal tax receipts	-.178	-.758	.018	.182	.640
4-6 month paper rate	-.301	.749	-.196	-.132	.707
3-6 month paper rate	-.325	.729	-.153	-.093	.670
bond yield	-.093	.663	.461	-.077	.667
discount rate (-1)	-.182	.649	-.008	.005	.446

VARIABLE[2]	Factor 1	Factor 2	Factor 3	Factor 4	R²
WPI	-.418 (27.63)	-.350 (21.88)	.372 (19.37)	-.416 (27.37)	.608 (32.05)
SULC	-.159	.459	.438	-.618	.810
defense/government expenditures	.282	-.017	-.293	.605	.532
lagged political dummy	.309	-.223	-.382	.576	.623
indirect tax rate	-.357	.109	.297	-.531	.510
variance added	.287	.123	.169	.081	
cumulative variance explained	.287	.410	.579	.660	

[1] Boxes indicate the factor to which the variable has been assigned.

[2] Variables are unassigned (but included in the components analysis) if there is no factor loading above |.39|. The unassigned variables are percent of labor force female, assets/liabilities-internal funds, corporate tax rate, inventory investment, UN↑, UN↓, full employment surplus, debt/GNP.

TABLE B-18 (continued)

VARIABLE[2]	Factor 1	Factor 2	Factor 3	Factor 4	R^2
WPI	.238 (6.03)	-.314 (10.50)	-.414 (18.25)	.302 (9.72)	.418 (14.84)
UN (-1)	-.024	-.578	-.022	.119	.349
$1/UN^2$ (-1)	.023	.576	.024	-.117	.346
defense/government expenditures	-.133	-.468	-.005	-.209	.281
$1/UN_{AL}$ (-1)	.167	.035	-.921	-.254	.942
$1/UN_{AL}$	.006	.118	-.884	-.364	.928
$1/UN_L$ (-1)	.125	.122	-.846	-.180	.778
CPI	.131	.005	-.846	.339	.847
UN_L (-1)	-.201	-.142	.831	.289	.835
$1/UN_L$	-.037	.056	-.823	-.345	.801
UN	.022	-.018	.793	.470	.850
materials cost	-.097	-.018	-.509	.041	.271
guidelines	-.040	-.022	.458	-.286	.294
SULC	.128	-.161	.210	.856	.819
political dummy	-.243	-.031	.126	-.757	.648
total employment	-.198	.344	-.120	-.747	.730
total employment (-1)	.047	.298	-.202	-.728	.661
lagged political dummy	-.134	.041	-.371	-.709	.660
AHE	-.118	-.018	-.583	.669	.801
government purchases	.063	-.044	-.132	-.642	.436
AWE	-.358	.158	-.360	.570	.607
WPI (-1)	.221	-.301	-.348	.433	.448
quit rate	-.231	.066	.023	-.411	.228
variance added	.169	.137	.091	.071	
cumulative variance explained	.169	.306	.397	.468	

[1] Boxes indicate the factor to which the variable has been assigned.

[2] Variables are unassigned (but included in the components analysis) if there is no factor loading above $|.39|$. The unassigned variables are UN, $1/UN^2$, percent of labor force female, investment in P & E, expected investment in P & E, assets/liabilities-internal funds, corporate tax rate, (ULC-SULC), inventory investment, stock price index, UN↓, UN↑, real GNP, unborrowed reserves, indirect tax rate, defense/government purchases, full employment surplus, debt/GNP, labor force participation rate.

TABLE B-19
Industry 29 Petroleum

Rotated Factor Loadings for 1959:1-1971:3 with the Wholesale Price Index
Current and Lagged - Percent Change over Four Quarters (F-ratio in Parentheses)[1]

VARIABLE[2]	Factor 1	Factor 2	Factor 3	Factor 4	R^2
WPI	.254 (12.36)	-.605 (70.17)	.534 (54.67)	-.135 (3.49)	.734 (46.90)
government purchases/national income	.833	-.091	.205	.204	.787
discount rate (-1)	.587	.035	.033	-.632	.746
cash flow	.530	-.173	-.119	.171	.354
profit/equity	.520	.088	-.402	.163	.467
M_1 (-1)	-.516	-.299	.468	.499	.824
real GNP	-.441	.310	-.186	.388	.475
output/previous peak	.401	.052	-.069	-.059	.172
government purchases (deflated)	.127	.886	.007	.242	.860
personal tax rate	.142	.863	-.005	.184	.800
GNP/potential GNP	-.303	-.863	.002	.231	.890
personal tax receipts	-.155	-.858	.267	.063	.836
unborrowed reserves	-.057	-.836	-.055	.175	.735
4-6 month paper rate	-.494	.710	.021	.286	.831
bond yield	-.121	.679	.567	.136	.815
WPI (-1)	.247	-.672	.529	-.084	.800
3-6 month paper rate	-.531	.651	-.012	.278	.783
materials cost	-.017	-.621	.506	.188	.678
quit rate	.122	.608	.076	.432	.577
accession rate	.187	.489	-.301	.337	.478
CPI	-.121	-.148	.880	-.040	.812
AHE	-.125	-.240	.815	-.071	.742
AWE	-.077	-.210	.770	-.031	.644
SULC	-.331	-.200	.755	-.214	.765
guidelines	-.047	.005	-.720	.099	.530

162

TABLE B-19 (continued)

VARIABLE[2]	Factor 1	Factor 2	Factor 3	Factor 4	R^2
WPI	.254 (12.36)	-.605 (70.17)	.534 (54.67)	-.135 (3.49)	.734 (46.90)
ULC	-.258	-.211	.701	-.026	.842
$1/UN_{AL}$ (-1)	-.002	.409	.701	.428	.861
$1/UN_{AL}$	-.050	.414	.589	.584	.348
total employment	-.023	.071	.584	.041	.399
defense/government purchases	.084	.102	.512	.345	
total employment (-1)	.053	.007	.482	-.052	.238
M_2 (-1)	-.186	-.339	-.096	.792	.787
money GNP	-.392	.133	.088	.779	.786
lagged political dummy	.084	.285	-.154	.758	.687
indirect tax rate	-.150	-.191	.020	-.730	.592
defense/government expenditures	.235	.057	.065	.650	.485
$1/UN_A$	-.307	.481	-.363	.629	.853
government purchases	.592	.235	.083	.625	.803
assets/liabilities-internal funds	-.077	.012	-.458	-.601	.577
political dummy	.420	.116	-.445	.552	.693
sales	.169	-.345	.332	.534	.543
layoff rate	.370	.045	-.010	-.508	.398
labor force participation rate	.244	-.247	.413	.486	.526
investment in P & E	.010	-.009	-.177	.433	.219
variance added	.079	.200	.157	.102	
cumulative variance explained	.079	.279	.436	.538	

[1]Boxes indicate the factor to which the variable has been assigned.

[2]Variables are unassigned (but included in the components analysis) if there is no factor loading above |.39|. The unassigned variables are percent of labor force female, output, expected investment in P & E, productivity, corporate tax rate, corporate tax receipts. (ULC-SLC), inventory investment, inventory/ sales, full employment surplus, debt/GNP.

TABLE B-20
Industry 29 Petroleum

Rotated Factor Loadings for 1959:1-1971:3 with the Wholesale Price Index
Current and Lagged - Quarterly Percent Change (F-ratio in Parentheses)[1]

VARIABLE[2]	Factor 1	Factor 2	Factor 3	Factor 4	R^2
WPI	.057	-.408	.452	-.413	.544
	(0.36)	(18.61)	(22.84)	(18.92)	(20.28)
output	.695	-.119	-.044	-.400	.650
productivity	.671	-.321	-.156	-.201	.617
ULC	.653	.157	.546	.087	.757
output/previous peak	.559	.072	-.013	-.490	.558
government purchases	.546	.144	-.034	.076	.326
lagged political dummy	.527	.326	.018	.329	.493
government purchases (deflated)	.097	.913	.021	-.199	.884
personal tax rate	.076	.892	.027	-.234	.856
GNP/potential GNP	-.021	-.868	-.011	.385	.903
personal tax rate	-.004	.855	-.048	.227	.784
bond yield	.062	.741	.293	.169	.668
materials cost	-.001	-.739	.283	.249	.688
4-6 month paper rate	-.005	.725	.076	.386	.681
3-6 month paper rate	.017	.687	.043	.385	.622
WPI (-1)	-.093	.597	.398	.019	.523
discount rate (-1)	-.046	.591	-.031	.095	.362
defense/government expenditures	.262	-.467	.016	.232	.341
CPI	.065	.019	.821	.065	.683
AHE	-.300	-.123	.709	-.011	.608
1/UN_{AL} (-1)	-.363	.221	.689	.090	.664
$SULC_{AL}$	-.155	-.114	.669	.053	.487
AWE	-.231	.035	.642	-.053	.495
1/UN_{AL}	-.404	.327	.613	.216	.692
guidelines	-.012	.089	-.609	.053	.382

TABLE B-20 (continued)

VARIABLE[2]	Factor 1	Factor 2	Factor 3	Factor 4	R^2
WPI	.057 (0.36)	-.408 (18.61)	.452 (22.84)	-.413 (18.92)	.544 (20.28)
money GNP	.192	-.062	-.092	.655	.479
$M_1(-1)$	.069	-.123	.448	.614	.597
1/UNA	.099	.426	-.286	.452	.478
cash flow	.101	.106	-.065	-.424	.206
variance added	.072	.140	.102	.077	
cumulative variance explained	.072	.212	.314	.391	

[1]Boxes indicate the factor to which the variable has been assigned.

[2]Variables are unassigned (but included in the components analysis) if there is no factor loading above |.39|. The unassigned variables are total employment, percent of labor force female, layoff rate, accession rate, quit rate, total employment (-1), investment in P & E, profit/equity, expected investment in P & E, sales, assets/liabilities-internal funds, corporate tax rate, corporate tax receipts, (ULC-SULC), inventory investment, inventory/sales, real GNP, unborrowed reserves, indirect tax rate, defense/government purchases, full employment surplus, debt/GNP, government purchases/national income, M_2 (-1), political dummy, labor force participation rate.

TABLE B-21

Industry 30 Rubber and Plastics

Rotated Factor Loadings for 1959:1-1971:3 with the Wholesale Price Index
Current and Lagged – Percent Change over Four Quarters (F-ratio in Parentheses)[1]

VARIABLE[2]	Factor 1	Factor 2	Factor 3	Factor 4	R^2
WPI	-.040 (0.31)	.053 (0.55)	.852 (141.90)	-.057 (0.64)	.734 (47.82)
profit/equity	.872	.142	-.204	.080	.828
cash flow	.867	.111	-.170	.032	.794
corporate tax receipts	.843	.093	.013	.173	.750
layoff rate	-.838	.006	.168	-.286	.812
AWE	.821	.101	.079	-.198	.731
output/previous peak	.804	-.098	-.151	-.006	.679
output	.779	.493	-.099	-.069	.864
sales	.779	.450	-.008	-.018	.809
M_2 (-1)	.763	.004	.210	.268	.697
money GNP	.699	.501	.338	.094	.863
inventory/sales	-.695	.053	.157	-.102	.521
stock price index	.692	.097	-.014	-.050	.491
productivity	.682	.496	.002	.085	.718
GNP/potential GNP	.640	-.468	.046	-.314	.729
4-6 month paper rate	.170	.894	.107	-.101	.850
3-6 month paper rate	.232	.857	.068	-.146	.814
total employment (-1)	-.042	.819	.095	.088	.786
discount rate	-.153	.811	.101	-.319	.792
1/UN	-.431	.791	-.161	.209	.882
total employment	.504	.766	.012	.085	.849
government purchases (deflated)	-.256	.745	.089	.422	.806
quit rate	.403	.728	-.166	.258	.786
investment in P & E	.211	.722	-.062	.103	.580
personal tax rate	.298	.714	.056	.398	.760
materials cost	.020	.678	.234	-.442	.711
expected investment in P & E	.114	.647	.033	.164	.460
real GNP	.177	.636	.120	-.183	.484

TABLE B-21 (continued)

VARIABLE[2]	Factor 1	Factor 2	Factor 3	Factor 4	R[2]
WPI	-.040 (0.31)	.053 (0.55)	.852 (141.90)	-.057 (0.64)	.734 (47.82)
personal tax receipts	.405	-.629	.236	-.297	.704
ULC	-.536	-.580	.174	-.206	.697
unborrowed reserves	.487	-.579	-.002	-.123	.588
debt/GNP	-.087	-.461	-.041	-.220	.270
WPI (-1)	-.073	-.047	.881	-.067	.788
CPI	-.122	-.212	.870	-.223	.866
$1/UN_{AL}$ (-1)	-.108	.358	.847	.266	.928
$1/UN_{AL}$	.076	.437	.788	.332	.928
M_1 (-1)	.620	.022	.665	-.191	.864
bond yield	-.095	.540	.552	.083	.612
AHE	.506	-.197	.550	-.357	.725
guidelines	.068	.136	-.549	.058	.328
labor force participation rate	-.102	.252	-.498	.438	.513
assets/liabilities–internal funds	.137	-.327	-.426	-.084	.314
corporate tax rate	-.074	-.106	.408	.216	.230
government purchases	.122	.089	.145	.898	.850
government purchases/national income	-.225	-.430	.150	.793	.887
political dummy	.213	.078	-.282	.790	.754
SULC	-.003	-.428	-.158	-.742	.758
defense/government expenditures	.287	.156	.064	.629	.507
accession rate	.415	.395	-.218	.566	.696
indirect tax rate	-.267	-.307	-.147	-.566	.507
lagged political dummy	.201	.421	.185	.554	.559
percent of labor force female	.354	-.174	-.337	.446	.469
variance added	.168	.271	.115	.097	
cumulative variance explained	.168	.439	.554	.651	

[1] Boxes indicate the factor to which the variable has been assigned.

[2] Variables are unassigned (but included in the components analysis) if there is no factor loading above |.39|. The unassigned variables are (ULC–SULC), inventory investment, defense/government purchases, full employment surplus.

TABLE B-22

Industry 30 Rubber and Plastics

Rotated Factor Loadings for 1959:1-1971:3 with the Wholesale Price Index
Current and Lagged – Quarterly Percent Change (F-ratio in Parentheses)[1]

VARIABLE[2]	Factor 1	Factor 2	Factor 3	Factor 4	R^2
WPI	-.009 (0.01)	-.025 (0.06)	.634 (35.91)	-.123 (1.35)	.418 (12.44)
output	.946	.058	-.046	.008	.900
productivity	.903	.128	.005	.091	.840
ULC	-.850	.143	.103	-.004	.753
total employment	.847	.330	-.018	-.068	.831
output/previous peak	.818	-.022	-.075	.282	.755
AWE	.786	-.161	.058	.029	.648
corporate tax receipts	.705	-.227	.298	.030	.634
AHE	.669	.010	.298	.359	.665
profit/equity	.661	-.546	-.006	-.196	.774
cash flow	.647	-.422	.023	-.235	.654
government purchases (deflated)	-.178	.873	.008	-.207	.837
GNP/potential GNP	.322	-.872	.043	-.051	.868
personal tax rate	-.179	.871	-.018	-.159	.817
personal tax receipts	.196	-.819	.104	-.092	.729
4-6 month paper rate	.337	.700	.159	-.257	.695
bond yield	.113	.686	.395	-.071	.645
3-6 month paper rate	.352	.664	.159	-.257	.641
discount rate (-1)	.077	.569	.084	-.197	.376
defense/government purchases	.080	-.470	.031	-.227	.280
layoff rate	-.375	.462	.081	.336	.473
corporate tax rate	-.175	.439	.154	.006	.247
CPI	-.077	.087	.817	.280	.759
1/UNAL (-1)	-.158	.232	.791	-.043	.707
1/UNAL	-.076	.296	.765	-.236	.734
guidelines	-.006	.059	-.488	-.215	.288
M_1 (-1)	.447	-.139	.485	-.119	.469

TABLE B-22 (continued)

VARIABLE[2]	Factor 1	Factor 2	Factor 3	Factor 4	R^2
WPI	-.009 (0.01)	-.025 (0.06)	.634 (35.91)	-.123 (1.35)	.418 (12.44)
quit rate	.070	.057	-.029	-.702	.502
1/UN$_A$	.302	.268	-.091	-.675	.627
money GNP	.311	-.239	-.190	-.669	.638
political dummy	.120	.140	-.276	-.617	.491
lagged political dummy	.018	.260	.215	-.555	.422
SULC	-.108	-.326	-.015	.522	.391
sales	.417	-.095	.049	-.517	.453
accession rate	.143	.092	.300	-.492	.361
indirect tax rate	.164	-.119	.046	.469	.234
total employment (-1)	-.183	.295	.065	-.446	.324
government purchases	-.133	.111	.031	-.431	.217
variance added	.162	.138	.068	.079	
cumulative variance explained	.162	.300	.368	.447	

[1] Boxes indicate the factor to which the variable has been assigned.

[2] Variables are unassigned (but included in the components analysis) if there is no factor loading above |.39|. The unassigned variables are percent of labor force female, investment in P & E, expected investment in P & E, assets/liabilities-internal funds, (ULC-SULC), inventory investment, stock price index, inventory/sales, material costs, real GNP, unborrowed reserves, defense/government expenditures, full employment surplus, debt/GNP, government purchases/national income, M_2 (-1), labor force participation rate.

169

TABLE B-23
Industry 31 Leather

Rotated Factor Loadings for 1959:1-1971:3 with the Wholesale Price Index
Current and Lagged – Percent Change over Four Quarters (F-ratio in Parentheses)[1]

VARIABLE[2]	Factor 1	Factor 2	Factor 3	Factor 4	R^2
WPI	-.658 (90.75)	.032 (0.21)	.473 (46.89)	-.336 (23.66)	.771 (53.86)
output	-.893	-.070	-.197	.204	.882
output/previous peak	-.862	-.130	-.215	.252	.869
total employment	-.850	.325	-.023	.107	.841
productivity	-.838	.083	.204	.217	.798
ULC	.825	-.124	.440	-.084	.897
profit/equity	-.790	-.049	-.013	-.039	.627
ULC-SULC	.784	.228	-.039	.075	.674
quit rate	-.783]	.356	.153	-.129	.780
corporate tax receipts	-.770	-.174	.161	.126	.664
1/UN$_A$	-.737	.482	.102	.105	.797
money GNP	-.720	.014	.563	.123	.850
layoff rate	.713	.140	.171	-.247	.632
sales	-.649	.235	.142	-.242	.555
3-6 month paper rate	-.648	.511	.311	-.303	.870
total employment (-1)	-.619	.559	.123	-.017	.712
inventory/sales	.559	.327	.186	-.189	.490
accession rate	-.549	.426	-.009	.227	.535
corporate tax rate	.534	-.121	.028	.149	.323
M$_2$ (-1)	-.493	-.342	.321	.432	.650
real GNP	-.476	.269	.171	-.138	.348
AWE	-.432	-.354	.342	.283	.509
cash flow	-.417	.028	-.059	.048	.180
personal tax rate	-.044	.894	.109	.177	.845
government purchases (deflated)	-.107	.888	.152	.207	.866
personal tax receipts	-.083	-.817	.238	-.114	.745
GNP/potential GNP	-.166	-.798	.128	-.114	.693
unborrowed reserves	.010	-.752	.004	.095	.575

TABLE B-23 (continued)

VARIABLE[2]	Factor 1	Factor 2	Factor 3	Factor 4	R^2
WPI	-.658 (90.75)	.032 (0.21)	.473 (46.89)	-.336 (23.66)	.771 (53.86)
SULC	.384	-.635	.506	-.213	.852
4-6 month paper rate	-.573	.590	.344	-.271	.868
discount rate	-.230	.588	.252	-.497	.710
debt/GNP	.181	-.462	-.172	-.080	.282
$1/UN_{AL}$ (-1)	.147	.343	.836	.241	.895
$1/UN_{AL}$	-.028	.349	.829	.311	.905
M_1 (-1)	-.283	-.423	.769	-.029	.850
CPI	.428	-.254	.766	-.131	.851
AHE	.210	-.135	.653	.276	.565
bond yield	-.187	.476	.621	-.078	.653
percent of labor force female	-.531	.039	.583	.071	.628
defense/government purchases	-.003	.185	.539	.166	.352
labor force participation rate	-.003	.346	.525	.264	.465
WPI (-1)	-.424	.246	.520	-.450	.714
guidelines	-.243	.028	-.506	.141	.335
assets/liabilities-internal funds	.011	-.194	.052	.831	.730
government purchases	-.114	.282	.213	.813	.798
political dummy	-.321	.147	-.260	.811	.850
government purchases/national income	.404	.017	.022	.782	.776
lagged political dummy	-.254	.300	.249	.610	.589
defense/government expenditures	-.245	.181	.281	.493	.414
indirect tax rate	.432	-.239	-.276	-.462	.533
variance added	.282	.120	.144	.103	
cumulative variance explained	.282	.402	.546	.649	

[1] Boxes indicate the factor to which the variable has been assigned.

[2] Variables are unassigned (but included in the components analysis) if there is no factor loading above $|.39|$. The unassigned variables are inventory investment, full employment surplus.

TABLE B-24
Industry 31 Leather

Rotated Factor Loadings for 1959:1-1971:3 with the Wholesale Price Index
Current and Lagged - Quarterly Percent Change (F-ratio in Parentheses)[1]

VARIABLE[2]	Factor 1	Factor 2	Factor 3	Factor 4	R^2
WPI	.548	-.132	.267	-.267	.460
output	.819	.122	-.193	.122	.738
output/previous peak	.798	.161	-.198	.144	.724
productivity	.773	.002	-.219	.111	.658
ULC	-.735	-.079	.457	.018	.755
total employment	.727	-.286	-.173	.080	.646
profit/equity	.663	.074	-.016	-.083	.448
money GNP	.651	.169	-.044	-.044	.459
$1/UN_A$	.641	-.409	-.114	.072	.596
percent of labor force female	-.478	-.016	.171	.052	.260
corporate tax rate	-.469	-.036	.032	.138	.241
quit rate	-.440	-.273	.027	.001	.268
layoff rate	-.410	-.131	.155	-.212	.255
government purchases (deflated)	-.110	-.891	-.046	.214	.854
personal tax rate	-.149	-.884	-.064	.183	.841
GNP/potential GNP	.309	.826	.108	-.190	.825
personal tax receipts	.191	.818	.132	-.183	.756
4-6 month paper rate	.343	-.729	.274	-.072	.730
3-6 month paper rate	.373	-.701	.244	-.108	.702
bond yield	.126	-.689	.406	.063	.660
discount rate (-1)	.122	-.662	.075	-.294	.545
total employment (-1)	.398	-.530	-.077	-.078	.452
defense/government expenditures	.118	.400	.064	.098	.188
CPI	-.221	.012	.873	.031	.812
$1/UN_{AL}$ (-1)	-.207	-.182	.734	.415	.787
$1/UN_{AL}$	-.035	-.286	.703	.449	.779
SULC	-.268	.409	.687	-.115	.724

172

TABLE B-24 (continued)

VARIABLE[2]	Factor 1	Factor 2	Factor 3	Factor 4	R^2
WPI	.548	-.132	.267	-.267	.460
M_1 (-1)	.408	.141	.665	-.027	.629
AHE	.033	.224	.603	.446	.614
guidelines	.103	-.034	-.523	.156	.310
political dummy	.385	-.121	-.297	.731	.786
lagged political dummy	.181	-.246	.147	.700	.605
government purchases	.025	-.131	-.021	.698	.505
government purchases/national income	-.457	.020	-.063	.614	.590
ULC-SULC	.047	-.191	.036	-.435	.230
variance added	.161	.121	.089	.066	
cumulative variance explained	.161	.282	.371	.437	

[1]Boxes indicate the factor to which the variable has been assigned.

[2]Variables are unassigned (but included in the components analysis) if there is no factor loading above |.39|. The unassigned variables are WPI (-1), accession rate, cash flow, sales, AWE, assets/liabilities-internal funds, corporate tax receipts, inventory investment, inventory/sales, real GNP, unborrowed reserves, indirect tax rate, defense/government purchases, full employment surplus, debt/GNP, M_2 (-1), labor force participation rate.

TABLE B-25

Industry 32 Stone, Clay, and Glass

Rotated Factor Loadings for 1959:1-1971:3 with the Wholesale Price Index
Current and Lagged - Percent Change over Four Quarters (F-ratio in Parentheses)[1]

VARIABLE[2]	Factor 1	Factor 2	Factor 3	Factor 4	R^2
WPI	.229 (65.28)	-.390 (189.34)	.802 (800.72)	-.320 (127.47)	.951 (394.63)
cash flow	.899	-.012	-.078	-.007	.814
corporate tax receipts	.886	.195	.024	.017	.823
output/previous peak	.878	.034	-.190	.007	.809
output	.848	.474	-.151	-.046	.969
productivity	.821	.519	.118	-.062	.961
inventory/sales	-.817	-.008	.175	-.016	.698
layoff rate	-.767	-.054	.174	.312	.719
M_2 (-1)	.755	-.083	.093	-.312	.776
AWE	.745	-.012	.508	.437	.867
sales	.743	.283	.014	-.233	.640
ULC	-.694	-.571	.397	.082	.967
money GNP	.687	.401	.278	-.042	.823
GNP/potential GNP	.602	-.458	.118	-.239	.643
total employment (-1)	.071	.907	.066	-.093	.842
4-6 month paper rate	.196	.886	.115	.075	.841
discount rate (-1)	-.106	.861	.163	-.206	.822
3-6 month paper rate	.262	.859	.085	.025	.815
total employment	.545	.796	-.024	-.066	.935
investment in P & E	.083	.774	-.066	-.048	.613
1/UN2	.328	.751	-.081	-.230	.730
UN	-.333	-.743	-.093	-.225	.722
UN(-1)	.098	-.741	.013	-.142	.579
1/UN2 (-1)	-.102	.741	-.004	.147	.581
1/UNA	.417	.710	-.227	.356	.857
government purchases (deflated)	-.221	.671	-.004	.466	.716

TABLE B-25 (continued)

VARIABLE[2]	Factor 1	Factor 2	Factor 3	Factor 4	R^2
WPI /	.229 (65.28)	-.390 (189.34)	.802 (800.72)	-.320 (127.47)	.951 (394.63)
personal tax rate	-.261	.650	-.023	.425	.672
quit rate	.460	.645	-.044	.440	.822
real GNP	.284	.611	.016	.003	.454
expected investment in P & E	-.136	.603	-.016	.043	.385
personal tax receipts	.364	-.597	.322	-.265	.663
unborrowed reserves	.434	-.586	.035	-.123	.549
debt/GNP	-.126	-.445	.009	-.341	.331
CPI	-.071	-.192	.924	-.095	.905
materials cost	-.033	-.249	.889	-.134	.871
WPI (-1)	.145	-.319	.819	-.370	.931
AHE	.272	-.220	.809	-.326	.894
$1/UN_{AL}$ (-1)	-.108	.285	.764	.458	.887
$1/UN_L$ (-1)	-.182	.334	.729	.337	.789
UN (-1)	.241	-.380	-.725	-.297	.816
$1/UN_{AL}$	.059	.337	.682	.549	.884
M_1 (-1)	.650	.101	.678	.045	.884
$1/UN_L$	.092	.381	.666	.420	.773
UN_L	-.066	-.458	-.665	-.375	.797
guidelines	-.170	.110	-.608	.013	.411
bond yield	-.144	.529	.530	.227	.633
SULC	.038	-.399	.505	-.499	.665
government purchases	-.057	-.060	-.012	.896	.810
political dummy	.083	-.071	-.489	.736	.793
lagged political dummy	.227	.278	-.006	.699	.617
indirect tax rate	-.270	-.247	.010	-.687	.606
defense/government expenditures	.090	.077	.001	.672	.465
government purchases/national income	-.395	-.520	.022	.680	.889
accession rate	.356	.309	-.251	.632	.685
labor force participation rate	-.158	.209	.381	.598	.565
assets/liabilities-internal funds	.051	-.063	-.315	-.498	.354
defense/government purchases	-.148	.109	.393	.443	.384

VARIABLE[2]	Factor 1	Factor 2	Factor 3	Factor 4	R^2
WPI	.229 (65.28)	-.390 (189.34)	.802 (800.72)	-.320 (127.47)	.951 (394.63)
variance added	.159	.262	.150	.090	
cumulative variance explained	.159	.421	.571	.661	

[1]Boxes indicate the factor to which the variable has been assigned.

[2]Variables are unassigned (but included in the components analysis) if there is no factor loading above $|.39|$. The unassigned variables are profit/equity, corporate tax rate, (ULC-SULC), inventory invest-
ment, UN↑, UN↓, full employment surplus.

TABLE B-26

Industry 32   Stone, Clay and Glass

Rotated Factor Loadings for 1959:1-1971:3 with the Wholesale Price Index
Current and Lagged - Quarterly Percent Change (F-ratio in Parentheses)[1]

VARIABLE[2]	Factor 1	Factor 2	Factor 3	Factor 4	R^2
WPI	-.115 (4.92)	-.450 (75.32)	-.772 (221.67)	-.156 (9.05)	.836 (103.65)
productivity	-.888	.023	.146	-.123	.825
output	-.877	.001	.143	-.210	.833
ULC	-.800	-.086	-.363	.062	.784
corporate tax receipts	-.778	-.215	-.033	-.136	.671
money GNP	-.768	-.062	-.149	.191	.652
total employment	-.762	.143	.079	-.065	.612
output/previous peak	-.745	-.239	-.138	-.114	.644
sales	-.669	.058	-.023	-.207	.495
$1/UN_A$	-.649	.411	.238	.045	.648
cash flow	-.621	-.053	-.039	-.321	.493
government purchases/national income	-.600	-.026	.051	.507	.620
UN	-.576	-.157	-.043	-.174	.388
$1/UN^2$	-.576	.154	.038	.169	.385
AWE	-.550	-.276	-.395	-.137	.553
layoff rate	.520	.209	-.165	-.229	.394
M_2 (-1)	-.466	.124	-.080	.091	.247
government purchases (deflated)	.041	.849	.070	.086	.735
personal tax rate	.065	.838	.073	.061	.715
GNP/potential GNP	-.310	-.779	-.102	-.008	.713
personal tax receipts	-.156	-.768	-.166	-.038	.642
UN (-1)	-.126	-.740	.030	.228	.617
1/UN (-1)	.116	.714	-.037	-.231	.578
4-6 month paper rate	-.307	.678	-.120	.068	.573
bond yield	-.106	.654	-.296	.081	.533
discount rate (-1)	-.153	.634	.003	-.194	.463
3-6 month paper rate	-.358	.612	-.086	.078	.517
UN↑	-.028	-.481	.183	.039	.267
total employment (-1)	-.218	.469	.0j7	-.142	.288

177

VARIABLES[2]	Factor 1	Factor 2	Factor 3	Factor 4	R^2
WPI	-.115 (4.92)	-.450 (75.32)	-.772 (221.67)	-.156 (9.05)	.836 (103.65)
CPI	.130	.039	-.904	.067	.840
materials cost	.096	.059	-.773	-.112	.623
WPI (-1)	-.021	-.198	-.757	-.267	.684
$1/UN_{AL}$ (-1)	.122	.267	-.720	.490	.845
$1/UN_L$ (-1)	.314	.328	-.678	.267	.742
$1/UN_{AL}$	-.057	.373	-.655	.520	.842
$1/UN_L$	-.096	.403	-.648	.449	.794
UN_L	.019	-.445	.634	-.442	.796
UN_L (-1)	-.344	-.296	.632	-.349	.728
AHE	-.163	-.218	-.623	-.173	.492
SULC	.204	-.351	-.608	-.328	.642
guidelines	-.090	.076	.563	.023	.331
M1 (-1)	-.544	-.094	-.559	.015	.618
(ULC-SULC)	.030	-.273	.431	.124	.276
government purchases	.093	.097	.118	.671	.482
lagged political dummy	-.224	.359	-.025	.632	.579
assets/liabilities-internal funds	-.048	.105	.023	-.588	.359
political dummy	-.243	.183	.453	.549	.599
inventory/sales	.099	-.221	.063	.495	.307
corporate tax rate	.217	-.108	.006	.413	.229
variance added	.153	.140	.113	.046	
cumulative variance explained	.153	.293	.406	.452	

[1] Boxes indicate the factor to which the variable has been assigned.

[2] Variables are unassigned (but included in the components analysis) if there is no factor loading above |.39|. The unassigned variables are percent of labor force female, accession rate, quit rate, investment in P & E, profit/equity, expected investment in P & E, inventory investment, UN↓, real GNP, unborrowed reserves, indirect tax rate, defense/government purchases, defense/government expenditures, full employment surplus, debt/GNP, labor force participation rate.

TABLE B-27

Industry 33 Primary Metals

Rotated Factor Loadings for 1959:1–1971:3 with the Wholesale Price Index
Current and Lagged – Percent Change over Four Quarters (F-ratio in Parentheses)[1]

VARIABLE[2]	Factor 1	Factor 2	Factor 3	Factor 4	R^2
WPI	.070 (0.89)	−.178 (5.76)	−.748 (101.72)	−.251 (11.45)	.659 (39.93)
output	.962	−.095	.013	.060	.939
output/previous peak	.950	−.025	.066	.087	.916
sales	.944	−.086	−.149	−.042	.922
inventory/sales	−.941	.156	.065	.097	.923
productivity	.921	−.067	.007	.066	.858
cash flow	.898	−.016	.090	.168	.843
corporate tax receipts	.893	−.153	.009	.206	.864
ULC	−.887	.132	−.112	−.118	.831
profit/equity	.883	−.139	.066	−.216	.849
AWE	.859	.069	−.252	−.139	.825
total employment	.764	−.453	−.097	−.110	.811
UN	−.624	.588	−.035	−.004	.736
AHE	.607	.363	−.529	−.241	.837
$1/UN^2$	.602	−.591	−.015	.018	.712
layoff rate	−.524	−.052	−.035	.027	.279
UN↓	.448	−.013	.132	.195	.257
UN↑	−.414	.097	.160	−.169	.235
UN (−1)	−.173	.859	.037	.079	.775
1/UN (−1)	.193	−.848	−.021	−.069	.761
4–6 month paper rate	.248	−.815	−.313	−.085	.831
discount rate (−1)	−.119	−.811	−.202	−.124	.729
3–6 month paper rate	.258	−.798	−.294	.025	.790
percent of labor force female	.191	−.685	−.147	.576	.859
real GNP	.189	−.679	−.144	−.014	.518
$1/UN_A$	.313	−.648	−.026	.344	.638
total employment (−1)	−.071	−.633	−.104	.050	.419
expected investment in P & E	−.274	−.616	.136	.200	.513

VARIABLE [2]	Factor 1	Factor 2	Factor 3	Factor 4	R^2
WPI	.070 (0.89)	-.178 (5.76)	-.748 (101.72)	-.251 (11.45)	.659 (39.93)
personal tax receipts	-.085	.595	-.244	-.453	.626
quit rate	.282	-.577	-.190	.130	.466
unborrowed reserves	-.011	.567	-.015	-.298	.410
GNP/potential GNP	.160	.470	-.150	-.440	.462
investment in P & E	-.039	-.439	.160	.177	.251
unfilled orders/sales	.102	-.426	-.321	-.117	.309
M_1 (-1)	.194	.144	-.822	-.149	.756
CPI	-.215	.278	-.793	-.189	.789
$1/UN_{AL}$ (-1)	-.158	-.168	-.776	.427	.838
materials cost	.251	-.174	-.774	.223	.742
$1/UN_{AL}$	-.011	-.198	-.767	.497	.875
$1/UN_L$ (-1)	-.048	-.300	-.735	.326	.739
$1/UN_L$ (-1)	-.005	.453	.704	-.080	.707
WPI (-1)	-.074	-.162	-.687	-.332	.614
$1/UN$ (-1)	.190	-.278	-.683	-.410	.747
UN_L (-1)	.427	-.291	.674	-.173	.751
bond yield	.021	-.448	-.622	.229	.640
assets/liabilities-internal funds	.009	-.019	.586	-.140	.363
money GNP	.463	-.276	-.570	.203	.656
guidelines	.271	-.250	.508	.038	.395
defense/government purchases	-.209	-.020	-.395	.329	.308
government purchases	-.013	.108	-.074	.854	.746
political dummy	.154	.003	.263	.727	.622
accession rate	.185	.035	.185	.672	.495
government purchases/national income	-.336	.489	.094	.660	.797
lagged political dummy	.216	-.270	-.205	.657	.593
indirect tax rate	.144	-.117	.225	-.647	.503
SULC	-.232	-.017	.096	-.615	.442

TABLE B-27 (continued)

VARIABLE[2]	Factor 1	Factor 2	Factor 3	Factor 4	R^2
WPI	.070 (0.89)	-.178 (5.76)	-.748 (101.45)	-.251 (11.45)	.659 (39.93)
government purchases (deflated)	.006	-.549	-.045	.608	.674
personal tax rate	-.039	-.526	.017	.576	.611
defense/government expenditures	-.017	-.020	-.107	.561	.327
labor force participation rate	-.161	-.091	-.457	.560	.557
debt/GNP	-.215	.257	.089	-.390	.273
variance added	.144	.258	.116	.090	
cumulative variance explained	.144	.402	.518	.608	

---

[1] Boxes indicate the factor to which the variable has been assigned.

[2] Variables are unassigned (but included in the components analysis) if there is no factor loading above $|.39|$. The unassigned variables are new orders/sales, corporate tax rate, inventory investment, full employment surplus, M_2 (-1).

TABLE B-28

Industry 33 Primary Metals

Rotated Factor Loadings for 1959:1 - 1971:3 with the Wholesale Price Index
Current and Lagged - Quarterly Percent Change (F-ratio in Parentheses)[1]

VARIABLE[2]	Factor 1	Factor 2	Factor 3	Factor 4	R^2
WPI	.100 (1.07)	-.046 (0.23)	.616 (40.58)	.137 (2.01)	.411 (14.65)
output	.983	.023	-.051	.034	.970
sales	.976	-.012	-.009	.002	.953
productivity	.972	.084	-.019	.048	.954
inventory/sales	-.962	.036	.050	-.028	.931
output/previous peak	.960	.074	-.068	.024	.931
ULC	-.958	-.084	.042	-.066	.932
cash flow	.958	.092	-.036	.030	.928
profit/equity	.947	.015	-.020	.011	.898
total employment	.940	-.083	.041	.137	.910
corporate tax receipts	.908	-.115	-.009	-.122	.853
AWE	.853	-.149	-.021	-.157	.775
AHE	.797	.079	.167	-.157	.694
money GNP	.599	-.370	.271	-.148	.590
$1/UN^2$	.558	-.497	-.082	.014	.566
UN	-.558	.491	.088	-.014	.561
new orders/sales	-.549	.123	-.022	-.184	.351
investment in P & E	.487	.008	.026	.261	.306
unfilled orders/sales	-.434	-.365	.084	-.210	.373
UN (-1)	.182	.767	-.070	-.080	.632
1/UN (-1)	-.182	-.766	.074	.083	.633
UN↑	-.191	.760	-.181	.058	.650
1/UN↑	.297	-.607	-.068	.344	.579
UN↓_A	.228	-.589	-.126	.067	.419
total employment (-1)	-.292	-.529	.048	.046	.369
government purchases/national income	-.426	.429	.053	.190	.404

TABLE B-28 (continued)

VARIABLE[2]	Factor 1	Factor 2	Factor 3	Factor 4	R^2
WPI	.100 (1.07)	-.046 (0.23)	.616 (40.58)	.137 (2.01)	.411 (14.65)
$1/UN_{AL}$ (-1)	-.047	.173	.890	.166	.851
$1/UN_{AL}$ (-1)	-.033	.020	.872	.253	.826
$1/UN_L$ (-1)	-.100	-.015	.847	.154	.751
CPI	-.105	.222	.806	-.103	.720
$1/UN_L$ (-1)	.189	-.235	.798	.158	.753
UN_L (-1)	.126	.086	-.794	-.080	.660
UN_L	-.159	.371	-.751	-.082	.733
$W\dot{P}I$ (-1)	.037	-.087	.583	-.049	.351
materials cost	.000	-.306	.521	-.108	.376
M_1 (-1)	.092	-.221	.465	-.341	.390
lagged political dummy	.117	-.252	.422	-.315	.354
guidelines	.053	-.304	-.401	.116	.269
government purchases (deflated)	-.051	-.029	.067	.930	.872
GNP/potential GNP	.200	-.090	-.013	-.912	.881
personal tax rate	-.073	-.014	.031	.912	.838
personal tax receipts	.107	.011	.042	-.882	.790
percent of labor force female	.346	-.277	.165	.788	.845
bond yield	.072	-.187	.437	.591	.581
4-6 month paper rate	.040	-.496	.262	.548	.616
3-6 month paper rate	.053	-.499	.216	.514	.563
discount rate (-1)	-.022	-.369	.081	.485	.379
variance added	.211	.070	.082	.136	
cumulative variance explained	.211	.281	.363	.499	

[1] Boxes indicate the factor to which the variable has been assigned.

[2] Variables are unassigned (but included in the components analysis) if there is no factor loading above |.39|. The unassigned variables are layoff rate, accession rate, quit rate, expected investment in P & E, assets/liabilities-internal funds, corporate tax rate, SULC, (ULC-SULC), inventory investment in real GNP, unborrowed reserves, indirect tax rate, government purchases, defense/government purchases, full employment surplus, debt/GNP, M_2 (-1), political dummy, labor force participation rate.

TABLE B-29

Industry 34 Fabricated Metals

Rotated Factor Loadings for 1959:1-1971:3 with the Wholesale Price Index
Current and Lagged - Percent Change over Four Quarters (F-ratio in Parentheses)[1]

VARIABLE[2]	Factor 1	Factor 2	Factor 3	Factor 4	R^2
WPI	-.338 (77.43)	.274 (50.88)	.833 (470.30)	.164 (18.22)	.910 (205.59)
profit/equity	.896	.052	-.121	.008	.821
output	.879	-.397	.136	.094	.957
corporate tax receipts	.864	-.076	-.115	.215	.812
ULC	-.850	.428	.061	-.126	.926
cash flow	.843	.138	-.106	.086	.749
productivity	.829	-.415	.204	.173	.931
output/previous peak	.821	-.238	.023	.211	.777
sales	.815	-.065	.081	.286	.756
quit rate	.809	-.413	-.040	.203	.868
layoff rate	-.807	-.196	.120	-.045	.706
$1/UN_A$	.776	-.480	-.117	.194	.884
money GNP	.771	-.096	.429	.351	.912
UN	-.735	.289	.199	-.033	.664
$1/UN^2$	.734	-.284	-.201	.039	.662
AWE	.655	-.187	.559	-.012	.776
M_2 (-1)	.653	.408	.127	.370	.746
accession rate	.607	-.283	-.284	.267	.601
corporate tax rate	-.595	-.022	.056	.129	.374
unborrowed reserves	.150	.792	-.075	-.135	.674
government purchases (deflated)	.107	-.779	-.173	.430	.832
personal tax receipts	.002	.776	.365	-.134	.753
personal tax rate	.052	-.771	-.207	.379	.784
GNP/potential GNP	.314	.759	-.293	-.239	.817
4-6 month paper rate	.475	-.753	.253	-.089	.865
discount rate (-1)	.136	-.723	.261	-.075	.615
3-6 month paper rate	.519	-.708	.251	.031	.834
bond yield	-.038	-.602	.423	.433	.731

TABLE B-29 (continued)

VARIABLE[2]	Factor 1	Factor 2	Factor 3	Factor 4	R^2
WPI	-.338 (77.43)	.274 (50.88)	.833 (470.30)	.164 (18.22)	.910 (205.59)
UN (-1)	-.452	.511	.295	-.199	.591
$1/UN^2$ (-1)	.462	-.494	-.293	.204	.585
real GNP	.422	-.440	.206	-.023	.414
AHE	-.101	.052	.892	.158	.834
materials cost	-.258	.096	.858	.130	.829
CPI	-.411	.147	.815	.277	.931
WPI (-1)	-.385	.345	.781	.165	.905
M_1 (-1)	-.378	.279	.758	.257	.861
assets/liabilities—internal funds	-.222	.405	-.657	.169	.674
political dummy	.369	.110	-.631	.499	.795
guidelines	.323	-.017	-.407	-.249	.333
SULC	-.251	.042	.066	-.843	.779
$1/UN_L$ (-1)	.065	-.264	.355	.829	.887
government purchases	.160	.028	-.357	.815	.817
UN_L (-1)	-.048	.319	-.291	-.802	.832
$1/UN_L$	.264	-.210	.326	.784	.835
$1/UN_{AL}$	.099	-.295	.482	.776	.932
$1/UN_{AL}$ (-1)	-.112	-.312	.524	.748	.944
UN_L	-.334	.243	-.289	-.739	.800
government purchases/national income	-.372	.327	-.431	.666	.874
labor force participation rate	-.076	-.176	.116	.653	.476
lagged political dummy	.440	-.134	.078	.623	.606
defense/government expenditures	.301	.087	-.246	.590	.508
indirect tax rate	-.427	.102	.118	-.583	.546
defense/government purchases	-.071	-.017	.081	.551	.316
total employment	.446	-.055	.108	.498	.462
unfilled orders/sales	-.071	-.036	.053	.465	.226
percent of labor force female	.275	.063	.309	.427	.358
total employment (-1)	.359	-.238	.232	.405	.404

185

VARIABLE[2]	Factor 1	Factor 2	Factor 3	Factor 4	R^2
WPI	-.338 (77.43)	.274 (50.88)	.833 (470.30)	.164 (18.22)	.910 (205.59)
variance added	.294	.090	.105	.159	
cumulative variance explained	.294	.384	.499	.648	

---

[1]Boxes indicate the factor to which the variable has been assigned.

[2]Variables are unassigned (but included in the components analysis) if there is no factor loading above |.39|. The unassigned variables are new orders/sales, (ULC-SULC), inventory investment, inventory/sales, UN↑, UN↓, full employment surplus, debt/GNP.

TABLE B-30
Industry 34 Fabricated Metals

Rotated Factor Loadings for 1959:1-1971:3 with the Wholesale Price Index
Current and Lagged - Quarterly Percent Change (F-ratio in Parentheses)[1]

VARIABLE[2]	Factor 1	Factor 2	Factor 3	Factor 4	R^2
WPI	-.041 (0.27)	-.020 (0.07)	.607 (59.93)	.505 (41.48)	.625 (33.88)
output	.937	-.211	.005	-.018	.923
productivity	.900	-.192	.065	-.007	.851
output/previous peak	.865	-.110	-.130	-.126	.793
ULC	-.835	.348	.085	-.104	.835
AWE	.780	.133	.188	-.125	.678
money GNP	.771	.050	.291	.036	.683
1/UNA	.714	-.414	-.094	.263	.759
UN	-.680	.096	.126	.040	.489
1/UN²	.678	-.101	-.133	-.041	.489
profit/equity	.675	.287	-.047	.338	.654
layoff rate	-.674	-.187	.014	-.058	.493
corporate tax receipts	.664	.307	.070	.298	.628
sales	.596	-.013	.130	.256	.438
government purchases/national income	-.558	.098	.163	.458	.558
AHE	.538	.259	.505	-.418	.787
cash flow	.534	.320	.019	.352	.511
quit rate	.502	-.328	-.010	.282	.440
assets/liabilities-internal funds	-.404	.155	-.056	.329	.298
government purchases (deflated)	-.046	-.878	.033	.147	.796
personal tax rate	-.070	-.863	.000	.123	.765
GNP/potential GNP	.305	.845	.053	-.069	.815
personal tax receipts	.158	.815	.102	-.133	.717
bond yield	.021	-.716	.365	-.068	.651
4-6 month paper rate	.226	-.712	.166	.072	.590
3-6 month paper rate	.250	-.673	.124	.070	.535
discount rate (-1)	.193	-.631	.058	-.103	.449
defense/government expenditures	.069	.482	.123	.280	.331

187

VARIABLE	Factor 1	Factor 2	Factor 3	Factor 4	R^2
WPI	-.041 (0.27)	-.020 (0.07)	.607 (59.93)	.505 (41.48)	.625 (33.88)
$1/UN_{AL}$ (-1)	-.184	-.186	.913	.016	.902
$1/UN_{AL}$	.008	-.286	.896	.102	.894
$1/UN_L$ (-1)	-.139	-.227	.875	.306	.930
$1/UN_L$	-.135	-.266	.821	.300	.853
UN_L (-1)	.277	.247	-.816	-.371	.941
CPI	-.232	-.051	.780	-.430	.850
UN_L	-.187	.314	-.759	-.328	.818
WPI (-1)	-.069	.151	.589	.482	.608
materials cost	.040	-.296	.513	.465	.568
M_1 (-1)	.279	.130	.490	-.048	.338
guidelines	.091	-.047	-.431	.334	.308
political dummy	.256	-.083	.028	.812	.733
SULC	-.211	.206	-.457	-.645	.713
government purchases	-.041	-.034	.258	.641	.480
lagged political dummy	.175	-.242	.460	.565	.620
accession rate	-.086	-.074	-.058	.540	.308
UN (-1)	.279	.222	.081	-.489	.373
$1/UN2$ (-1)	-.266	-.229	-.088	.487	.368
variance added	.168	.141	.096	.076	
cumulative variance added	.168	.309	.405	.481	

[1] Boxes indicate the factor to which the variable has been assigned.

[2] Variables are unassigned (but included in the components analysis) if there is no factor loading above $|.39|$. The unassigned variables are total employment, percent of labor force female, total employment (-1), unfilled orders/sales, new orders/sales, corporate tax rate, (ULC-SULC), inventory investment, inventory/sales, UN↑, UN↓, real GNP, unborrowed reserves, indirect tax rate, defense/government purchases, full employment surplus, debt/GNP, M_2 (-1), labor force participation rate.

188

TABLE B-31
Industry 35   Machinery, except electrical

Rotated Factor Loadings for 1959:1–1971:3 with the Wholesale Price Index
Current and Lagged – Percent Change over Four Quarters (F-ratio in Parentheses)[1]

VARIABLE[2]	Factor 1	Factor 2	Factor 3	Factor 4	R^2
WPI	.207 (21.42)	-.165 (13.61)	.893 (398.72)	.084 (3.53)	.874 (145.66)
profit/equity	-.904	-.049	-.228	.026	.872
AWE	-.888	-.028	.271	-.112	.875
corporate tax receipts	-.882	-.036	-.111	-.226	.843
output	-.878	.349	-.141	.186	.947
UN	.862	-.255	.169	-.091	.846
$1/UN^2$	-.862	.249	-.161	.103	.842
$1/UN_A$	-.842	.262	-.100	.287	.870
cash flow	-.841	-.103	-.186	.258	.820
output/previous peak	-.838	.203	-.154	-.169	.796
productivity	-.809	.415	.118	.247	.902
3-6 month paper rate	-.786	.414	.236	-.094	.854
sales	-.785	.191	.023	.443	.848
layoff rate	.784	.359	.232	-.166	.824
4-6 month paper rate	-.756	.485	.264	-.062	.881
accession rate	-.756	.036	-.153	.253	.661
inventory/sales	.752	.398	.229	-.187	.881
ULC	.750	-.435	.272	-.268	.897
money GNP	-.727	-.127	.420	.360	.850
total employment	-.687	.657	-.027	.244	.965
quit rate	-.675	.170	-.009	.235	.539
real GNP	-.539	.258	.146	-.001	.378
corporate tax rate	.473	-.024	.252	.110	.300
total employment (-1)	-.337	.849	.001	.240	.893
GNP/potential GNP	-.115	-.816	.127	-.074	.702
unborrowed reserves	.071	-.759	-.014	.044	.583
personal tax receipts	.180	-.741	.272	-.078	.662
government purchases (deflated)	-.256	.715	.020	.299	.667

VARIABLE[2]	Factor 1	Factor 2	Factor 3	Factor 4	R^2
WPI	.207 (21.42)	-.165 (13.61)	.893 (398.72)	.084 (3.53)	.874 (145.66)
personal tax rate	-.209	.710	-.016	.254	.612
investment in P & E	-.525	.698	-.104	-.040	.775
UN_L (-1)	.155	.675	-.460	-.455	.899
expected investment in P & E	-.049	.664	-.086	.199	.491
UN (-1)	.619	-.636	.140	-.024	.807
assets/liabilities-internal funds	-.091	-.624	-.575	.007	.728
$1/UN^2$ (-1)	-.622	.618	-.132	.038	.787
discount rate (-1)	-.468	.582	.255	-.285	.705
unfilled orders/sales	-.328	.420	.185	-.096	.327
UN↑	.358	-.404	.135	-.176	.340
CPI	.345	-.098	.897	-.054	.937
AHE	-.180	-.189	.890	-.165	.888
materials cost	.142	.022	.881	-.188	.833
WPI (-1)	.314	-.144	.848	.049	.841
$1/UN_{AL}$ (-1)	.005	.368	.777	.429	.924
M_1 (-1)	-.333	-.470	.744	.134	.903
$1/UN_{AL}$	-.154	.308	.720	.519	.907
bond yield	-.201	.529	.584	.115	.676
$1/UN_L$ (-1)	-.062	.501	.547	.610	.927
percent of labor force female	.200	-.010	.523	.338	.428
guidelines	-.300	-.037	-.505	.012	.346
government purchases	-.010	.127	-.056	.880	.793
SULC	.203	-.297	-.016	-.856	.862
political dummy	-.130	.016	-.468	.752	.802
government purchases/national income	.569	.000	-.127	.714	.849
lagged political dummy	-.342	.195	.082	.690	.639
$1/UN_L$	-.282	.386	.485	.674	.918
defense/government expenditures	-.240	.011	-.024	.667	.504
indirect tax rate	.439	-.092	-.040	-.647	.621

TABLE B-31 (continued)

VARIABLE[2]	Factor 1	Factor 2	Factor 3	Factor 4	R^2
WPI	.207	-.165	.893	.084	.874
	(21.42)	(13.61)	(398.72)	(3.53)	(145.66)
M$_2$ (-1)	-.434	-.532	.144	.539	.783
UN$_L$	.454	-.488	.409	-.514	.875
labor force participation rate	-.054	.327	.363	.509	.500
variance added	.337	.107	.162	.085	
cumulative variance explained	.337	.444	.606	.691	

[1] Boxes indicate the factor to which the variable has been assigned.

[2] Variables are unassigned (but included in the components analysis) if there is no factor loading above $|.39|$. The unassigned variables are new orders/sales, (ULC-SULC), inventory investment, UN↓, defense/government purchases, full employment surplus, debt/GNP.

TABLE B-32
Industry 35 Machinery, except electrical

Rotated Factor Loadings for 1959:1-1971:3 with the Wholesale Price Index
Current and Lagged - Quarterly Percent Change (F-ratio in Parentheses)[1]

VARIABLE[2]	Factor 1	Factor 2	Factor 3	Factor 4	R^2
WPI	-.182 (5.08)	.092 (1.30)	-.688 (72.55)	.271 (11.25)	.589 (30.09)
output	.910	-.270	.053	-.010	.904
productivity	.867	-.186	.130	.161	.829
ULC	-.825	.265	-.283	-.152	.853
profit/equity	.783	.011	.100	-.155	.647
sales	.766	-.045	-.029	.137	.608
$1/UN^2$	.753	-.034	.080	.066	.579
UN	-.753	.034	-.078	.068	.579
$1/UN_A$	.743	-.270	.012	.065	.043
output/previous peak	.736	-.246	-.033	-.275	.680
total employment	.729	-.448	.096	.279	.819
cash flow	.728	.104	.069	-.058	.549
corporate tax receipts	.725	.064	.086	.064	.541
money GNP	.638	.251	-.342	.131	.604
layoff rate	-.622	-.240	.081	.252	.515
AWE	.620	-.135	-.446	-.135	.684
accession rate	.536	.050	.037	-.027	.292
UN↓	.418	-.147	.172	.064	.230
investment in P & E	.416	-.345	.126	.094	.317
UN↑	-.154	.873	-.170	-.162	.841
GNP/potential GNP	.157	.871	.128	-.103	.810
government purchases (deflated)	.066	-.842	.047	.169	.744
personal tax rate	.022	-.838	.057	.133	.723
personal tax receipts	-.007	.801	-.135	.050	.662
bond yield	.110	-.608	-.289	.006	.683
4-6 month paper rate	.464	-.655	-.308	.049	.742
discount rate (-1)	.312	-.623	-.121	-.117	.514
3-6 month paper rate	.500	-.608	-.289	.006	.703
total employment (-1)	.423	-.575	.202	.423	.730

TABLE B-32 (continued)

VARIABLE[2]	Factor 1	Factor 2	Factor 3	Factor 4	R^2
WPI	-.182 (5.08)	.092 (1.30)	-.688 (72.55)	.271 (11.25)	.589 (30.09)
defense/government expenditures	.296	.551	.086	.223	.449
UN (-1)	-.378	.466	-.116	-.095	.382
$1/UN^2$ (-1)	.379	-.464	.116	.095	.381
AHE	.224	.108	-.842	-.085	.779
CPI	-.339	-.016	-.837	.235	.871
materials cost	-.048	-.203	-.762	.022	.625
WPI (-1)	-.102	.215	-.687	.195	.567
M_1 (-1)	.278	.263	-.683	-.006	.613
guidelines	.232	-.032	.504	-.021	.309
$1/UN_L$	.144	-.190	-.239	.894	.913
$1/UN_L$ (-1)	-.126	-.196	-.294	.883	.920
UN_L (-1)	.184	.269	.140	-.878	.897
UN_L	-.200	.326	.149	-.848	.887
SULC	-.357	.094	-.245	-.777	.799
$1/UN_{AL}$	-.003	-.207	-.534	.766	.915
lagged political dummy	.303	.114	.012	.757	.679
$1/UN_{AL}$ (-1)	-.205	-.149	-.541	.745	.913
government purchases	.157	.040	.206	.566	.389
political dummy	.394	.047	.424	.507	.594
government purchases/national income	-.374	.054	.285	.452	.043
variance added	.206	.090	.072	.135	
cumulative variance explained	.206	.296	.368	.503	

[1]Boxes indicate the factor to which the variable has been assigned.

[2]Variables are unassigned (but included in the components analysis) if there is no factor loading above |.39|. The unassigned variables are percent of labor force female, quit rate, unfilled orders/sales, new orders/sales, expected investment in P & E, assets/liabilities-internal funds, corporate tax rate, (ULC-SULC), inventory investment, inventory/sales, real GNP, unborrowed reserves, indirect tax rate, defense/government purchases, full employment surplus, debt/GNP, M_2 (-1), labor force participation rate.

TABLE B-33

Industry 36 Electrical Equipment

Rotated Factor Loadings for 1959:1-1971:3 with the Wholesale Price Index
Current and Lagged – Percent Change over Four Quarters (F-ratio in Parentheses)[1]

VARIABLE[2]	Factor 1	Factor 2	Factor 3	Factor 4	R^2
WPI	-.208 (10.73)	.243 (14.64)	.789 (154.40)	-.147 (5.36)	.746 (61.67)
$1/UN^2$	.934	-.056	.005	.022	.876
UN	-.933	.061	-.004	-.018	.874
$1/UN_A$	.896	-.170	.018	.233	.885
output	.862	-.239	-.098	.161	.836
corporate tax receipts	.847	.380	.025	.173	.893
productivity	.806	-.332	.054	.183	.796
cash flow	.802	.304	.000	.157	.759
ULC	-.799	.374	.157	-.228	.855
3-6 month paper rate	.783	-.247	.270	-.197	.785
percent of labor force female	.766	.015	.316	.033	.688
accession rate	.766	.033	-.113	.359	.729
$1/UN^2$ (-1)	.765	-.407	.161	-.001	.777
UN (-1)	-.762	.416	-.160	.005	.779
output/previous peak	.761	.168	-.244	-.062	.671
4-6 month paper rate	.760	-.316	.323	-.165	.809
profit/equity	.760	.417	-.212	.107	.807
total employment	.753	-.436	.177	.246	.850
sales	.751	-.119	.527	.096	.866
GNP	.730	.357	.386	.181	.842
layoff rate	-.674	-.462	.214	-.186	.748
discount rate (-1)	.542	-.440	.348	-.392	.763
real GNP	.524	-.158	.169	-.147	.350
quit rate	.518	-.136	-.030	.293	.374
inventory investment	.490	-.009	.089	.046	.250
UN↓	.478	-.006	-.092	.106	.248
UN↑	-.475	-.169	-.067	-.310	.355
debt/GNP	-.405	.182	.154	-.166	.249

TABLE B-33 (continued)

VARIABLE[2]	Factor 1	Factor 2	Factor 3	Factor 4	R^2
WPI	-.208 (10.73)	.243 (14.64)	.789 (154.40)	-.147 (5.36)	.746 (61.67)
GNP/potential GNP	.016	.789	-.087	-.104	.642
personal tax rate	-.250	.737	.084	.128	.629
M_1 (-1)	.260	.724	.560	.075	.912
unborrowed reserves	-.143	.689	-.175	.069	.531
AWE	.186	.681	.315	-.339	.712
personal tax receipts	.385	-.675	.246	.222	.713
M_2 (-1)	.398	.659	.079	.418	.774
total employment (-1)	.503	-.651	.260	.233	.799
government purchases (deflated)	.424	-.643	.275	.256	.735
inventory/sales	-.543	-.626	.143	.083	.715
investment in P & E	.122	-.563	.322	.060	.439
expected investment in P & E	-.066	-.447	.387	.415	.527
$1/UN_{AL}$ (-1)	.048	-.102	.903	.220	.877
$1/UN_{AL}$	.218	-.032	.849	.310	.867
$1/UN_L$ (-1)	.201	-.241	.806	.337	.861
CPI	-.386	.296	.786	-.240	.911
UN_L (-1)	-.229	.390	-.765	-.283	.870
materials cost	-.163	.000	.743	-.307	.673
WPI (-1)	-.309	.243	.724	-.174	.709
$1/UN_L$	.421	-.110	.719	.375	.847
bond yield	.255	-.286	.691	-.022	.625
UN_L	-.502	.226	-.675	-.330	.868
new orders/sales	-.074	.287	-.624	-.132	.495
assets/liabilities/internal funds	-.270	.340	-.622	-.002	.576
labor force participation rate	.105	-.202	.593	.432	.590
AHE	-.477	.424	.576	-.345	.858
guidelines	.156	.083	-.554	.066	.343
defense/government purchases	.070	-.058	.527	.376	.428

VARIABLE[2]	Factor 1	Factor 2	Factor 3	Factor 4	R^2
WPI	-.208	.243	.789	-.147	.746
	(10.73)	(14.64)	(54.40)	(5.36)	(61.67)
government purchases	.086	-.118	.198	.872	.821
political dummy	.156	-.046	-.314	.814	.788
SULC	-.209	.363	.202	-.776	.819
government purchases/national income	-.518	-.097	.088	.763	.868
defense/government expenditures	.289	.002	.200	.669	.572
indirect tax rate	-.402	-.015	-.201	-.600	.562
unfilled orders/sales	-.213	-.063	-.132	.587	.411
lagged political dummy	.338	-.048	.205	.578	.493
variance added	.309	.119	.156	.083	
cumulative variance explained	.309	.428	.584	.667	

[1] Boxes indicate the factor to which the variable has been assigned.

[2] Variables are unassigned (but included in the components analysis) if there is no factor loading above $|.39|$. The unassigned variables are corporate tax rate, (ULC-SULC), full employment surplus.

TABLE B-34
Industry 36 Electrical Equipment

Rotated Factor Loadings for 1959:1-1971:3 with the Wholesale Price Index
Current and Lagged - Quarterly Percent Change (F-ratio in Parentheses)[1]

VARIABLE[2]	Factor 1	Factor 2	Factor 3	Factor 4	R^2
WPI	.062	-.117	.642	-.035	.432
	(0.43)	(1.52)	(45.71)	(0.14)	(15.97)
output	-.833	.174	-.149	.091	.755
productivity	-.728	.269	-.180	.238	.692
ULC	-.728	-.294	.288	-.265	.770
total employment	-.703	.390	-.013	.324	.751
$1/UN^2$	-.676	-.037	-.032	.145	.481
UN	.671	-.040	.032	-.145	.474
corporate tax receipts	-.670	-.010	-.062	-.144	.474
output/previous peak	-.667	-.067	-.151	-.214	.518
$1/UN_A$	-.665	.261	-.144	.212	.576
money GNP	-.651	-.264	.245	.175	.585
cash flow	-.587	.016	-.028	-.201	.385
profit/equity	-.586	-.109	-.124	-.263	.440
sales	-.571	.179	.268	.192	.466
layoff rate	.549	.456	.065	-.032	.515
UN	.540	.385	-.091	-.134	.465
government purchases/national income	.534	.110	-.043	.453	.505
accession rate	-.503	.099	-.185	.170	.325
percent of labor force female	-.480	.231	.143	.033	.306
M_2 (-1)	-.444	-.081	.068	-.102	.219
UN↓	-.400	.144	-.068	.310	.281
GNP/potential GNP	-.153	-.887	.099	.065	.824
government purchases (deflated)	-.140	.873	-.018	.078	.788
personal tax rate	-.113	.865	-.030	.063	.766
personal tax receipts	-.017	-.799	.157	.037	.664
bond yield	-.184	.663	.383	-.057	.624
4-6 month paper rate	-.487	.610	.179	.003	.641
investment in P & E	.075	.597	.098	.081	.378
discount rate (-1)	-.341	.572	.060	-.182	.480
3-6 month paper rate	-.510	.541	.141	-.022	.573

VARIABLE[2]	Factor 1	Factor 2	Factor 3	Factor 4	R^2
WPI	.062 (0.43)	-.117 (1.52)	.642 (45.71)	-.035 (0.14)	.432 (15.97)
defense/government expenditure	-.102	-.525	.039	.481	.518
total employment (-1)	-.343	.524	-.010	.432	.579
$1/UN^2$ (-1)	-.394	-.426	-.019	.025	.337
UN (-1)	.392	-.422	.019	-.022	.333
CPI	.213	.042	.872	-.206	.849
$1/UN_{AL}$ (-1)	.184	.224	.848	.336	.916
$1/UN_{AL}$	.004	.283	.811	.413	.908
$1/UN_L$ (-1)	.154	.371	.674	.484	.850
$1/UN_L$	-.198	.318	.656	.569	.895
AHE	-.287	-.339	.638	-.271	.678
UN_L (-1)	-.200	-.435	-.612	-.517	.871
UN_L	-.145	-.444	-.594	-.577	.903
WPI (-1)	.213	.007	.564	-.108	.375
M_1 (-1)	-.415	-.278	.539	-.295	.627
guidelines	-.032	.027	-.539	-.120	.307
materials cost	.052	.383	.531	-.166	.459
SULC	.180	-.246	.359	-.694	.703
government purchases	.024	.113	-.014	.659	.448
lagged political dummy	-.132	.212	.214	.615	.486
political dummy	-.299	.063	-.274	.556	.467
assets/liabilities-internal funds	.184	-.001	-.277	-.444	.308
AWE	-.371	-.313	.358	-.415	.536
variance added	.185	.084	.129	.066	
cumulative variance explained	.185	.269	.398	.464	

[1] Boxes indicate the factor to which the variable has been assigned.

[2] Variables are unassigned (but included in the components analysis) if there is no factor loading above $|.39|$. The unassigned variables are quit rate, unfilled orders/sales, new orders/sales, expected investment in P & E, corporate tax rate, (ULC-SULC), inventory investment, inventory/sales, real GNP, unborrowed reserves, indirect tax rate, defense/government purchases, full employment surplus, debt/GNP, labor force participation rate.

TABLE B-35

Industry 37 Transportation

Rotated Factor Loadings for 1959:1-1971:3 with the Wholesale Price Index
Current and Lagged – Percent Change over Four Quarters (F-ratio in Parentheses)[1]

VARIABLE[2]	Factor 1	Factor 2	Factor 3	Factor 4	R^2
WPI	.043 (0.77)	.189 (17.17)	.910 (398.24)	.189 (1.73)	.869 (139.30)
profit/equity	-.928	-.028	.115	-.042	.877
corporate tax receipts	-.909	-.068	.139	-.019	.850
sales	-.894	-.257	.102	.154	.899
cash flow	-.879	-.064	.216	.002	.824
UN	.863	.280	.172	-.151	.875
$1/UN^2$	-.857	-.277	-.185	.155	.870
output/previous peak	-.851	-.349	-.163	.003	.873
inventory/sales	-.845	-.084	.198	.335	.872
output	-.837	-.338	.230	.303	.960
productivity	-.763	-.365	-.268	.380	.932
AWE	-.706	-.111	.451	-.072	.719
ULC	.691	.342	.434	-.375	.924
layoff rate	.669	.252	-.062	-.041	.517
UN↓	-.661	.173	.021	-.074	.473
$1/UN_A$	-.599	-.532	-.276	.444	.916
UN (-1)	.510	.446	.328	-.242	.625
1/UN (-1)	-.507	-.439	-.337	.246	.624
UN↑	.507	-.267	.213	.106	.384
quit rate	-.473	-.372	-.126	-.417	.552
new orders/sales	-.419	-.118	.051	-.213	.238
4-6 month paper rate	-.172	-.858	-.072	.299	.861
discount rate (-1)	.048	-.856	-.059	.075	.744
3-6 month paper rate	-.235	-.839	-.033	.251	.823
government purchases/national income	.278	.682	-.217	.447	.790
real GNP	-.346	-.602	-.033	.232	.537
investment in P & E	-.261	-.586	-.574	.012	.741
bond yield	.353	-.578	.167	.443	.683
unborrowed reserves	-.395	.537	.403	-.123	.622

VARIABLE[2]	Factor 1	Factor 2	Factor 3	Factor 4	R^2
WPI	.043	.189	.910	.189	.869
	(0.77)	(17.17)	(398.24)	(1.73)	(139.30)
government purchases (deflated)	.111	-.528	-.447	.480	.722
personal tax rate	.126	-.515	-.466	.418	.673
WPI (-1)	-.028	.044	.911	-.086	.840
AHE	-.290	-.061	.845	-.006	.802
M_1 (-1)	-.152	-.111	.800	.385	.823
CPI	.530	-.032	.754	.188	.885
personal tax receipts	-.215	.448	.697	-.168	.760
GNP/potential GNP	-.489	.364	.574	-.157	.726
expected investment in P & E	-.206	-.287	-.567	-.146	.467
guidelines	-.370	.027	-.449	-.104	.350
$1/UN_L$ (-1)	.094	-.208	.091	.909	.886
$1/UN_L$	-.129	-.173	.084	.890	.846
$1/UN_{AL}$	.188	-.319	.296	.824	.904
SULC	.099	.049	.371	-.819	.821
UN_L (-1)	-.081	.327	-.040	-.809	.769
UN_L	.234	.298	-.074	-.803	.793
lagged political dummy	.234	-.073	-.205	.771	.697
government purchases	-.092	.303	-.264	.760	.747
$1/UN_{AL}$ (-1)	.370	-.308	.323	.740	.883
indirect tax rate	.178	.023	.204	-.702	.567
total employment (-1)	-.158	-.429	-.364	.701	.833
assets/liabilities-internal funds	-.263	.281	-.128	-.687	.636
labor force participation rate	-.310	-.101	-.061	.658	.543
total employment	-.619	-.315	-.203	.646	.941
defense/government expenditures	-.242	-.141	-.118	.610	.464
money GNP	.540	-.353	.349	.589	.884
M_2 (-1)	-.515	.199	.294	.543	.686
political dummy	-.312	.377	.530	.536	.802
unfilled orders/sales	.521	.173	-.419	.525	.752
defense/government purchases	.286	-.009	.105	.498	.341

TABLE B-35 (continued)

VARIABLE[2]	Factor 1	Factor 2	Factor 3	Factor 4	R^2
WPI	.043	.189	.910	.189	.869
	(0.77)	(17.17)	(398.24)	(1.73)	(139.30)
variance added	.187	.075	.119	.282	
cumulative variance explained	.187	.262	.381	.663	

[1]Boxes indicate the factor to which the variable has been assigned.

[2]Variables are unassigned (but included in the components analysis) if there is no factor loading above |.39|. The unassigned variables are percent of labor force female, accession rate, corporate tax rate, (ULC-SULC), inventory investment, materials cost, full employment surplus, debt/GNP.

Table B-36
Industry 37 Transportation

Rotated Factor Loadings for 1959:1-1971:3 with the Wholesale Price Index
Current and Lagged - Quarterly Percent Change (F-ratio in Parentheses)[1]

VARIABLE[2]	Factor 1	Factor 2	Factor 3	Factor 4	R^2
WPI	-.150 (1.84)	.138 (1.56)	-.435 (15.50)	.010 (0.01)	.231 (6.31)
output	.953	.175	.136	.081	.963
output/previous peak	.944	.175	.040	-.030	.925
sales	.929	.210	-.036	.037	.910
productivity	.920	.156	.171	.133	.918
corporate tax receipts	.893	.354	-.030	-.008	.924
ULC	-.866	-.032	-.262	-.104	.831
total employment	.836	.228	.229	.311	.900
profit/equity	.822	.459	-.022	.027	.887
unfilled orders/sales	-.783	-.139	.230	.189	.721
cash flow	.766	.220	-.131	.021	.653
UN	-.744	.110	-.303	.069	.662
1/UN²	.742	-.108	.307	-.073	.662
AWE	.697	.382	-.111	-.033	.645
money GNP	.694	.063	.041	.377	.630
AHE	.631	.560	-.256	.121	.480
government purchases/national income	-.595	.207	.199	.209	.369
layoff rate	-.594	-.123	-.009	.023	.306
investment in P & E	.480	-.125	.238	-.060	.233
expected investment in P & E	.441	.111	.150	.058	.257
real GNP	.407	-.220	.110	.177	.201
accession rate	-.397	.032	.189	.080	
government purchases (deflated)	-.180	-.826	.215	.188	.796
personal tax rate	-.196	-.818	.199	.149	.770
GNP/potential GNP	.410	.807	-.130	-.017	.837
personal tax receipts	.329	.723	-.237	-.046	.749
bond yield	-.061	-.728	-.242	.343	.709
4-6 month paper rate	-.170	-.714	.081	.288	.628
3-6 month paper rate	.192	-.675	.100	.249	.564

TABLE B-36 (continued)

VARIABLE[2]	Factor 1	Factor 2	Factor 3	Factor 4	R^2
WPI	-.150 (1.84)	.138 (1.56)	-.435 (15.50)	.010 (0.01)	.231 (6.31)
defense/government expenditures	.123	.610	.156	.235	.467
discount rate (-1)	.140	-.608	.111	.031	.402
total employment (-1)	-.234	-.548	.442	.291	.635
WPI (-1)	.062	.546	-.326	.025	.409
corporate tax rate	-.187	-.539	-.077	-.134	.349
new orders/sales	.056	.426	.170	-.017	.214
CPI	-.230	-.075	-.739	.413	.775
political dummy	.072	.031	.640	.442	.612
guidelines	.023	-.006	.541	-.103	.304
$1/UN^2$ (-1)	-.173	-.070	.576	.109	.378
UN (-1)	.182	.066	-.571	-.112	.376
$UN\uparrow$	-.350	-.092	-.537	.164	.445
$UN\downarrow$	.370	.166	.530	-.033	.447
$1/UN_A$	.475	-.365	.514	.223	.672
$1/UN$ (-1)	-.154	-.104	-.065	.947	.936
$1/UN_L$	.093	-.130	.082	.928	.893
UN_L (-1)	.265	.095	.011	-.885	.862
UN_L	-.190	.185	-.103	-.875	.847
$1/N_{AL}$	-.061	-.187	-.313	.874	.901
$1/UN_{AL}$ (-1)	-.187	-.104	-.461	.799	.897
lagged political dummy	.041	-.086	-.325	.798	.751
SULC	-.161	.156	-.465	-.675	.723
government purchases	-.146	.101	.394	.466	.404
variance added	.221	.144	.062	.088	
cumulative variance explained	.187	.262	.381	.663	

---

[1]Boxes indicate the factor to which the variable has been assigned.

[2]Variables are unassigned (but included in the components analysis) if there is no factor loading above |.39|. The unassigned variables are percent of labor force female, quit rate, assets/liabilities-internal funds, (ULC-SULC), inventory investment, inventory/sales, materials cost, unborrowed reserves, indirect tax rate, defense/government purchases, full employment surplus, debt/GNP, M_1 (-1), M_2 (-1), labor force participation

TABLE B-37
Industry 38 Instruments

Rotated Factor Loadings for 1959:1-1971:3 with the Wholesale Price Index
Current and Lagged – Percent Change over Four Quarters (F-ratio in Parentheses)[1]

VARIABLE[2]	Factor 1	Factor 2	Factor 3	Factor 4	R^2
WPI	-.453 (15.14)	.007 (0.00)	.238 (4.22)	.271 (5.42)	.336 (8.27)
inventory/sales	-.828	-.084	-.236	.072	.754
money GNP	.810	-.256	-.063	.309	.020
cash flow	.790	-.235	.155	.137	.724
percent of labor force female	.769	.051	-.080	.202	.643
corporate tax receipts	.739	-.443	.000	.197	.781
M_1 (-1)	.738	.193	-.473	.071	.812
profit/equity	.726	-.304	.391	.006	.773
M_2 (-1)	.697	-.238	.172	.404	.738
AWE	.636	-.178	-.443	-.080	.639
layoff rate	-.616	.112	.112	.155	.429
accession rate	.552	-.319	.329	.124	.533
sales	.525	-.415	-.176	.323	.585
output/previous peak	.517	-.323	.479	-.854	.607
full employment surplus	-.452	-.044	.172	.069	.241
WPI (-1)	-.449	.072	.326	.269	.386
4-6 month paper rate	.391	-.833	-.056	-.036	.852
government purchases (deflated)	-.113	-.827	-.032	.331	.807
personal tax receipts	.171	-.806	.025	.297	.767
total employment (-1)	.006	-.792	-.006	.454	.385
3-6 month paper rate	.428	-.785	-.009	-.075	.807
total employment	.307	-.773	.126	.443	.904
personal tax receipts (-1)	.271	.762	-.195	-.048	.698
discount rate (-1)	.177	-.758	-.102	-.247	.680
unborrowed reserves	.287	.752	-.123	-.051	.665
GNP/potential GNP	.529	.704	.050	-.096	.787
output	.558	-.691	.257	.199	.896
ULC	-.426	.689	-.389	-.235	.862
manhour productivity	.473	-.674	.161	.270	.779

204

TABLE B-37 (continued)

VARIABLE[2]	Factor 1	Factor 2	Factor 3	Factor 4	R^2
WPI	-.453 (15.14)	.007 (0.00)	.238 (4.22)	.271 (5.42)	.336 (8.27)
bond yield	.064	-.638	.558	.196	.761
1/UNA	.514	-.622	.386	.279	.877
quit rate	.505	-.620	.161	.255	.728
real GNP	.357	-.519	.151	-.065	.424
debt/GNP	-.282	-.414	-.026	-.164	.280
CPI	.063	.196	-.933	-.029	.915
AHE	.090	.245	-.915	-.064	.913
materials cost	.177	-.049	-.862	.190	.815
1/UN$_{AL}$ (-1)	.107	-.370	-.713	.461	.869
guidelines	.011	-.039	.653	-.116	.442
1/UN$_{AL}$	.256	-.398	-.584	.533	.851
assets/liabilities-internal funds	.404	.097	.433	.138	.379
government purchases	-.071	-.097	.067	.929	.881
SULC	-.114	-.399	.140	-.773	.791
defense/government expenditures	-.155	-.083	.111	.769	.633
government purchases/national income	-.497	.298	-.056	.767	.929
political dummy	-.023	-.035	.560	.661	.754
indirect tax rate	-.418	.233	-.102	-.592	.589
lagged political dummy	.267	-.297	.152	.581	.521
labor force participation rate	.153	-.271	-.391	.560	.564
defense/government purchases	.064	-.125	-.353	.542	.438
variance added	.136	.303	.128	.092	
cumulative variance explained	.136	.439	.567	.659	

[1] Boxes indicate the factor to which the variable has been assigned.

[2] Variables are unassigned (but included in the components analysis) if there is no factor loading above |.39|. The unassigned variables are corporate tax rate, (ULC-SULC), inventory investment.

TABLE B-38
Industry 38 Instruments

Rotated Factor Loadings for 1959:1-1971:3 with the Wholesale Price Index
Current and Lagged - Quarterly Percent Change (F-ratio in Parentheses)[1]

VARIABLE[2]	Factor 1	Factor 2	Factor 3	Factor 4	R^2
WPI	-.032 (0.06)	.210 (2.49)	-.281 (4.46)	-.090 (0.46)	.132 (2.48)
total employment	.809	-.153	.046	-.306	.773
ULC	-.783	.278	.176	.112	.736
productivity	.774	-.265	-.037	.129	.689
output	.750	-.374	-.017	-.126	.720
SULC	-.729	-.387	-.162	.182	.741
political dummy	.703	.167	-.280	.039	.603
total employment (-1)	.684	.123	.009	-.420	.659
lagged political dummy	.661	.315	.162	-.080	.572
1/UNA	.657	-.361	-.088	-.223	.621
money GNP	.566	-.362	.273	.264	.595
quit rate	.500	-.189	.102	-.141	.314
sales	.416	-.246	.316	-.035	.336
government purchases/national income	-.035	.720	-.087	-.020	.526
profit/equity	.302	-.693	-.008	-.237	.630
cash flow	.262	-.617	.120	-.194	.501
government purchases	.475	.520	-.024	-.000	.498
AWE	.074	-.501	.484	-.082	.499
corporate tax receipts	.288	-.482	.363	-.122	.463
assets/liabilities-internal funds	.059	-.406	-.023	.083	.174
CPI	-.278	.180	.856	-.099	.851
AHE	-.310	-.015	.783	.032	.710
1/UNAL	.163	.517	.735	-.177	.865
1/UNAL (-1)	.351	.431	.712	-.221	.869
M1 (-1)	.166	.361	.662	.238	.655
materials cost	-.180	-.100	.655	-.343	.591
guidelines	.179	-.089	-.522	.031	.312

TABLE B-38 (continued)

VARIABLE[2]	Factor 1	Factor 2	Factor 3	Factor 4	R^2
WPI	-.032 (0.06)	.210 (2.49)	-.281 (4.46)	-.090 (0.46)	.132 (2.48)
GNP/potential GNP	.016	-.227	-.105	.918	.904
government purchases (deflated)	.262	.108	-.015	-.871	.838
personal tax rate	.216	.098	-.025	-.870	.812
personal tax receipts	-.074	-.089	.108	.854	.753
bond yield	.210	.066	.379	-.695	.678
4-6 month paper rate	.416	-.185	.212	-.614	.629
defense/government expenditures	.277	.207	.048	.591	.473
3-6 month paper rate	.405	-.200	.180	.570	.562
discount rate (-1)	.246	-.329	.030	-.569	.494
variance added	.191	.073	.093	.101	
cumulative variance explained	.191	.264	.357	.458	

[1] Boxes indicate the factor to which the variable has been assigned.

[2] Variables are unassigned (but included in the components analysis) if there is no factor loading above |.39|. The unassigned variables are WPI (-1), percent of labor force female, layoff rate, accession rate, output/previous peak, corporate tax rate, (ULC-SULC), inventory investment, inventory/sales, real GNP, unborrowed reserves, indirect tax rate, defense/government purchases, full employment surplus, debt/GNP, M_2 (-1), labor force participation rate.

Bibliography

Adelman, Irma, and Cynthia Taft Morris. *Society, Politics and Economic Development*. Baltimore: Johns Hopkins Press, 1967.

Ando, Faith Halfter. *The Cyclical Behavior of Materials Prices in United States Industry*. Unpublished doctoral dissertation. Cambridge, Mass.: Harvard University, 1966.

Barrett, Nancy S. *The Theory of Macroeconomic Policy*. Englewood Cliffs, N.J.: Prentice-Hall, Inc. 1972.

Baumol, William J. *Business Behavior, Value and Growth*. New York: Harcourt, Brace & World, Inc., 1967.

Bhatia, Rattan J. "Profits and the Rate of Change in Money Earnings in the United States, 1935-1959." *Economica*, n.s., 29 (August 1962), pp. 255-62.

———. "Unemployment and the Rate of Change of Money Earnings in the United States 1900-1958." *Economica*, n.s., 28 (August 1961), pp. 286-96.

Bosworth, Barry. "Phase II: The U.S. Experiment with an Incomes Policy." *Brookings Papers on Economic Activity* (1972:2), pp. 343-83.

Bowen, William G. *Wage Behavior in the Postwar Period: An Empirical Analysis*. Princeton, N.J.: Princeton University Press, 1960.

Bronfenbrenner, Martin, and Franklyn D. Holzman. "Survey of Inflation Theory." *The American Economic Review*, 53 (September 1963), pp. 593-661.

Dicks-Mireaux, L.A., and J.C.R. Dow. "The Determinants of Wage Inflation: United Kingdom 1946-1956." *Journal of the Royal Statistical Society*, Series A, 22 (1959:2), pp. 145-74.

Dicks-Mireaux, L.A. "The Interrelationship Between Cost and Price Change." *Oxford Economic Papers*, 13 (October 1961), pp. 267-92.

Eckstein, Otto. "A Theory of the Wage-Price Process in Modern Industry." *The Review of Economic Studies*, 30 (October 1964), pp. 267-86.

Eckstein, Otto, and Thomas A. Wilson. "The Determination of Money Wages in American Industry." *The Quarterly Journal of Economics*, 72 (August 1962), pp. 379-414.

Eckstein, Otto, and Gary Fromm. "The Price Equation." *The American Economic Review*, 58 (December 1968), pp. 1159-83.

Eckstein, Otto, and David Wyss. "Industry Price Equations." *Conference on the Econometrics of Price Determination*. Washington, D.C., 30-31 October 1970.

Eckstein, Otto, and Roger Brinner. *The Inflation Process in the United States*. A study prepared for the use of the Joint Economic Committee. Washington, D.C., 1972.

Fuchs, Victor R. *The Service Economy*. New York: National Bureau of Economic Research, 1968.

Garbarino, Joseph W. "Unionism and the General Wage Level." *The American Economic Review*, 40 (December 1950), pp. 893-96.

Gordon, Robert J. "Inflation in Recession and Recovery." *Brookings Papers on Economic Activity* (1971:1), pp. 105-58.

_____. "Wage-Price Controls and the Shifting Phillips Curve." *Brookings Papers on Economic Activity* (1972:2), pp. 385-421.

Harman, H.H. *Modern Factor Analysis.* Chicago: University of Chicago Press, 1960.

Hines, A.G. "Trade Unions and Wage Inflation in the United Kingdom, 1893-1961." *The Review of Economic Studies*, 31 (October 1964), pp. 221-52.

Kendall, Maurice. *A Course in Multivariate Analysis.* New York: Hafner Publishing Company, 1960.

Kerr, Clark. "Labor Markets: Their Character and Consequences." *American Economic Association Papers and Proceedings*, 40 (May 1950), pp. 278-91.

Keynes, John Maynard. *The General Theory of Employment, Interest, and Money.* New York: Harcourt Brace Jovanovich, Inc. 1965.

Klein, L.R., and R.J. Ball, "Some Econometrics of the Determination of Absolute Prices and Wages." *The Economic Journal*, 69 (September 1959), pp. 465-82.

Kuh, Edwin. "Profits, Profit Markups, and Productivity." In *Study of Employment, Growth and Price Levels*, Study Paper No. 15, Joint Economic Committee, Washington, D.C., 1959.

Lekachman, Robert. *The Age of Keynes.* New York: Random House, 1966.

Levinson, Harold M. "Postwar Movement of Prices and Wages in Manufacturing Industries." In *Study of Employment Growth, and Price Levels*, Study Paper No. 21, Joint Economic Committee, Washington, D.C., 1960.

Lipsey, Richard G. "The Relation Between Unemployment and the Rate of Change of Money Wage Rates in the United Kingdom 1862-1957: A Further Analysis." *Economica* n.s., 17 (February 1960), pp. 1-31.

Mansfield, Edwin M. *Monopoly Power and Economic Performance.* New York: W.W. Norton and Company, Inc., 1968.

Perry, George L. "Changing Labor Markets and Inflation." *Brookings Papers on Economic Activity* (1970:3), pp. 411-48.

_____. *Unemployment, Money Wage Rates, and Inflation.* Cambridge, Mass.: The M.I.T. Press, 1966.

_____. "Wages and the Guideposts." *The American Economic Review*, 57 (September 1967), pp. 897-904.

Phelps, Edmund S. *Inflation Policy and Unemployment Theory.* London: Macmillan and Company, Ltd., 1972.

Phelps, Edmund S., et. al. *Microeconomic Foundations of Employment and Inflation Theory.* London: Macmillan and Company, Ltd., 1970.

Phillips, A.W. "The Relation Between Unemployment and the Rate of Change of

Money Wage Rates in the United Kingdom, 1861-1957." *Economica*, 25 (November 1958), pp. 283-99.

Pierson, Gail. "The Effect of Union Strength on the U.S. 'Phillips Curve'." *The American Economic Review*, 58 (June 1968), pp. 456-67.

Reder, M.W. "The Theory of Frictional Unemployment." *Economica* (February 1969), pp. 1-28.

Romans, J.T. "Moral Suasion as an Instrument of Economic Policy." *The American Economic Review*, 56 (December 1966), pp. 1220-26.

Samuelson, Paul. "Wage-Price Guideposts and the Need for Informal Controls in a Mixed Economy." In *Full Employment, Guideposts, and Economic Stability: Rationale Debate Seminars*, Washington, D.C., 1967.

Samuelson, Paul, and Robert Solow. "Analytical Aspects of Anti-Inflation Policy." *The American Economic Review*, 50 (May 1960), pp. 177-94.

Schultze, C.L. "Recent Inflation in the United States." In *Study of Employment, Growth and Price Levels*, Study Paper No. 1, Joint Economic Committee, Washington, D.C., 1959.

Schultze, C.L., and J.L. Tryon. "Prices and Wages." In *Brookings Quarterly Econometric Model of the United States*. Chicago: Rand McNally, Inc., 1965.

Weiss, Leonard W. "Concentration and Labor Earnings." *The American Economic Review*, 56 (March 1966), pp. 96-117.

Index

Accelerationist theory of inflation, 7–9, 25, 97, 102–103
Aggregate demand remedies, 1–11, 60–63, 67–68, 94–98 (see also Keynesian policy)
  evaluation of, 67–68
  interindustry impact of, 97–98
  and markup pricing, 60
  neutrality of, 97–98
  and the profit rate, 94
  secular changes in effectiveness of, 62–63
Ando, Faith Halfter, 24

Ball, R.J., 106
Brinner, Roger, 14

Capacity ulitization, 107
Comparative statics, 3
Compensatory pricing, 54, 61–63, 72, 92, 95–97, 106–107
Concentration of industry, 10
Concentration ratio, 93–96
Cost variables, 24–25, 114–15
Countervailing power, 59, 61, 68
Cyclical behavior of prices, 52

Data, discussion of, 21–28, 113–16
Data problems, 25–26
Demand variables, 23, 113–14
Demographic factors in the labor market, 7, 43
Durable manufacturing, 29–68
  price equation, 52–54
  statistical analysis of, 29–68
  wage equation, 56–59
  wage-price interaction, 61–62

Eckstein, Otto, 14, 21, 24, 46, 106–108
Empirical models of inflation, 13–20
Equilibrium analysis, 3

Factor analysis, 15–20
Factor pattern, defined, 19
Factors, interpretation of, 29–42–45, 70–71
  in industry analysis, 70–71
Financial variables, 23–24, 114
Firm, theory of, 9–10 (see also Microeconomic tehory)
Fiscal policy, 25, 54, 64–67, 98–99
  evaluated, 98–99
  statistical analysis of, 64–67
Fromm, Gary, 14, 21, 46, 106

Gordon, Robert, 13–14, 106–107

Incomes policy, 8 (see also Wage-price guidelines)
Industries, classification of, 69–70
Industry analysis, 9–10, 69–100, 107–108
  cross section regressions, 91–96
  factors in, 70–71
  price equations, 71–91
  wage equations, 75–91
Inflation, 1–20, 27–28, 51
  empirical studies of, 13–20
  industry analysis of, 9–10, 69–100
  and market structure, 10, 91–96
  secular trend in, 51
  theory of, 1–11, 27–28
    comparative statics methodology in, 3
    demand pull versus cost push, 9, 27–28
Inflationary gap, 2–4

Kendall, Maurice, 20
Kendall coefficient, 20, 62n., 63n., 97
  defined, 20
Keynes, 1–11, 23–24, 64 (see also Keynesian policy)
  theory of inflation, 1–11, 64
    described, 2–4
    and the labor market, 2
Keynesian policy, 67–68, 97–109 (see also Aggregate demand remedies
  evaluation of, 67–68, 101–109
  neutrality of, 97–97
  versus wage-price guidelines, 103–109
Klein, L.R., 106

Labor market analysis, 2–7
Labor market variables, 21–22, 113
Labor markets, spillover effects in, 70–71, 97–98
Labor unions, 10, 59, 97 (see also Unionization)
  and inflation, 10
  and wage stability, 97
  and wages, 59
Lags, 27, 46, 54, 60, 97, 101–102, 107
  in industry analyses, 97, 107
  specification of, 27
Laissez faire, 2
Leijonhufvud, Axel, 3n.
Linkages, 70–71, 99, 102, 108
  between markets, 108
  in product markets, 70–71, 99, 102, 108

Lipsey, Richard, 105

Macroeconomic policy, 99–105
  evaluated, 101–105
  neutrality of, 99, 104–105
Manufacturing, total, 29–68
  price equation, 45–52
  statistical analysis of, 29–68
  wage equation, 55–56
  wage-price interaction, 60–61
Market level, 94–96
Market structure, 10, 69–100, 107–108
Markup pricing, 60, 72, 97, 102, 106–107
Materials costs, 24, 106–107
Methodology, 1–2, 13–20
Microeconomic basis of price behavior,
  106–107
Microeconomic models, 14
Microeconomic theory, 9–10, 71–72
Monetary policy, 3, 23–24, 54, 64–67,
  98–99
  evaluation of, 98–99
  statistical analysis of, 64–67
Money illusion, 6–9, 62, 97
Multicollinearity, 1, 13–20, 26, 43, 108
  and hypothesis testing, 1
  in wage equations, 43

Natural rate of unemployment, 9
Neoclassical theory, 6, 60
  of inflation, 60
  of unemployment, 6
Nixon, Richard M., 8, 103

Oligopoly, 71–72

Perry, George, 7–9, 13–14, 21–22, 25, 105
  empirical study of inflation, 13–14
  theory of inflation, 7–9
Phase II price policy, 8 (see also Wage-price
  guidelines)
Phillips, A.W., 1–11, 21–22, 105
  empirical study of inflation, 5, 105
  and inflation theory, 1–11
Phillips curve, 5–7, 43–44, 60, 67, 102,
  105, 108
Policy factor, 44
Policy instruments, 1
Policy variables, 25, 64–67, 98, 99, 115
  (see also Fiscal policy, Macroeconomic

policy, Monetary policy, Wage-price
  guidelines)
  in industry analyses, 98–99
  statistical analysis of, 64–67
Political factors in inflation, 1, 25–28, 51–52,
  61
Price behavior, types of, 97–98
Price leadership, 72
Primary products, 10
Principal components analysis, 1–2, 14–20
Product classification, 69–70
Productivity, 60, 103–104
Profit rate, 93–96
Psychology of inflation, 6–9

Seasonal adjustment, 26
Secular trend in the inflationary process,
  51, 61–63
Simultaneity, 43, 46, 59, 104–106
  bias from, 105–106
  in the wage-price process, 43
Spillover effects in labor markets, 70–71,
  97–98
Stabilization policy, 1–11 (see also Keyne-
  sian policy, Macroeconomic policy)
Stagflation, 54, 56, 63
Standard Industrial Classification, 69–70
Structural models, 1–20

Target return pricing, 54, 106–107

Unemployment, 1–11, 102–109
  versus inflation, 1–11, 102–109
  natural rate of, 9
Union-firm interaction, 94–96
Unionization, 94–96 (see also Labor
  unions)
Unit labor costs, 2–4, 44

Variables, described, 21–26, 113–116

Wage-price guidelines, 1, 8, 10, 44, 64–67,
  99, 103–109
  evaluation of, 103–109
  versus Keynesian policy, 103–109
  statistical analysis of, 64–67
Wages, 2–9
  and inflation, 2–7
  real versus money, 6–9
Weiss, Leonard W., 94
Wyss, David, 24, 107–108

About the Authors

Nancy S. Barrett is associate professor of economics at the American University in Washington, D.C. She received the Ph.D. in economics from Harvard University. She is the author of textbooks in both macroeconomic and microeconomic theory as well as numerous journal articles.

Geraldine Gerardi is an economist with the Bureau of Economic Analysis.

Thomas P. Hart is a doctoral candidate at the American University.